XENOPHON'S MARCH

Xenophon's MARCH
INTO THE LAIR OF THE PERSIAN LION

JOHN PREVAS

DA CAPO PRESS

Published by Da Capo Press
A member of the Perseus Books Group
http://www.dacapopress.com

ISBN 0-306-81117-0

Da Capo Press books are available at special discounts for bulk purchases in the
U.S. by corporations, institutions, and other organizations. For more information,
please contact the Special Markets Department at the
Perseus Books Group, 11 Cambridge Center, Cambridge, MA 02142,
or call (800) 255-1514 or (617) 252-5298
or email j.mccrary@perseusbooks.com

Cataloging-in-Publication data is available from the
Library of Congress.

First edition, first printing.

PRINTED AND BOUND IN THE UNITED STATES OF AMERICA.
1 2 3 4 5 6 7 8 9–06 05 04 03 02

CONTENTS

MAPS

CHRONOLOGY

800-700 B.C.	Iliad and Odyssey of Homer
750-500 B.C.	Greek Archaic Period
594	Solon becomes archon at Athens
546	Peisistratus establishes a benevolent tyranny at Athens
540	Persians conquer Greek cities of Asia Minor (Ionian coastline)
539	Persia conquers Babylon
513	Persians conquer Thrace
508	Cleisthenes establishes democracy in Athens
499	Ionian revolt against Persian rule
494	Miletus destroyed and Ionian revolt crushed by Persia
493	Themistocles becomes archon at Athens
490	Athenians defeat Persians at Marathon
480	Battles of Thermopylae, Artemisium, and Salamis
478	Creation of the Delian League
461-446	First Peloponnesian War
450s-430s	Prominence of Pericles at Athens
445	Thirty-year peace treaty between Athens and Sparta
431	Second Peloponnesian War begins
430	Plague at Athens; approximate date of Xenophon's birth
429	Death of Pericles
415-413	Athenian expedition to Sicily
411	Oligarchy of the Four Hundred at Athens
410	Democracy restored at Athens
404	Athens surrenders to Sparta
404-403	Thirty Tyrants rule in Athens
402	Democracy restored in Athens
401	Cyrus undertakes the expedition against Artaxerxes
400	The expedition of the Greeks begins
399	Thibron begins a new war against the Persians; trial of Socrates
394	Xenophon fights with Spartans at battle of Coronea
380s-370s	Xenophon settles in Olympia, later in Corinth
333	Alexander the Great defeats Darius at Issus
331	Alexander enters Babylon
323	Death of Alexander at Babylon

PREFACE

When I retraced the steps of Xenophon and the Greeks in preparation for this book I found many things throughout Turkey to be remarkably similar to what is described in the ancient Greek and Latin manuscripts. Many of the names of towns and cities through which the mercenaries marched twenty-four hundred years ago can be found today in slightly altered form in the modern town and city appellations. So many place names bear a remarkable similarity to the ancient names and the distances between them correspond almost exactly to the distances described in the ancient sources. There remain many archaeological sites to visit from this period in history. Customs of the people remain unchanged as well. The marketplace still plays a dominant role in the life of every village, town, and city just as it did in ancient times. One can find everything imaginable to purchase there, from silks and spices to tank parts and Viagra. Animals are still sold, slaughtered, and butchered by the roadside in the same manner as they have been for centuries. Women, in the eastern part of the country at least, are still subservient to men and lead lives of hard physical toil.

Vast areas of the Persian Empire in Asia Minor are described in the ancient manuscripts as being a virtual garden. I found that Turkey today is the same garden that is described in those manuscripts and nearly all the work in that garden is still done by hand. From one end of the country to the other the land is a cornucopia of olives, grapes, fruit, and grains that are harvested by villagers. The main road through central Turkey follows the ancient spice route from the orient and today trucks of every size and description haul goods along it just as caravans did centuries ago.

Traveling through the eastern part of Turkey it is disheartening to observe how little some things in that part of the world have improved from the descriptions found in the ancient manuscripts. Poverty and the specter of war still loom over the lives of the common people. Thugs and terrorists control significant sectors of the economy and countryside while progress has added additional burdens to the backs of the poor in the forms of population density and industrial pollution. Among areas of genuine progress, I was impressed with the efforts to which the Turkish government has gone to insure that each village or town, no matter how remote or poor, has a school staffed with teachers and books for the children. While armed soldiers have to escort some of those children to school, and heavily fortified military outposts are in evidence in nearly every town and village, there is a genuine commitment to education of the young in the country.

Terrorists are still a concern in parts of the countryside just as marauding bands were in ancient times. While one is able to tour most of eastern Turkey with minimal hindrance and in relative safety, the borders with Armenia, Iran, Iraq, and Syria can be dangerous and unstable places. In the current political climate it is unfortunately impossible to duplicate the entire trek of Xenophon and the Ten Thousand. Nevertheless, I was able to complete the majority of the route and gain a perspective that proved invaluable in the writing of this book. It is my hope that the reader will enjoy the book as much as I enjoyed researching and writing it.

John Prevas
Washington, D.C.
March 2001

INTRODUCTION

In the eastern part of the ancient Mediterranean world most people were slaves in one way or another. Either they were owned by others in the classic definition of slavery or they were controlled to the point where they had little say over their own lives. Most people paid a high percentage of what little they raised as tribute to emperors, kings, governors, and a host of other petty tyrants and local thugs more powerful than they were. In that way they might be left alone to live out in relative peace what remained of their short lives. Many fell victim to the incessant wars and conflicts that raged throughout the ancient world and few would have reached their natural lifespans. People had a difficult existence in the ancient world that tended, as the philosopher Hobbes once wrote, to be "short, nasty, and brutish." It was not, in general, a pleasant time to be alive and nowhere does that statement find greater validity than in the story that will follow in the pages of this book.

This is the story of a brief but violent conflict in the ancient world that began when two brothers vied for the throne of Persia. Greeks were drawn into the conflict when the younger brother hired a large contingent of them as mercenaries to spearhead the army he had raised to fight against his older sibling, the king. This was a short conflict as wars go in ancient history and it is not well-known outside the circles of military specialists and classicists. However, it was a conflict that set into motion a massive shift in the balance of power in the century that followed and eventually affected the fate of civilizations.

The Greek mercenaries who joined the younger brother, Cyrus, showed the world that the Persian Empire was not the invincible monolith everyone had believed it to be. When the Greeks went into Persia they demonstrated to the world what a small but well-organized and disciplined force of professional soldiers could achieve against the largest land power on earth. The Greeks, against all odds, penetrated nearly fifteen hundred miles into the heart of the Persian Empire and caused the mighty "king of kings," Artaxerxes II, to retreat from the field of battle. For over a year these Greeks, who became known as the "Ten Thousand," wandered nearly two thousand miles more through the king's empire trying to find a way home. Along the way they burned, looted, and pillaged countless villages and towns. They took slaves and intimidated each army of Persian soldiers that was sent to stop them.

From the broad plains of western Asia Minor to the scorching deserts of Syria, and through the snow-covered mountains of Armenia to the shores of the Black Sea, this small army fought nature and man to survive. Through all their hardships these Greeks remained a "marching democracy," fighting and voting their way through the darkest recesses of the Persian Empire. They suffered casualties of nearly 60 percent lost or killed, and yet they showed the world that courage, endurance, and a commitment to independence could prevail over the strongest forms of Oriental despotism.

These were free Greeks who marched against Persia and they would only be governed by their own consent, following leaders of their own choosing. Each man, from private to general, insisted on his right to be heard in assembly and to be consulted in matters of common interest. They were men who loved to be persuaded by the logic of an argument and yet, in an instant, could succumb to the power of their collective emotions and stone to death the very men they had chosen to lead them. At times they embodied what the Athenian philosopher Socrates feared most about a democracy: its propensity to degenerate into a mob. Yet all the power of the Persian Empire was unable to subdue this democratic army.

The leader of the Greek mercenaries was Xenophon, an Athenian among Spartans and a philosopher among soldiers. His name has never been placed on the list of history's great commanders. In fact, Xenophon was not a soldier by training, experience, or inclination, but came forward only when the Greeks endured their greatest crises. He kept them together and brought them through their darkest hours. He was an educated man who became general of an army of hardened mercenaries, and he was a leader who relied on reason and persuasion rather than force or fear.

What follows in this book is the story of the "Ten Thousand" and it is one of the greatest adventures ever told. It is a story that every eighteenth- and nineteenth-century British and American schoolboy once knew by heart in a time when Greek and Latin were required subjects in schools and considered the mark of a well-educated person. Times have changed and the study of ancient Greek has all but disappeared from public and most private school curricula. Latin has fared a little better than Greek but remains more for show in the few public schools that offer it rather than as a serious academic pursuit.

The story of these Greeks was recorded by their leader Xenophon in the fourth century B.C. in a work called the *Anabasis,* which is Greek for "expedition." It is one of the greatest treatises ever written on the conduct of ancient warfare, the strategy and tactics of retreat, the skill and difficulty of command, the treachery of politics and the complexity of human behavior. The manuscript was written in a form that characterizes the golden period of Greek literature. It is a simple yet elegant Greek that falls almost in the center of the period between the language of Homer and that of the New Testament. For that reason Xenophon was, until our own time, standard reading for students beginning the study of ancient Greek, just as Caesar's *Gallic Wars* was once the standard introduction to the literature of Latin.

The story of Xenophon and the Greek mercenaries who marched and fought their way through the Persian Empire deserves to be told once more in the hopes that younger generations might, at the very least, become motivated enough by reading it to consider taking something more than a brief glimpse into the vast treasure chest that is classical literature. Older readers are sure to enjoy rereading a classic from their youth that reminds us how little has changed over the centuries when it comes to war, politics, and human nature.

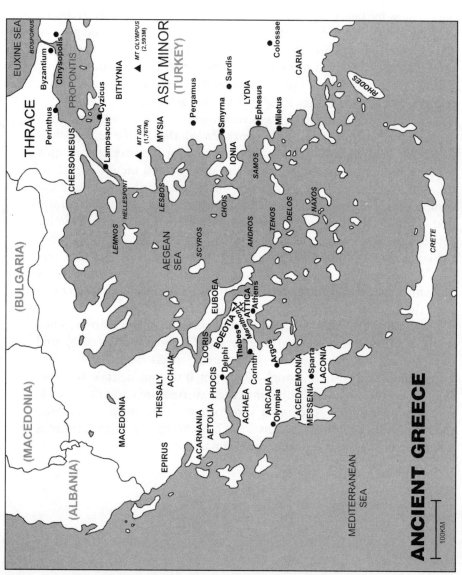

ANCIENT GREECE

The Regions and City-States of Fifth-Century Greece

I
THE GREEKS AND THE PERSIANS

By the end of the fifth century B.C., two civilizations stood apart from the rest of the Mediterranean world. One, under the rule of great kings, had achieved unprecedented wealth and power through conquest. The other consisted of citizens who resisted subjugation to any sovereign. One was monolithic, its continuing expansion driven from palaces in the territorial center of its empire. The other was fractious, divided into quarreling city-states that fought among themselves. One civilization flared briefly on the stage of history, leaving behind little but windswept stone or marble ruins to signify its former grandeur. The other left behind concepts of humanism and individualism that have endured as the philosophical foundations of political freedom to this day. When Xenophon and the Greek "Ten Thousand" began their march through the Persian Empire, few could have guessed the final outcome of the clash between these two civilizations, one which epitomized the ruling culture of the East and the other which founded the guiding principles of the West. But it was largely due to Xenophon that the mixture of awe and fear with which the Greeks viewed the Persians began to dissipate.

The Persians and the Greeks were the major players in the civilized world at this crucial stage of history, yet both peoples stemmed from modest roots and emerged rather suddenly into prominence. The significance of Xenophon can hardly be appreciated without a brief survey of the background of both the Persian Empire and Classical Greece and a mention of some of the important events that took place just prior to the epic march of the Ten Thousand.

What we know of Greek civilization extends much farther back in time than our knowledge of the Persians. Originally a branch of the Indo-European peoples, as traced by linguists, the first Greeks migrated south from the Danube region and became predominate in the third millennium B.C. in what is today the nation of Greece. Once they had arrived at the Mediterranean they encountered the Minoan culture, the origins of which are unknown but which had established a wealthy, advanced civilization based on the Aegean island of Crete. Archaeologists named this ancient civilization after King Minos, who, among other legendary deeds, reputedly kept a Minotaur in a labyrinth under his palace—perhaps located at Knossos on Crete. The Minoan culture was suddenly destroyed in the fifteenth century B.C. after a series of calamities that remain mysterious to modern scholars. Evidence points to earthquakes, followed by tidal waves that wiped out cities along the Cretan coast. Earlier, a huge volcanic eruption had caused most of the Minoan island of Thera to be buried by the sea— an event that some believe to be the germ of truth behind the legend of Atlantis. Thus weakened, the Minoans became easy prey for outside predators, and in 1430 B.C. even the city of Knossos with its vast palace complex was destroyed.

On the mainland, the early Greeks had benefited from close contacts with the Minoans to establish an advanced society of their own called the Mycenaean civilization, named after the city of Mycenae in the Peloponnese, the large peninsula that forms southern Greece. This bronze-age warrior culture was characterized by strong, fortified cities and kings who took elaborate weapons, armor, and treasure with them to the grave. The Mycenaeans inherited the Minoan trading network with the Egyptians and others on the Mediterranean rim, and they became great seafarers. Archaeologists can attest that the Mycenaean civilization was destroyed more gradually than the Minoan, but the cause, or combination of causes, is no less elusive. A catastrophic famine or drought leading to social upheaval cannot be ruled out; nor can the possibility that the civilization simply fought itself to death through internecine conflict. But the great destructive catalyst appears to have been a new wave of invaders from the north, called the Dorians. These Greeks, from the same branch of Indo-Europeans as the Mycenaeans, arrived in stages, and by 1200 B.C. had become culturally and linguistically dominant on the peninsula. The Ionic city of Athens, perhaps singularly, was able to resist the invaders, but the remainder of the Greek mainland was overrun. The foremost Doric city, which took shape from a confederation of five villages in the Peloponnese, was called Sparta.

At the same time the Mycenaeans were being overwhelmed, the

Hittite Empire in Anatolia (modern Turkey) was destroyed by waves of invaders, indicating that some form of upheaval farther north in Eurasia was forcing a widespread migration of nomadic peoples from their homelands. In the east, the invaders continued along the Mediterranean coast until they were finally stopped by the Egyptian Pharoah Rameses III at the Nile.

After the violent submergence of the Mycenaean civilization, Greece entered a long period of strife and poverty, called its Dark Age. These hundreds of years of vicious turmoil have remained largely impenetrable to historians, except for clear evidence of the destruction of Mycenaean splendor and a lack of new art or architecture. The practice of writing was lost, and men were said to have gone about their daily tasks armed with weapons. While gravesites from the older Mycenaean period reveal fine riches buried with the dead, graves from the Greek Dark Age contain only bones or modest belongings, frequently made of clay. During this period many Greeks took to the sea, founding new communities far from the Greek mainland. Egyptian accounts of piratical "sea peoples" during this time may refer in part to Mycenaean Greeks who raided and plundered Mediterranean coastal cities en route to finding new homes. Athens became the "mother city" to many new Greek communities founded in the Aegean and on the coast of Asia Minor.

The torch that finally illuminated the Greek Dark Age took the form of a blind poet named Homer, whose epic poems, told around 750 B.C., reminded everyone of the earlier glory of the Mycenaean era, which has often been called the Heroic Age. The primary focus of Homer's stories was a war fought by the united Greeks against a foreign city, Troy, one of whose princes had abducted the beautiful queen of Sparta. His tales evoked Greek heroism and patriotism in a common cause, and they provided vivid depictions of the Greek gods fully engaged with the world of mortals. His subthemes of individualism, self-determination, and the power of reason, particularly in his account of Odysseus's struggles against man, gods, monsters, and nature, ignited what were to emerge as the basic tenets of Greek culture.

Ironically, Homer, as well as the Greeks who listened to him, were all products of the Dark Age, and the oral history of a war fought half a millennium earlier was no doubt filtered through their cultural values. The Heroic Age, therefore, was an interpretation of the Mycenaean era as the Dorians viewed it through the prism of their own ideals. For centuries, historians assumed that the Trojan War, like many other tales in the rich trove of Greek mythology, was a legend, until in 1871 a German archaeologist, Heinrich Schliemann, identified the remains of Troy in Asia Minor near the Hellespont, a key trade route. His excavations proved that Troy had indeed been violently destroyed during the Mycenaean era, and many surrounding geographic features fit the descriptions in the epic poems. Homer was certainly taken seriously by his Greek audiences and by others for centuries after he wrote. In his *Histories*, Herodotus solemnly analyzes how Helen could not possibly have been present in Troy during the ten-year war (otherwise the Trojans would have handed her over); Alexander of Macedon took pains, upon entering Asia Minor in 336 B.C., to visit the Greek hero Achilles' grave.

It was around this time, too, that the Greeks rediscovered writing. They adopted the Phoenician alphabet, improving upon it by adding vowels, so that written Greek became the most accessible of the ancient world's written languages. In 776 B.C., the first Olympic Games were held, to which all Greeks, and only they, were invited. Politically, the Greeks were not a nation, but through language, custom, religion, and—through Homer—common heritage, they had gained a sense of cultural unity.

The period from 750 to 500 B.C. is called the Archaic Age, during which the Greeks became organized into a loose coalition of independent city-states that was unique to the Mediterranean world. The concept of monarchy rapidly died out and political power began to be transferred to individual citizens. Though there are estimated to have been hundreds of small cities and towns in Greece that were politically independent and managed their affairs with considerable participation by their citizens, five principal ones stood out among the rest and came to dominate the Greek mainland: Athens, Sparta, Thebes, Argos, and Corinth. The subsequent history of domestic Greece from the time of the Iliad and Odyssey of Homer in the eighth century B.C. until the time of the Roman conquest in the second century B.C. was to be the history of the interrelations of these five.

Each city-state was called a polis, a political arrangement whereby a large town or city was linked with its surrounding countryside to form a sovereign state. These city-states ranged in size from a few hundred people in the more rural areas of Greece to as many as 40,000 adult male citizens in the largest cities—the figure estimated for the citizen population of Athens in 450 B.C. Each of these political entities within Greece had its own militia army, its own unique customs and laws, and its own governing bodies. Over the centuries the city-states developed various forms of semi-democratic government unique to their particular circumstances. Some developed into oligarchies ruled by landed aristocrats but most created councils of citizens to formulate their policies and laws.

As the "demos," or common people, in Greece gained more of a voice in the sixth century B.C., more broadly representative forms of democratic government began to emerge. The definition of "citizen," however, remained strict. Within each city-state, regardless of size, there was a basic distinction between citizens and the rest of the population: women, slaves, and foreigners. The citizens were the adult, property-owning males who dominated the polis and who in essence constituted the state.

While the city-states of mainland Greece often squabbled and fought among themselves, Greek society in general consisted of free men held together by a common philosophy and a strong sense of ethnic identity. The Greeks shared the same religious beliefs, worshiped the same gods at the sanctuaries of Delphi and Olympia, and came together for the Olympics and other periodic festivals to which all the city-states sent contestants. There was a sense among Greeks that while each of them belonged to his own city-state, they also enjoyed a broader sense of national identity. This cultural bond, with its underlying belief in individual freedom, set the Greeks apart from the monarchical or despotic world that surrounded them. The Greeks alone considered themselves free in the ancient world, and when their philosophy and way of life became threatened by hostile outside forces they put aside their regional differences and came together as one people to defend their culture and their country.

By the end of the sixth century B.C., the greatest threat to Greek freedom came from an ominous monolith that had risen far to the east and which had subsequently conquered every civilization in its path. This was the Persian Empire, and by the year 500 B.C. the greater part of the civilized world had come under its domination. The largest empire ever seen at that time, its borders had spilled from Asia into Africa, and then into Europe, to the Macedonian highlands that lay above Greece itself. In the east it stretched to India, and in the north to the central Asian steppes. In only half a century, the Persians had come to control the most developed, fertile, and wealthiest areas of the known world.

The Persians and their way of life symbolized all that was philosophically repulsive to the Greeks. The Greeks referred to the Persians contemptuously as "barbarians" and believed that "in Persia everyone is educated to be a slave and nobody stands up for himself." The Persian Empire was maintained by a system that exploited its subjects, channeled all wealth toward its center, and kept each man in his place through fear. To the Greeks the empire was a sea of nameless, faceless peasants prostrate before the image of one man. The entire political culture of the empire was oriented toward the support and exaltation of the "king of kings." The king was the center of the Persian universe and to him the lives of his subjects were a cheap and disposable commodity. Punishment for crimes against the person of the king, his family, his representatives, or his property was swift and severe. The concepts of citizenhood, democracy, or trial by jury were unknown to the Persians. Instead, the entire population was subject to death, flogging, or mutilation at the whim of a despotic sovereign. Only the wealth and pleasure of the king and the small circle that supported him mattered. All else was of little or no consequence beyond its value to be exploited.

It is seldom remembered today that the Persian Empire, described with awe in the works of Greek historians, in the Bible, and in countless ancient inscriptions from Egypt to India, was always a young empire, failing to exceed in longevity, for example, ancient Rome. Its formalistic monarchy did not leave behind a large trail of written history, so that most of what we know about Persia comes from outside observers, especially the Greeks, many of whom had a patriotic axe to grind. In fact, though the empire became unprecedented in its time for size, wealth, and strength, the Persians themselves were parvenues in ancient historical terms, a small people who made it big, primarily through the efforts of one family, and especially one individual.

Originally an Aryan people from the central Asian steppes, the Persians were nomads who by the early seventh century B.C. had established a kingdom called Persis, along the Zagros Mountains in southwestern Iran. There they fell into the sphere of a related Iranian people, the Medes, who had established a considerable empire. The

Persians became able subjects of the Medes, whose land stretched far to the north and east while its army pressed against the Babylonian and Lydian Empires to the west.

In 550 B.C., a Persian king, Cyrus, who may have had royal Median blood through his mother, revolted against the Median king, Astyages. The Persians were heavily outnumbered but had the advantage that Cyrus was a dynamic, charismatic leader, while Astyages was corrupt and strongly disliked by his people. At the climactic battle of the war, among the heights of the Zagros Mountains, much of the Median army defected to Cyrus. Astyages was captured and forced to cede his throne. Cyrus, whose Persian family was called the Achaemenes, assumed sovereignty over Media, and though he placed Persian nobles into positions of responsibility, he kept most of the Median infrastructure intact. To all outside appearances, the Median Empire had not been conquered by its ethnic cousins but it had clearly acquired aggressive new leadership. The words "Persian" and "Mede" are often cited together or interchangeably in ancient sources, and some contemporary writers, unfamiliar with the Persians, persistently referred to them as Medes.

Cyrus immediately took up Media's longstanding conflict with the Lydian Empire, whose territory lay in Anatolia, modern-day Turkey. The Lydian king, Croesus, whose wealth was said to be fabulous, fought the Persians to a standstill in a battle on the frontier. He then retired to his capital, Sardis, to wait out the winter. But Cyrus surprised him by following with his army, and the Persians took Sardis in 547 B.C. after a short siege. Croesus was reported to have burned himself alive on his throne when he realized all was lost. At that time a vital part of the Lydian Empire was the string of Ionian Greek cities along the coast of Asia Minor. Most of these offered to submit to Cyrus, but the Persian king dispatched troops to forcibly seize them.

After campaigning to the northeast, where he established the border of his empire on the Jaxartes River in the Eurasian steppe, Cyrus turned to Babylonia, the most formidable commercial and military power in the "cradle of civilization." The Babylonians had anticipated the threat by constructing the "Median Wall," twenty-feet thick and ninety-feet high, between the Tigris and Euphrates Rivers in the north. Cyrus got behind the wall and spent some time diverting the Tigris into a series of easily passable canals that would abet his further progress.

The king of Babylon at this time was an unpopular sovereign

named Nabonidus, who had stayed away from his kingdom for ten years, ostensibly on campaigns to the south. When he returned for the crisis, he further alienated his subjects by importing every statuary idol of a foreign god he could find, rather than trusting in the Babylonians's own god, Marduk. In 539 B.C. Cyrus met the Babylonian army at Opis, between the rivers, and defeated it. He then instructed a rebel Babylonian general to enter the capital to intimidate its population before his arrival. When Cyrus entered Babylon he was greeted as a savior, releasing the people from inept rule and restoring respect for their true god. Showing as much skill at diplomacy as on the battlefield, Cyrus publicly professed veneration for Marduk. He also released the Hebrew captives who had been held in the city as slaves. They were allowed to return to their homes in Canaan along with the treasures the Babylonians had looted from their temple in Jerusalem.

Babylon's empire had included much of the defunct Assyrian one, and its conquest gained the Persians an important bonus: the eastern Mediterranean coastline and its skilled maritime culture, collectively termed the Phoenicians. Just as the Greeks had extended their civilization across the northern rim of the Mediterranean, Aegean, and Black Seas, the Phoenicians had countered with maritime expansion along the southern Mediterranean, from North Africa to the Straits of Gibraltar, and thence backward along the southern coast of Spain. One of the Phoenician colonies, Carthage, would eventually threaten to dominate the entire Mediterranen world. In terms of shipbuilding, seamanship, and navigational skill, the Phoenicians ceded little to the Greeks, and in fact had taught them much of their expertise. And as the Phoenician cities came under Cyrus's rule, the formerly landlocked Persians gained the potential to become the foremost naval power in the Mediterranean.

Cyrus constructed his capital at Pasargadae in the Zagros Mountains of Iran, on the site of his initial victory over the Medes. It was built on a plateau at 6,000 feet above sea level, where stiff winds still chill to the bone and snow falls early and stays late. The imperial palace was an architectural marvel with walled parks, lodge gates guarded by great Assyrian winged bulls of stone, and an audience hall that was nearly two hundred feet in length. It was from here that Cyrus ruled his empire and inscribed above the entrance to his palace in three languages his tribute to himself and his own glory: "I am Cyrus, the King, the Achaemenid."

As the empire grew, Cyrus instituted a system of royal satraps or governors to rule each area on his behalf. To ensure the honesty and loyalty of his satraps, Cyrus kept their children at court, ostensibly to provide for their education, but in reality as hostages. In addition, he organized a network of spies throughout the empire known as the "eyes and ears of the king." These spies reported directly to the king on how efficiently and loyally matters were being administered to his benefit within each of the satrapies. Often these spies were financial officers assigned to the satrap, but answerable only to the king.

Cyrus died in 530 B.C. in a fight at the northeastern edge of his empire, termed by Herodotus the "most terrible battle ever fought." He was buried at Pasargadae in a somewhat modest tomb that remains to this day. Cyrus's career of conquest was one of the most spectacular in history and he fully deserved to be termed "the Great." Two centuries later, young King Alexander of Macedon, who would earn the same appellation, made a pilgrimage to his predecessor's tomb. The scope of Alexander's conquests more or less followed the blueprint first achieved by Cyrus, with the important exception that the Macedonian also conquered the Greeks. (It's tempting to get further ahead of our chronology at this point by mentioning that Alexander's impressions of Cyrus came largely from the written works of the Athenian warrior, historian, and philosopher Xenophon.)

Cyrus the Great was succeeded by his son, Cambyses, who lacked his father's charismatic personality and was said to be cruel. In one incident he killed the son of one of his courtiers just to show off his skill in archery. Nevertheless, Cambyses followed through on his father's plans and launched an invasion of Egypt, the oldest and most secure of the Mediterranean world's empires. With the fall of Egypt in 525 B.C., the Greek colony of Cyrene in Libya and the island of Cyprus fell into his hands. Cambyses also marched his army far enough south into Africa to receive tribute from the kingdom of Kush (Nubia). His three-year expedition was successful and the mighty Egyptians, along with the Medes, Babylonians, Lydians, the remains of the Assyrians, and countless other peoples sullenly succumbed to Persian rule.

Cambyses died before he could return from his Egyptian expedition, triggering the first of a number of bloody succession intrigues that would eventually weaken the empire. Since he had not left an heir and his brother had been murdered (perhaps by Cambyses himself before he left for Egypt), his throne was occupied by an Achaemenid

cousin, Darius, who went to great pains to propagandize his legiti-
macy, but whose first task was to put down a series of revolts against
his rule. Fortunately for the Persians, Darius proved to be fully worthy of Cyrus's mantle.

Darius improved upon the administrative foundation established
by Cyrus and Cambyses. He codified Persian law and issued an
"Ordinance of Good Regulations" to provide consistent administrative practices throughout the empire. This was a code of imperial
edicts intended to organize and regulate the many provinces or
satrapies of the domain. Darius took great pride in his laws and maintained they were superior to the ones issued centuries earlier by the
Babylonian King Hammurabi. (Most scholars have no doubt but that
he copied much of Hammurabi's Code.) To provide for his own personal security and that of successor Persian kings, Darius formed an
elite military unit called the "Immortals." These were soldiers dedicated to the protection of the king who pledged their lives to serve as
his bodyguard.

Darius established a single monetary unit for the empire, the daric,
and instituted a system of weights and measures for the regulation of
commerce. In addition he improved the infrastructure of the empire
through a series of irrigation projects and paved royal roads. The road
system was designed to unite the empire, and just as five centuries later
"all roads would lead to Rome," so with the Persians, all roads were
designed to bring wealth into the center of the empire and extend military might to its fringes. The longest stretch of road, almost 1,700
miles, became the royal highway from Sardis in Asia Minor to Susa in
Iran. These roads, together with a royal courier service (the ancestor
of the American West's Pony Express), facilitated communication and
enabled Darius to ensure an uninterrupted flow of tribute from even
the most remote satrapies to his capital.

The most important task of Cyrus's successors, however, remained
that of expanding the empire. Shortly after consolidating his power in
521 B.C., Darius fought a successful campaign against barbarians to
the northeast, near the Caspian Sea. He then turned to India, establishing his border along the Indus River. Afterward, this area became
the empire's greatest source of wealth, especially in gold.

In 513 B.C., Darius crossed the Bosporus Strait into Europe and
marched through present-day Bulgaria. He flirted with calamity, however, when he led the Persian army north of the Danube River in order

to subdue the Scythian "horse people" who had constantly annoyed and raided civilized territory. Steppe warriors, among whom the Scythians were only precursors to greater scourges such as the Mongols, possessed deadly skill at arms while having no settled culture of their own to protect. They could retreat day upon day, leaving nothing but the dung of their horses and the tracks of their wagons behind, while a marching army of civilized pursuers found itself more isolated, beleaguered, and weaker with each step. For two months the Persians disappeared in the steppe along the Black Sea, perhaps going as far as the southern Ukraine. The Ionian Greeks, whom Darius had ordered to build and hold his bridge across the Danube, were about to withdraw, harried by Scythians and having assumed the Persian army had been destroyed, when Darius suddenly appeared, returning from the north. If Darius had returned one day later, his army would have been trapped against the Danube and he would have joined Crassus of Rome, Boris of Constantinople, and other commanders to come, who saw their civilized armies obliterated by the mobile horse-archer armies of the steppe.

The Greek historian Herodotus derided the wisdom of Darius's invasion of the Scythians's domain, but the fact that the Persian army emerged from its ordeal across the Danube intact engendered respect. Darius had marched as far north in Europe as his predecessor, Cambyses, had marched south in Africa, and he had secured the Bosporus, extending Persia's border hundreds of miles. There were no lands or people on earth, it appeared, that could feel safe from the might of the Persian king.

The Persians had proven adept at conquering the older empires of the Mediterranean world, but they had no significant civilization of their own to layer it with a new culture. Instead, they rode herd as martial overlords of artisans, craftsmen, bureaucrats, and accountants of civilizations that had come before. Of their great cities, Babylon had been a commercial and political center for centuries; Ecbatana had been the Median capital; Susa the capital of the former Elamite Empire; and Sardis the imperial seat of the Lydians. When Darius decided to establish a new imperial city at Persepolis, its architecture reflected a hodgepodge of styles from Assyrian to Egyptian to Ionic and Doric Greek. Persepolis, constructed near to, but at a more comfortable altitude than, Cyrus's capital Pasargadae in the Zagros, nevertheless rose as an awe-inspiring tribute to Persian grandeur. It was

not meant to be a cosmopolitan city but rather an imperial retreat and
storehouse of Persian wealth. Later, after being sacked and burned by
Alexander's Greek army in 331 B.C., its remote location discouraged
the founding of additional cities on the site, so that the ruins of
Persepolis, carefully nurtured by archaeologists, are among the most
impressive that remain today from this period of history.

Economically, subjugation by the Persians resulted in initial benefits to the conquered peoples. The conquests had dissolved borders
between previous states and commerce now proceeded unobstructed
from India to the Mediterranean. The Persians were tolerant of other
nations' religions (witness how reluctantly Darius threw Daniel into
the lions' den) and were more interested in prosperity than repress-
sion. The Phoenician cities that had chafed under Babylonian rule now
found free rein under the Persians. Shipbuilding, trade, and its consequent expansion of wealth and empire were heartily encouraged under
the Achaemenids. As the decades passed and the Persian Empire
reached its zenith, it became, as at least two reliable ancient sources
have written, "the meeting ground of the great cultures of the ancient
world."

The one cultural element that the Persians enforced upon their
huge empire was veneration for their king. In private ceremonies at
Pasargadae when assuming the throne, Persian kings donned Cyrus's
old robes and ate a fig and sour milk, symbols of their humble past.
But in public, the Persians insisted on a level of obeisance designed to
enhance their newfound stature. Elaborate court ceremonies were
devised, beginning with the notorious requirement, despised by the
Greeks, that visitors prostrate themselves in the royal presence.

From the Greeks' perspective, one man's prostration before another was antithetical to their philosophy. From a modern perspective, it
is difficult to see how a Persian king was able to rule if his subjects
were perpetually on their hands and knees, or afraid to laugh, cough,
or even look at him directly. Without a doubt, Cyrus, Cambyses, and
Darius had all engaged in heated debates with their advisers while on
military maneuvers and even in administrative matters on how best to
govern the empire. The great king, if he was effective, was not an
unapproachable demigod but an active innovator or arbiter of new
initiatives, projects, and campaigns. Still, from the point of view of
foreign emissaries, the image of the king of Persia—almighty and
placidly infallible—was real enough and has endured through history.

This was an image the Persians themselves sought for their king, and their demand for obeisance, as well as riches, was the primary demand they made upon the older civilizations they now possessed. The Persians had been able to harness the power of several ancient empires, a number of formidable peoples, and countless smaller tribes into the greatest empire ever known. By the year 500 B.C. they controlled all but the farthest reaches of the known world. And one of those far reaches, the Balkan Peninsula, across the Aegean Sea from Asia Minor, was the homeland of the Greeks.

In the same century that saw Persia envelop the civilizations of the East with its relentless autocracy, the Greeks were undergoing their own political and cultural transformations in the West. There the trend continued toward empowering individuals, and absolute monarchy had all but disappeared. In part, the experience in Greece stemmed from its geography. Unlike the flat, fertile plains of Near Asia—the breeding ground for countless empires and just as many ancient conquerors—Greece was a rough, mountainous country, naturally divided into segments, with little natural wealth. The soil that nurtured democracy and allowed philosophy to take root has never been able to feed the people who live on it; Greece in ancient times as well as today is a land of rocks, often susceptible to poverty. But the same nature that created Greece's mountains also carved harbors and inlets, providing access to maritime trade. Unable to live off their own land, the ancient Greeks, like their modern descendants, turned to the sea to make a living and to distant lands to find their fortunes.

Trade by sea for the Greeks flourished during the seventh and sixth centuries B.C. and they began to establish colonies along the coasts of the more prosperous and fertile lands that their ships visited. When they expanded west, the Persians would find strong, established Greek cities along the fringe of their empire. There are indications of Greek settlements along the Aegean coast of Turkey and the nearby islands as early as 750 B.C. The Greeks settled as well along the Turkish shores of the Black Sea and along the coasts of southern Russia, where they established thriving towns as early as 600 B.C. Greek colonies were created as far south as the coasts of Syria, Egypt, and Libya, and as far west as southern Italy, the island of Sicily, and the Mediterranean coasts of France and Spain.

Over the years, many of these colonies and trading posts developed into prosperous cities, yet they retained a strong sense of ethnic identity and cultural ties with the mainland Greeks. The democratic winds that swept the mainland also reached the colonies that were situated closer to the lands of the barbarians. Wherever they lived, Greeks came to consider themselves free men, who could only be governed by their own consent.

By the fifth century B.C., many of these cities, especially those along the western and northern coastlines of modern-day Turkey, had advanced in terms of culture and architecture to such an extent that they rivaled and may even have surpassed most of the famous cities on the Greek mainland. Nothing makes this point more dramatically than a visit to any of the Greek ruins in southwestern Turkey, such as Ephesus, Sardis, or Hierapolis. These sites are magnificent and rival in scale and architectural beauty anything one can see in Greece.

The largest Greek city, however, and the one that led the evolution of Greek political thought, was Athens, situated near the east coast of mainland Greece, north of the Peloponnese. Like many of the city-states, Athens in the very early years of her political development had been ruled by kings. Sometime in the early part of the seventh century the last king was replaced with an elected magistrate, and within a few decades the government had expanded to include nine magistrates or *archons*. In 594 B.C. the Athenians elected an astute archon, Solon, and entrusted him with extraordinary dictatorial powers. Solon published an entire *juris corpus*, adding his own suggestions to the existing body of Athenian laws and customs. He organized the Athenians into four propertied classes with political criterion based on holdings and income rather than on hereditary titles of nobility. From the upper classes a council was formed called the Areopagus after the large rock in the center of Athens on which it met to debate the course of government.

Solon took the first steps in leading the Athenians toward democracy. He recognized the grievances of the poor and provided mechanisms within the state to resolve or at least accommodate them. The remarkable thing about Solon is that he had no army at his disposal and fulfilled his mission of restructuring the Athenian government through arbitration and persuasion. When his work was done Solon placed himself in voluntary exile for ten years and made the Athenians swear they would not change or modify his laws during his absence.

The rule of Solon was followed by the tyranny of Peisistratus from 560 to 527 B.C., roughly concurrent with Cyrus's reign as king of Persia. An Athenian general who governed Athens with an iron hand, Peisistratus proved over the years to be a humane ruler, patron of the arts, and urban developer. As a tyrant he held power without legal sanction but he could not be termed an oppressor. He drew his support largely from the poorer classes and undertook a popular redistribution of land that he had seized from his political opponents. Under his rule the Athenians continued to use their democratic institutions, the archons continued in office, and the council continued to meet on the Areopagus. What Peisistratus developed for Athens during his long tenure was a form of paternalistic "guided democracy." He stood at the helm as the Athenian ship of state sailed through the then-uncharted political waters toward democracy.

Another ruler, Cleisthenes, came to power several years later and established a lower council of five hundred members to exist beside the Areopagus council. In time, the lower council came to overshadow the Areopagus in importance. By the fifth century B.C., the number of male citizens qualified by income to serve in the lower council is estimated to have been around 15,000. This meant that there was a fair chance that every eligible man in Athens would serve on the council once during his lifetime. This gave every citizen a personal interest in supporting and participating in the democratic process.

Once a year the Athenians invoked a procedure known as ostracism. In this the Athenians voted on broken pieces of pottery called *ostraca* to condemn the man they considered the greatest threat to the city for that year. The unfortunate citizen was then sent into exile for ten years while his family and property remained in the hands of the Athenians. He could reclaim both family and property if he fulfilled the terms of his exile and returned to Athens.

In military service, the Athenians provided for the election of ten generals each year to direct their armed forces. Once elected general a citizen could retain this post year after year. The dominance in Athenian military life of men like Cimon, Pericles, and Nicias for long periods was based on their reelection to this important post.

The Athenian legal system revolved around a system of juries chosen from a panel of many citizens. This panel supplied the various courts with their necessary jurors and the jurors were paid a modest sum each day for their service. The juries were omnipotent as there was no controlling body of statute law and no judge who could direct their verdicts. There was no appeal from the jury of peers. The decisions of the citizens were final.

The political evolution in Athens—from kings, to tyrants and oligarchs, to democracy—was duplicated elsewhere in Greece, and by the end of the sixth century B.C. all the major Greek cities had adopted some form of democratic government. One city, however, had undergone a parallel social evolution of its own, and would emerge as Athens's greatest rival for supremacy in the Greek world.

Sparta was a polis that continued to have two hereditary kings, each of whose family was said to have descended from Hercules. But the Spartans, while anachronistic in some respects, were revolutionary in others, in a militaristic vein, and were admired by many Greeks. The city had a full assembly of citizens, a council of twenty-eight elders, which joined the two kings in deliberations, and, most powerful of all, a board of five citizens called ephors elected by the assembly who were the true policymakers of the state. The kings, rather than governing, were expected to perform religious ceremonies and be generals of the army, though if they proved inadequate in warfare the Spartans would not hesitate to elevate other generals.

The Spartans attributed their system to a ninth-century B.C. lawgiver named Lycurgus, whose life is shrouded in myth. But the Lycurgian system proved to be the most stable in Greece, and Sparta, unlike Athens, never suffered tyrants or oligarchic coups. Sparta's credos were order and discipline; its men were required to devote their lives to the army, and its infantry came to epitomize military skill. The Spartans were a people whose rigid character made it difficult for them to function comfortably in a fully democratic society such as developed in Athens, yet they did not stand completely apart from the Greek ethos of individual freedom. As one historian has commented, the Spartans accepted an "inoculation of democracy" to guard against an outbreak of the full disease.

The factor underlying Sparta's militarization was its decision to hold down a vast slave population that included fellow Greeks. While other Greek city-states sought prosperity through trade or by establishing colonies overseas, Sparta simply conquered its neighboring region, Messene, and held the Messenians, termed helots, as serfs to work the land and feed the Spartan population. This not only freed Spartan citizens to develop skill at arms but forced them to do so, because the helots often rose in bloody rebellions. Each year the

Spartans made a formal declaration of war against the helots, and Spartan men never stopped training in order to be strong enough to keep their slave population in its degraded status.

The Spartan systems of education and military training were incredibly rigid, and private life or family life apart from the state was practically nonexistent. Life was regulated by the state from birth to death. Infants were inspected by government officials shortly after they were born and those deemed not strong enough to make good soldiers or healthy mothers when they matured were left to die on top of a mountain. Spartans were taught from early childhood that theft was an art to be cultivated and practiced. Those who were caught stealing were severely punished, not for the theft but for the crime of getting caught. As part of their training, boys were sent as spies among the helot population to identify potential rebel leaders.

A Spartan male spent almost his entire life in the military. From the age of seven, when he first entered a troop, until the age of sixty, when he retired and was at last freed from military obligations, a Spartan's entire life was oriented toward war. The males ate and lived together in barracks during their prime. They ate a bland form of gruel, kept conversation to a minimum, and the younger ones were forced to sleep naked outdoors. The Spartans valued a man who spoke little and accomplished much. (The modern word "laconic" derives from Laconia, the region that surrounded Sparta, just as Attica surrounded Athens. The territory immediately around the city of Sparta was called Lacedaemon so that ancient sources frequently refer to the Spartans as Lacedaemonians.) People who lived in Sparta's territories were called *perioki* ("those who dwell about") and were free men but without the rights of citizens. The perioki would flesh out the ranks of a Spartan army in battle.

Helots had no rights whatsoever but could be used as baggage handlers or camp slaves. In times of crisis, as during the Persian invasion, they could even be made to serve with the army as soldiers. This may sound like a dangerous option for the Spartans, but it was safer to bring helots with the army on campaign than leave them at home unattended where they might rebel again. Even the Spartan women were required to keep in excellent physical condition in order to bear healthy children for the state. Ironically, in a society known for repression, Spartan females were what one today would call the most "liberated" in the Greek world.

The Spartans gained a fierce reputation as fighters, as their iron-clad discipline and non-stop training gave them a distinct advantage over other armies. Their warrior ethos also provided a certain psychological edge. For a Spártan in war there were only two choices: either to return home carrying his shield in victory or to be brought home upon it in death. The Spartan system, though harsh, was unquestionably effective. By the fifth century B.C. the Spartans had become the most feared ground soldiers in the ancient world. Their system made no allowance for individuality and it stifled artistic creativity and intellectual endeavor. Whereas the Athenian system had its flaws and eccentricities, it produced magnificent examples of literature, architecture, art, philosophy, and science. Sparta, in contrast, became a military machine that produced warriors who lived only to fight. The Spartan infantry, however, was only the most formidable in a Greece that had collectively revolutionized the ancient world's combat tactics.

Just as important as political developments and the growing economic strength of city-states during the sixth century B.C. was the evolution of Greek warfare. Previously, and as continued to be practiced in the East, combat took place largely at a distance, waged with missile weapons on a fluid battlefield where each side probed and parried, hesitant to come to close grips unless an opponent was vulnerable. The Greek innovation was to institutionalize shock tactics: direct, close-quarters combat wedded to strict unit discipline and state-of-the-art equipment. The geography of Greece had an important influence on tactics. During centuries of warfare between city-states in a land that was 90 percent mountainous, the Greeks found little use for long-range projectiles, cavalry, or prolonged battles of maneuver. Instead, opposing Greek forces would simply meet on a suitable field and decide the issue at close hand in a quick, violent test of strength. These direct confrontational tactics, honed after decades of incessant warfare with fellow Greeks, proved overwhelming when the Greeks turned to fight the more traditional armies of other lands.

A Greek army during this period was composed primarily of infantry called hoplites, after the *hoplon*, a round shield some three feet in diameter. In addition to the large, convex shield strapped to his left arm, each hoplite carried a spear of six to seven feet in length and wore armor consisting of a helmet, breastplate, and greaves (below the knees). A short sword for close combat was carried as an auxiliary weapon. During the Trojan War, similarly armed heroes would ride to battle in chariots and then dash among the enemy, or flee and then advance again according to wild swings of combat fortune. By the sixth century B.C., Greek individualism in warfare had been sublimated into the unit, and the key to hoplite warfare had become maintaining strict discipline in a tactical formation called the phalanx.

Looked at head-on, a phalanx was a long, moving wall of shields and armor, with iron-barbed spears protruding forward. Each man would be protected not only by his own shield, but in part by the shield of the man next to him, while his right hand was free to thrust his spear at the enemy with all his strength. It was vital that close formation be maintained so as not to leave any openings for the enemy to exploit, and to apply pressure across the entire enemy line. The phalanx would typically consist of eight successive ranks of soldiers, though its depth could vary depending on terrain or tactics. The first two ranks of the phalanx were the ones that participated in the combat while the remaining ranks served as replacements for the dead and wounded. In addition, the supporting ranks provided moral encouragement for the men who were fighting and, if need be, physical pressure through shoving to advance the line of battle. Thus a deeper phalanx could hope to overcome a more shallow one when push came to shove, even if both sides had the same number of men in actual combat.

Tactically, the phalanx was relatively inflexible, though commanders could apportion more depth to the center or flanks in advance. Once combat was joined, the outcome would be a matter of strength, endurance, or whichever side was best able to conquer its fear with fierce determination. The men in the rear ranks of the phalanx, who would almost never arrive at the point of combat, probably did not wear the complete protective armament of the soldiers in front. It was in the rear ranks that the weaker and more inexperienced soldiers, and even slaves, would be placed for their value in giving the phalanx mass. The rear ranks were also of use in helping to care for the wounded, and by killing any of the enemy who had fallen beneath the crowd or who by chance had broken through.

Greek armies also included light troops, called peltasts, armed with bows, slings, or javelins, as well as small shields and hand weapons. The peltasts would act as a skirmish line to harass an approaching enemy, but once the opposing phalanxes met they would slip to the flanks. During the clash of hoplites the peltasts would jostle with their counterparts on the other side, unless or until the enemy's phalanx broke, and then, being unencumbered by armor, they would be quickest to pursue the beaten foe. Horses were fairly rare in Greece so what small cavalry forces existed would be useful in reconnaissance or pursuit rather than during the main clash of arms. The Greek hoplite had a heavy load of equipment to carry and he was responsible for his own supplies while on the march. The hoplite was usually accompanied by a slave or porter. These porters, armed at most with a dagger in their belt or perhaps a light spear, foraged for their masters, cooked, cleaned clothes, and repaired weapons.

From ancient art, we have a clear idea of what a phalanx looked like. The wild, individualistic paintings on the shields, sharp, plumed helmets, glistening bronze armor, and iron weapons must have made a more fearsome impression than could be described in words. But the degree to which intra-Greek warfare was determined by protocol, or ritual, remains a matter of conjecture. In one battle between Sparta and Argos, both sides designated three hundred men to fight, as if it were a lethal sporting match. In more typical clashes, both sides would perform animal sacrifices before battle, and ground may often have been chosen by mutual consent in advance. Surprise attacks, ambushes, night attacks, or even flanking maneuvers were rare. When two armies met in an open field, one commander might choose to thin the depth of his phalanx in order to gain greater width, but the corresponding commander would be compelled to do likewise. Phalanx formations were extremely vulnerable in the flank, so in confrontational battles it was essential to match the enemy's breadth of front. In intra-Greek warfare, pursuit of a beaten enemy was not a high priority; winning the brief, violent test of strength was considered enough, rather than attempting to annihilate defeated countrymen. Of course, passion knows no rules and in some wars between city-states utter ruthlessness held sway.

When describing Greek warfare, it is essential to distinguish between battles among Greeks, in which certain conventions normally applied, and those between Greeks and others, such as the Persians. To the Persians, who relied heavily on archery, the grim determination of a Greek phalanx relentlessly closing to arm's length was terrifying. If the Greek shield wall could underrun the initial rain of arrows—a process that might take four minutes—utter carnage would ensue.

Eastern infantry, as a rule, were not as heavily armored as the Greeks and, more important, were untrained to withstand the psychological travail of standing in tight, disciplined ranks, hacking and killing until the opposing line broke. But the Persians, unconstrained by the conventions of intra-Greek warfare, had certain advantages. Their bowmen and other missile throwers could fight without coming to actual grips. To counter them, Greek peltasts may have played a more valuable role in foreign expeditions than they did in hoplite battles. The Persians were not adverse to surprise, and they also possessed a large cavalry arm, drawing on the Bactrians, Parthians, and other skilled horse warriors, to which the Greeks were vulnerable because cavalry could easily turn the flanks of a phalanx. Persian elites such as the Immortals were as well-equipped as any opponent, and Persian armies were invariably larger than Greek ones.

The greatest danger to a foreign army would occur if the Greeks were allowed to close, because no other armies in the ancient world preferred such violent, close-quarters combat. Once in the face of an enemy, a Greek phalanx started forward slowly, to the rhythm of drums or flutes. The hoplites would chant a paean in unison, calling upon one of their gods for victory. They would move forward methodically, the shield wall keeping in one straight line. Then, as the phalanx came near the enemy, the Greeks would break into a run, shouting their fierce war cry. By that time, a foreign enemy to their front was usually in flight.

In Asia, the Persian achievement of forging the largest empire in the history of the known world was not mysterious, except insofar as the qualities that comprise dynamic leadership will always remain elusive. The Persians's success had an arithmetic logic, in that the more peoples they conquered, either through leverage or "hostile takeovers," the stronger they became and thus the more vulnerable their next prey. The fact that they did not have an oppressive culture or religion of their own to force upon their subjects, but instead looked to take advantage of the skills of older civilizations to enhance their empire, helped them to consolidate power. In modern business terms, the Persians were a conglomerate that absorbed older, more skillful regional powers on the sole condition that the bulk of revenue flow back to headquarters. Their main expertise was administrative, ensuring the capital flow. As long as the empire expanded it would be healthy. The greatest danger to the Persians was inertia: the prospect that they would stop striving for new goals and instead fall back comfortably on the wealth and status they had already earned.

The Greeks were no less expansionist than the Persians, but their growth could be measured not just in territorial or economic terms but in the growth of their cultural and political institutions, and their new method of waging war. If Persia was an acquisitive conglomerate, the Greek world was a burgeoning, original enterprise, not building upon prior achievements but with a vast, untapped potential that sprung from within.

History has provided a number of examples of peoples living in remote, poor, mountainous lands who developed both a high degree of martial skill and a taste for freedom, even to the point of remaining internally divided. The Highland clans of Scotland, the cantons of Switzerland, and the tribes of Afghanistan all reflect this dual characteristic of cultures nurtured in mountainous terrain. But the homeland of the Greeks featured a twist. Their rocky, forbidding territory was replete with excellent harbors, and was situated at the maritime crossroads of the ancient world. The Greeks could remain irascible and unconquerable among their heights but at the same time could become rich, and enriched, by the commerce, culture, art, and philosophy of other civilizations. A fierce mountain people in one aspect, they were in a unique position to use their foundation of freedom to become the most advanced artistic and political culture of the ancient world.

Greek culture, or Hellenism, however, would have to pass through two crucibles before it could become the basic foundation of Western Civilization. One challenge would arise from the Persian Empire, the largest concentration of power the ancient world had ever seen; the other would come from the Greeks' own inability to stop fighting among themselves.

II
THE TUMULTUOUS
FIFTH CENTURY B.C.

It was inevitable that when the Persian Empire began to overlap the burgeoning world of Greek trading cities, bitter conflict would follow. Long before the Persians had embarked on their string of conquests, the Greeks had become firmly established throughout the Aegean Sea and along the coast of Asia Minor. These cities, as a visit to modern Turkey will attest, were no less impressive than city-states on the Greek peninsula, and their citizens at the time were no less imbued with Hellenic values. Today, the political map of Greece still spans the Aegean and includes islands off the coast of Turkey, from Lesbos and Kos to Rhodes, and as far south as Cyprus. In the fifth century B.C., the Greek world also encompassed large footholds on the Asian mainland.

The impetus of Greek expansion was more commercial than imperical. Anywhere on a foreign shore that a convenient harbor could be established for merchant ships, along with a conduit for trade from inland, Greeks were quick to seize the opportunity, supplanting existing villages, if necessary, and subsequently creating prosperous towns and cities. Copper and tin (the elements of bronze), iron, and timber were important resources to be found abroad, thence shipped to the city-states on the Greek mainland. Wine, dyes, salt, incense, textiles, pottery, and, of course, gold and silver, also did a flourishing trade. Many colonists chose sites abroad for rich farmland, a rarity in Greece, and the mainland came to rely on imported food. The richest were the source of foodstuffs in colonies established along the Black Sea coast. For this reason, the narrow straits that form the entrance to the Black Sea from the Aegean were of vital importance.

The Greek cities of Asia Minor, or the Ionian Coast, had come under Lydian rule in the sixth century B.C., but the Lydians were unoppressive. They had, in fact, invented minted coins, an innovation that the Ionian Greeks helped to spread throughout the ancient world. But when Cyrus the Great defeated wealthy King Croesus, and militant Persians from the East supplanted the Lydians, the Ionian Greeks grew restless. The Persian system was to delegate rule in their provinces to satraps, who had a high degree of autonomy. Within a province the satrap would designate tyrants to rule specific cities, and officials to oversee trade. Their primary goals were tax collection for the king and enrichment for the local ruling class. Just when mainland Greece began to blossom in terms of its innate power and its politics devoted to citizens' rights, the Ionian cities were forced to chafe beneath the rule of autocratic eastern barbarians. In 499 B.C. they rebelled.

The city of Miletus, which had never given in to the Lydians, and had been taken only with difficulty by Cyrus, led the revolt. It soon spread along the coast and even the Carians in southern Asia Minor joined in. Prior to taking up arms against the Persians, the Ionians had sent emissaries to the Greek mainland to ask for support, and Athens and the city of Eretria had responded with ships and troops. The rebels, assisted by their fellow Greeks, attacked Sardis, the primary Persian city in Anatolia, and burned it.

The mainland Greeks who came to the aid of their kinsmen on the coast of Turkey were not entirely motivated by altruism. The Greeks of the fifth century B.C., both on the mainland and elsewhere, had developed their own concept of Hellenism. This spirit held that the entire Greek world, though internally divided, was culturally and politically inviolable to barbarians. Communally they viewed the outside world as uncivilized, and notions of Greek cultural and intellectual superiority were used to justify expansion, both east and west. In the east, Persian control of the straits leading to the Black Sea, accomplished with Darius's march to the Danube in 513 B.C., was considered a dangerous development. The Athenians and Eretrians called back their forces after the fall of Sardis, but it remained of keen interest to all Greeks whether the Ionians could succeed in their revolt.

Darius was no stranger to uprisings in his domain, and by 494 B.C. he had crushed the rebellion. At first he left the matter to local satraps, but then the empire began to pour in troops who engaged in a number of sieges. The peninsular city of Miletus was strongly barricaded on the land side, so it relied on sea power for sustenance and battle defense. When the Ionian fleet was decisively defeated by the Persians navy, the backbone of the rebellion was broken. The Persian fleet sailed up the coast, all the way to Byzantium at the mouth of the Black Sea, bringing each successive Greek city to heel.

Once victorious, Darius had the good sense to revamp his bureaucracy in Asia Minor, replacing some local tyrants with more flexible rulers, and he even encouraged democracy in Greek cities that had risen in revolt under tyrants. The Persians often displayed tolerance toward their subjects' local culture, politics, or religion, as long as obedience to the king was observed and tax revenue flowed uninterrupted. But in this case, Darius was looking to pacify and solidify a new base of operations. It had become clear that the empire's western borders would never be secure as long as Athens and other city-states across the Aegean were free to meddle in Persian affairs. The bloody experience in Ionia aroused in Darius a desire for revenge on the Greeks across the Aegean who had supported the revolt and whose homeland had thus far remained beyond Persian grasp.

In 492 B.C., Darius dispatched Mardonius, a young kinsman who was one of his best generals, to seize Thrace, the region along the north of the Aegean, and Macedonia, a large territory populated by rustic Greeks that lay just above the Hellenic city-states. Mardonius accomplished his task and Darius then sent envoys to the Greek city-states to demand recognition of his authority. Their request was for "earth and water," symbolic signs of submission to the king.

In fractious Greece, a number of city-states complied with the envoys' demands, on the theory that the faraway Persian king could have little influence on their lives, and might even prove to be a valuable ally in their local feuds or in matters of trade. The two most powerful Greek city-states, however, were defiant. When the Persian ambassadors arrived in Athens with Darius's demand for earth, the Athenians threw them into a pit and told them to dig for the Persian king. When a Persian delegation arrived in Sparta to present the great king's demands for water, the Spartans threw them into a well and told them to drink their fill. Darius had received his answer, and the Persians and Greeks were now at war.

In 490 B.C. Darius dispatched a huge fleet across the Aegean Sea. It conquered the Greek island of Naxos, and stopped at other islands on the way to take slaves and seize young children as hostages. It then descended on Eretria, on the large island of Euboea, just off the Greek mainland. The Persian army sacked Eretria, killed all the Greek defenders, and took the women and children who survived as slaves. The Persian expeditionary force then landed on the mainland, near a place called Marathon, just a day's march north of Athens.

The Athenians and Spartans had agreed to jointly defend their homeland against the foreign invasion. But when the Athenians sent urgent word to their allies in the Peloponnese that the Persians had landed, the Spartans were in the midst of a religious ceremony and said they could not leave their city for another week. About 9,000 Athenian hoplites, joined by a thousand men from a nearby ally, Plataea, marched out to confront the Persians by themselves.

The sight of the Persian host must have been astounding to the citizen soldiers of Athens. It was an army far larger than their own (estimates begin at 15,000 troops) and its exotic dress, variety of weapons, and mix of different peoples inspired awe. The Persians had also brought cavalry, in specially built horse transports, and the size of their fleet far exceeded any that the Greeks could assemble. Most impressive was that the Persians, once aroused, could land a multinational army of trained warriors on Greek soil merely at the whim of the great king. The Greeks, in contrast, had no formal unity and the citizens of Athens, along with the few men from Plataea, had been left to contest the invasion alone. In observing the Greek army mingling before them, the Persians were probably not as impressed. It had no cavalry, few archers, and the men who camped to their front looked unaggressive and outnumbered.

The Athenians had the option to wait for the Spartans to arrive, but in the meantime Persian diplomacy or intimidation might work its way through the oligarchists in Athens, and earn new allies among other city-states. The Athenian system of placing their army under ten elected generals caused further hesitation. Finally, the leadership of the army fell to a general named Miltiades and he saw that the Persian cavalry had left its main force and were either off foraging or put back aboard ships. He decided to attack. In the early morning hours, the Greek hoplites donned their helmets and armor, strapped on their shields and formed into a phalanx. In order to match the length of the Persian front, Miltiades thinned out his center so that the Greek formation was strongest on its wings.

The Athenians began to stalk across the plain toward the enemy. When they approached arrow range they broke into a run. They maintained a tight formation, seemingly oblivious to the clouds of missiles urgently dispatched by the Persian archers and slingers. The Persians had never seen this kind of attack and thought a "madness" had inspired the Greeks. The wall of shields and spears raced straight toward them, and amid the din of ten thousand voices shouting the Greek war cry it crashed into their front.

The Persian expeditionary force consisted of good troops, and in the center held its own, even threatening to break through the Greek line. But on the flanks the Athenians were overwhelming. The key to the battle was that the triumphant Greek wings maintained their cohesion, and rather than pursue fleeing Persians they wheeled inward to trap the enemy center, which then became a scene of carnage. The entire Persian front broke in a stampede back to the ships, a scene each of the Greek hoplites had envisioned from stories learned since childhood of the war against Troy. Many Persians were driven into a nearby swamp where they were killed, but most scrambled back to their fleet. The Athenians pursued, and were even able to hold on to the cables of seven Persian ships, preventing them from leaving the shoreline.

Afterward the casualties were announced as 192 Greek dead, all of whom were buried in a mound that is visible to this day, and 6,400 Persian dead. The total of Persian dead is subject to query, especially when one calculates that precisely 33.33333 (etc.) Persians were reputed to have been slain for every one Greek. Nevertheless, Marathon was a stupendous victory for the Greeks, and regardless of whether Persian casualties were three-to-one or thirty-three-to-one, Darius's troops were seen to run from the field. The long-feared might of the Persian Empire had finally been encountered, and the Greeks had proven superior.

Once back aboard their ships, the Persian expeditionary force sailed for Athens, hoping it would be undefended. But the Athenian army quickly marched back to their city to defend it against a renewed onslaught. Earlier, a messenger had raced at full speed the twenty-six miles to Athens to relay news of the victory, thus inspiring a modern endurance race, the marathon. Upon finding the Greek army once more arrayed before them at Athens, the Persians sailed for home, their expedition a failure. Significantly, the Athenians had turned back the Persians almost single-handed, without help from the Spartans, who arrived later and were given a tour of the battlefield.

Darius died of natural causes in 486 B.C. after a forty-year reign that, notwithstanding the failure of his large-scale raid at Marathon, was impressive. He had followed in Cyrus's footsteps by continuing to conquer new lands and had also, through road, canal, and irrigation projects, brought increased wealth and efficiency to Persia's gigantic domain. Darius was succeeded by his son, Xerxes, who inherited not only an empire at the height of its power but the unfinished business of revenge against the Greeks. Fortunately for the latter, revolts broke out in Egypt and Babylonia that required the new king's immediate attention. The delay was vital for the Greeks because in 482 B.C. the Athenians discovered a rich vein of silver in Attica. Rather than spread the newfound wealth among the population, a leader named Themistocles persuaded the city to increase the size of the Athenian navy. New state-of-the-art triremes began pouring from the shipyards just in time to face the Persian onslaught, for once Xerxes had ruthlessly quelled the rebellions in the empire he returned to the problem of Greece. This time the task would not be left to a marine expeditionary force; the entire Persian army and fleet would launch a full-scale invasion.

In 480 B.C., Xerxes personally led his army into Europe across the Hellespont, over a massive pontoon bridge constructed by his engineers. His navy of some eight hundred warships sailed along the coast, protecting the seaborne flank of the army. To forestall naval aid to the Greeks from their powerful colony of Syracuse in the western Mediterranean, the Phoenician colony of Carthage attacked Sicily. In Europe, Xerxes' father had already conquered Thrace and Macedonia. As the huge army descended on Greece, Persian emissaries were dispatched ahead to demand the surrender of Greek cities in its path, and many, including Thebes, the rest of Boeotia, and the city-states of Thessaly, surrendered.

Farther to the south, representatives from Greek city-states met at Corinth to devise a common strategy against the invasion. To some, the only logical course was to defend the narrow isthmus that led to the Peloponnese. Corinth, Sparta, Olympia, and other places could thus easily be defended. But Athens lay north of the isthmus and would obviously be the initial target of the Persians's wrath. The Spartans, still red-faced over their inactivity during the first Persian invasion, took on the leadership role of the combined Greek forces. They agreed to place a blocking force north of Athens, at a narrow pass between the mountains and the sea called Thermopylae.

About six thousand Greeks held the pass, led by three hundred Spartans under one of their kings, Leonidas. Xerxes sent in wave after wave of troops, and at one point his Immortals, in order to force the way. But their bodies only piled up before the wall the Greeks had built to block their passage. It was a Thessalian who finally betrayed the Spartan position to the Persian king. The Greek traitor led a large Persian contingent secretly over the mountains and they came down unexpectedly behind the Spartans. Faced by overwhelming numbers on both sides, Leonidas prepared his men for the impending massacre. He addressed his troops that morning and advised them all to eat a hearty breakfast for it would be a long day, and that night they would all "dine in hell." Leonidas ordered the other Greek contingents to retreat, but he and his men would stand where they were because Spartans never withdrew in the face of an enemy. He and his men were killed, not in defense of their city-state, but in defense of Greece.

The Spartans had retrieved, with blood, the status within the Greek world they had lost to the Athenians at Marathon. And Xerxes, surveying the wreckage of his elite troops in the pass, had seen further proof of Greek formidability.

After the Persians destroyed the small Spartan force they moved south against Athens unchallenged. They entered the city in 480 B.C. and burned the Acropolis. They needed to kill a number of Athenian diehards who had held out in defense of the temples; the bulk of Athens's population had been evacuated before their arrival. With the sacking of Athens, Xerxes avenged the reputation of the Persian royal house, but he was still far from home and the war was far from being over.

The Greek fleet—half Athenian, with large contingents from Corinth and the island of Aegina plus other vessels—had skirmished with the Persian fleet while the battle of Thermopylae was taking place, without decisive results. The Persian fleet consisted of navies from the Phoenicians, the Egyptians, and the Ionian Greeks, but it had been ravaged by a storm in the unfamiliar waters off Euboea and severely weakened. Athens having fallen to the enemy, the Greek quandary was now whether to withdraw their fleet to the Peloponnese or to maintain it at the island of Salamis, just across from Athens. The Spartans were in favor of pulling it away from the straits of Salamis, where the ships were in danger of being trapped and destroyed. The

Athenian leader Themistocles, however, was convinced that if the ships withdrew, Athens would be lost for good. He slipped word to Xerxes that the Greeks were about to fall into their usual disunity and that if the Persians struck into the narrows that divided Salamis from the mainland they would win a great victory. Xerxes fell for the bait and ordered an Egyptian contingent to sail around the island to block the Greek escape route to the west. He ordered the main strength of his fleet to attack into the strait head-on. In anticipation of victory, Xerxes had his throne set up along the shoreline so he could watch the battle. He soon realized that the bulk of the Greek fleet had been concealed behind a promontory in the strait. When the Persian ships charged in, the Greek ships suddenly emerged to give battle.

The Greeks had just over three hundred ships and the Persians five hundred to six hundred. The method of combat was partly marine, because every ship carried soldiers. The ram, however, was the most effective weapon, and each warship was equipped with a metal prow just beneath its waterline to destroy an opponent. The Phoenicians, as the first line of the enemy attack, were assailed by the Greeks and cornered against the shore in the narrow strait. Their ships were lighter and more maneuverable than the Greek ones, but in the confined space off Salamis they couldn't move and were methodically destroyed. The Egyptian ships were hardly recognized in the battle by ancient sources, though their marine fighters were greatly feared; the Ionian Greek ships, fighting under duress, may have had their own agendas. Persian warriors put aboard ships couldn't swim, and when their vessels foundered they drowned. Xerxes, on his throne, saw the wreckage of his ships and the bodies of his men pile up on the shore at his feet. One of the few successful Persian ships was commanded by a female, Artemesia, and at one point Xerxes exclaimed, "My men have turned into women and my women into men!"

Salamis became, along with Marathon, one of the most important battles in world history. The relentless Greeks wrecked ship after enemy ship, and afterward they reported forty losses as opposed to two hundred of the enemy. Many Greek oarsmen or sailors from crippled ships survived, whereas entire Persian crews were lost. In addition, the Greeks who held the strait retrieved most of the damaged vessels. They were triumphant while the Persian fleet had been rendered a timid shadow of its former self.

With the Greek fleet ascendant, Xerxes was in peril. The enemy ships could race across the Aegean to cut his bridge across the Hellespont, blockading the strait. He needed to retreat while he still could. For propaganda purposes the Persians declared that the sack of Athens had been the culminating point of the king's campaign. Meanwhile, Xerxes withdrew with the bulk of his army, along with the immense horde of servants, extended family, concubines, and treasure he had brought with him on the trek. He left behind, however, a third of his fighting troops, about 60,000 men under Mardonius, to continue the war.

After Xerxes had gone, Mardonius acted skillfully, using Boeotia as a base of operations. His combination of diplomacy and attempted bribery failed to sever Athens from the Greek coalition, though to the Peloponnesians it seemed a near-run thing. As a result, Attica was ravaged again in the spring of 479 B.C. Mardonius had been given the pick of the empire's fighting troops and his army was further buttressed by Thebans and other Greek hoplite warriors who joined the Persian cause, preferring it over subordination to Athens or Sparta.

In August 479 B.C., the Spartans led the allied forces out of the isthmus of Corinth to confront Mardonius. As the armies jostled, Persian cavalry wreaked havoc in the Greek rear, but then the Greeks finally caught the Persian infantry in the open where their phalanx could be brought to bear. The Spartan hoplites served as the hammer in the battle of Plataea, in which Mardonius was killed and the Persian army routed. It had taken a year, but the coalition from the Peloponnese had finally risen to defeat the invader. Across the Aegean Sea, the Greek fleet, primarily Athenian, caught the Persian one unawares at Mycale on the coast of Asia Minor. When the soldiers and sailors fled inland they were caught between newly aroused Ionian Greek forces and the pursuing Athenians. These two nearly simultaneous victories destroyed forever the Persian ambition of conquering Greece. It had instead become apparent that the perpetually feuding Greeks, forced to unite in common cause, would emerge as a dangerous threat to the Persian Empire.

The Greeks followed up their decisive defeat of Xerxes' invasion by rolling back the empire's gains in Macedonia and Thrace, all the way to the Hellespont, which they now controlled. Naval and expeditionary forces from the Greek mainland assisted the Ionian cities in throwing off the Persian yoke. Aegean islands that had been seized by the Persians were retaken, one by one, by the powerful Greek fleet.

Once the crisis had passed, the Spartans returned to the Peloponnese, to their perpetual problem of keeping the Messenians under-
foot. Athens, a larger and more ambitious city-state, resolved to continue the war against the Persians. It became the fulcrum of a coalition
called the Delian League, so-called because representatives met on the
sacred island of Delos in the Aegean. The purpose of the league was
to "ravage the lands of the Persian king." The alliance soon swept the
Aegean clean of Persian ships and bases, while comprising a prohibi-
tive deterrent against a renewed enemy offensive. It also suppressed
the many pirates who had long interfered with seaborne commerce.

City-states could contribute either ships or money, but the vast
majority of the 150 members the Delian League claimed at its height
chose the latter. It was far easier for populous Athens, once funded, to
build and man the ships, and as a consequence the city enjoyed full
employment and a thriving maritime construction trade. As the years
passed, Athens came to dominate the League, using it as a vast base of
power to pursue its own agenda. Commercial disputes had to be
solved before Athenian juries, who were Athenian citizens paid for
their time; Athens also intervened in political disputes in member
states, nominally in support of democrats but more pragmatically in
support of Athenian policy. Local subversives who pursued power
under the democratic banner could be confident of overwhelming military support.

In the 450s B.C., during an Egyptian revolt against the Persians,
the Athenians dispatched a fleet to the Nile. But a counterattacking
Persian fleet trapped it there and in 454 B.C. achieved its destruction.
The Athenians used the crisis to justify moving the gigantic Delian
League treasury from Delos to Athens, where it would be safer. In
449 B.C., the Greeks and Persians, both having tired of the war, agreed
to a truce, yet Athens insisted that members of the Delian League
continue paying tribute. When some city-states objected and tried to
withdraw from the alliance, Athens sent forces to brutally force their
submission. What had begun as a mutual defense pact had evolved
into a coalition from which members were not allowed to leave. The
city-states of the Delian League were forced to continue paying tribute
to what had become an Athenian empire.

Once the Athenians had taken possession of the League's treasury,
they launched the most ambitious building campaign in Greek history.
Earlier, in 480 B.C., the Persians had burned the temples on the

Acropolis, the high, stone butte that dominates the center of Athens. Now the Athenians would restore the site with beautiful, elaborate structures such as the Parthenon and Erechtheum, temples to the gods, and a large, magnificent statue of Athena. The building program also had the advantage of maintaining full employment now that a large standing navy was no longer necessary. Using Delian League funds, Athens was transformed into one of the most beautiful cities in the ancient world. In addition, it entered into a period of intellectual, cultural, and artistic development unparalleled in human history. During the half century from the defeat of the Persian invasion until the beginning of the Peloponnesian War, Greek civilization at Athens rose to its greatest heights.

The Greek classical period began with the premise that in spite of material wealth a man could never be truly happy until he could evaluate his life and assign some purpose to it. The Greeks inquired into why the world was as it was and what role man was expected to play. An Athenian teacher, Socrates, brought philosophy in its most pragmatic form down from heaven and placed it in the Greek cities. He asked his fellow Greeks to consider what was "right" and "just" in life and in what way men could come to know the "good life." Another philosopher, Protagoras, proclaimed for all in the ancient world to hear that *man* was the only true measure of all things. All that existed in the world did so because man confirmed and validated that existence and nothing should be accepted unless it had been first filtered through the human senses.

The followers of Socrates, in their philosophical approach, developed a "man-centered" culture that tried to chart a course toward a good life through logical analysis and argument. They believed that true wisdom could only be found, first, in the modest realization of how little one really knows and, second, in looking for moral guidance through the development of an inner voice that instinctively warned when one was about to do something wrong and strove to bring one back onto the right path. Discussion and debate became the Greek method of philosophical and political discourse and eventually the foundation of Western modes of government.

Plato, a student of Socrates, continued the work of his teacher and produced a number of famous books that touch nearly every problem of moral, political, and ethical behavior. He wrote about mathematics, music, and psychology. His most widely read work, the *Republic*, outlined the ideal society and the perfect form of government. Plato promoted enlightened rule of the masses by philosopher kings who instinctively and through moral training would do what was right for their people. He outlined the components of an ideal society and the duties of each person to ensure the harmonious existence of all. Socrates promoted the need for enlightened government among the Greeks and Plato urged his fellow citizens to strive toward attaining the perfect society. This intellectual tradition was passed on to Aristotle, a pupil of Plato, who in turn became the tutor and mentor of the young prince Alexander of Macedon in the fourth century B.C.

The city of Athens became a center for literary and artistic advancements. In no other city of the ancient world could be found such a concentration of artistic, political, scientific, and philosophical genius. In addition to the three great philosophers, Socrates, Plato, and Aristotle, there were playwrights like Aeschylus, Sophocles, and Euripides, who wrote the most heartbreaking tragedies revealing the flawed nature of man. Another Greek of the classical era, Aristophanes, wrote comedies of biting wit and satire that retain their value as political commentaries to this day. Herodotus and Thucydides defined the scope and writing of history while Hippocrates established the foundations of medicine. The Athenians of this time also defined the ideals of architecture, showing the world the marvels of their buildings and, led by the genius of Phidias, how the human form could be brought to a state of perfection in the sculptures of masters.

During this period, the city of Sparta achieved none of the grandeur of Athens. Art, architecture, and philosophy were low priorities for the Lacedaemonian state, which still used iron bars as a medium of exchange instead of coins. Yet, as Athens flourished as the most visible purveyor of the greatness of Greek civilization, many city-states still looked to Sparta as their moral and constitutional leader. In the middle of the fifth century B.C., the Athenian and Spartan spheres of influence had scraped against each other with tentative military campaigns, almost as if to keep each generation of Greek hoplites in a high state of readiness. In 431 B.C., the tension that had been building between Athens and Sparta and their respective allies burst into full-scale war.

A number of historians have drawn a comparison between the Peloponnesian War in Greece and World War I in Europe. The two conflicts were equally ruinous on their respective scales, and both began similarly, because the main combatants were drawn into direct warfare through minor allies. But as with the Great War, which similarly followed a long period of prosperous peace, the situation in fifth-century B.C. Greece may only have needed a spark to set off a smoldering conflagration. In 431 B.C., two small islands off the west coast of Greece fell into a dispute. One looked to Athens for support, the other to Corinth. The Athenians jumped in, notwithstanding that Sparta was committed to Corinth as an ally. Soon, the entire Greek world was at war. Athens and all its allies opposed Sparta and its coalition from the Peloponnese, which was soon joined by Thebes and most of the states of Boeotia.

The first phase, which lasted for ten years, has become known as the Archidamian War. Sparta and its allies marched into Attica and laid waste its crops and farmland. The Athenians, however, had provided for the security of their city by erecting a series of strong walls that stretched from the Acropolis to their seaport at Piraeus. Thus their city was secured and could be supplied indefinitely. Their navy could meanwhile strike at will along enemy coastlines.

An unforeseen event occurred after Athens's entire population had sought shelter behind the city's "long walls." Plague broke out in the crowded city, spread quickly, and almost a third of Athenians perished. Among the many victims was Pericles, Athens's most brilliant leader of the classical period. But the Spartans were unable to maintain a siege, and as the war developed, each year they would march into Attica, destroy as much as they could, and withdraw again. With citizen armies short campaigns were the only option because Sparta's allies had their own crops to harvest and the Spartans themselves needed to tend to their slave population.

The Athenians were aware of the Spartans's Achilles' heel and under the leadership of Cleon they sent an expeditionary force under one of their best generals, Demosthenes, to incite uprisings among Sparta's helots. The war went back and forth with victories and defeats for both sides but with no resolution in sight. This phase of the war ended in 421 B.C., when the Athenians elected Nicias, the leader of the aristocratic peace party, as general. The Athenians and Spartans signed the Treaty of Nicias, which resulted in an uneasy truce. But neither side had been humbled and the issue of supremacy on the Greek mainland had yet to be solved.

In 415 B.C. the Athenians, incited by the charismatic personality of one of their young leaders, Alcibiades, decided to employ their best weapon, their fleet, against Syracuse, the powerful Greek city-state in the western Mediterranean. Success there would enhance Athenian power and the Spartans would be further diminished. Syracuse lay on the eastern shores of Sicily and was central to control of the western Mediterranean sea lanes. Alcibiades, however, defected to Sparta and divulged the Athenians's plans. The Spartans sent a contingent to Syracuse and the Athenian fleet became trapped inside the city's harbor. After a tense standoff they were defeated in a desperate attempt to break out. Most of the Athenian sailors and soldiers abandoned their ships and fled into the interior of Sicily, but the enemy hunted them down and those Athenians who survived the ensuing massacre became slaves in the island's stone quarries.

In 413 B.C., after the catastrophe in Sicily, the full Peloponnesian War resumed in a phase called the Ionian War. With the decimation of its vaunted navy, Athens had become vulnerable in the Aegean, and some of its allies began to break away. On land, the Spartans had already marched through Thessaly into Thrace, seizing many of the Delian coastal states. Sparta finally set up a permanent base in Attica, which soon became the receptacle of up to 20,000 Athenian slaves who sought freedom, or at least escape from their brutal toil in the silver mines. As the Athenian empire began to disintegrate, strife broke out within the city walls. In 411 B.C. an oligarchic party seized power and delegated rule to a narrow group of citizens, the "Four Hundred." Alcibiades returned from exile in 407 B.C. and entered the fray loyal to the democratic cause. The Four Hundred fell from power and were murdered or executed. They were replaced by the "Five Thousand." Athenian democracy, in vindictive form, had been restored. From the Athenian view, however, the war was to take still another turn for the worse.

In Persia, King Xerxes had died in 464 B.C. and was succeeded by his son, Artaxerxes, who ruled for thirty-nine years, until 425 B.C. Artaxerxes thus oversaw the Peace of Callias, which ended direct hostilities with Athens in 449 B.C., and lived to see the first stage of the Peloponnesian War, in which Athens was assailed by the other city-states of the Greek mainland. That Athens and its Ionian empire were being fought down by other Greeks was by no means displeasing to the Persians. Artaxerxes was succeeded by Xerxes II, who was murdered after forty-five days in an alarming development for the Persian monarchy. The problem with a family concern such as the Achaemenes was that successive generations of kings could not continually be expected to be worthy of rule. In the Greek world, leaders were replaced, voted down, or ostracized according to their performance or popular will. In Persia one had to trust that kings' offspring would prove worthy of leadership. Around the throne bureaucrats, generals, and eunuchs could be more astute, experienced, and ruthless than the children born into the royal family. Darius II quickly succeeded Xerxes II, and when the Peloponnesian War resumed, in 413 B.C., he took an active interest.

As the Athenians and Spartans and their allies engaged in total war, Persian wealth was available to assist either side. In Asia Minor, the Persian satraps Tissaphernes and Pharnabazus, respectful of Greek military prowess, played a balancing game. But in 407 B.C., the king's brother, Cyrus, assumed control of Persia's territory in western Anatolia. He unabashedly admired the Spartans and was eager to see the Athenian grip on the Ionian coast broken. Persian funds began to pour into Spartan coffers for the purpose of constructing a fleet. Phoenician expertise and resources were put at the Spartans's disposal. Over the years Athens, protected by its walls, had been able to draw upon the strength of its vast network of Aegean city-states in order to pursue the war. The Spartans had been unworried by land attack but had been unable to challenge Athens's supremacy in the Aegean. Now the Spartans acquired a powerful fleet of their own. The final phase of the war was primarily naval, as the Spartans with their new empowerment probed the Ionian coast for Athenian weakness.

The Athenians depended for their food supply on imports from Greek colonies along the Black Sea. They thus maintained a fleet of 180 ships to hold open the Hellespont and Bosporus, the two narrow passages between Europe and Asia that provide access to the Black Sea from the Aegean. By 405 B.C., however, the Spartans had gained an equivalent naval force, created thanks to Persian largesse and contributions from Syracuse, and, in a general named Lysander, a talented leader to command it.

In the late summer of 405 B.C., the Spartan fleet was positioned on one side of the Hellespont and the Athenian fleet on the other. For four straight days, the Athenians voyaged across the strait to challenge the Spartans to fight. Each time, the Spartans refused. On the fifth day the Athenians repeated the exercise and retired lackadaisically to their base, confident that the Spartans had no stomach for a naval battle.

That evening, however, Lysander led the Spartan fleet to sea, following the Athenian fleet just over the horizon. From out of the dusk, he
fell upon the enemy ships that were swaying at anchor or had been
carelessly beached on shore. In the battle of Aegospotami, the
Spartans destroyed or captured almost the entire Athenian fleet, and
ruthlessly slaughtered the fleeing seamen. Athens's food supply was
cut off. The Spartan fleet made its next appearance off Athens's port
of Piraeus, where it applied a tight blockade. Surrounded from both
land and sea, Athens made it through the winter, but in the spring of
404 B.C. the starving city had no choice but to surrender. The
Peloponnesian War had ended, with the utter degradation of Athens
as the result.

Sparta's allies, most vocally Corinth and Thebes, urged that
Athens be destroyed. But the Spartans, in spite of years of fighting the
Athenians, could not bring themselves to destroy a city that had rendered such patriotic service to Greece in the past. They also realized
that a prostrate Athens was a greater asset to them than a vacuum of
power that could only benefit Corinth and Thebes. The Spartans
ordered the Athenians to dismantle their "long walls" that had con-
nected the city to the sea, and they imposed a government of thirty oligarchic citizens to preserve compliance with Spartan policy.

The "Thirty Tyrants" (as they were called) were members of aristocratic Athenian families, some of whom had been exiled for their
pro-Spartan sympathies. They returned to their city with the Spartan
occupying forces and undertook a bloody purge of their enemies. The
Athenians endured the rule of the Thirty Tyrants for nearly a year
before rebelling and driving them out of the city in 403/402 B.C..
Democracy was once more established, but Athens was not the same
city it had been before the wars. Its resources had been depleted from
long years of fighting, its navy destroyed, its empire dismantled, and
its people devastated from war and plague.

The Spartans, too, had suffered from the long years of fighting
but they were the new masters of mainland Greece. They imposed oligarchies favorable to their policies throughout the Greek world. The
Persians, claiming their part of the bargain, reoccupied the Ionian
Greek cities along the coast of Asia Minor. Almost all of them had
been members of the Delian League, but now that Athens had been
defeated they resumed their former status as subjects of the Persian
king.

The devastation of the long Peloponnesian War made mainland Greece an unsettled country as the fifth century B.C. came to a close. The wars were over and thousands of Greeks had been released from military service. An entire generation of men had been born into warfare, and as they reached maturity knew no other life except fighting for their city-state. Arms and armor were the only tools they had been taught to use, and they had no business or other livelihood to return to.

Greek society did not know what to do with them. There was little good land in Greece to begin with and none left to absorb these men. The economy and trade routes were fragile after so many years of war and there was little work for them in the already overcrowded cities. Many of the adrift warriors were from the lower ranks of Greek society and not easy to integrate into the peaceful pursuit of commerce. In addition, large numbers of these men had tasted the benefits—plunder and a certain freedom based on lawlessness—that could come from war. On the Greek mainland, the mercenary population disrupted traditional relationships between city-states. A small city could employ mercenaries to suddenly overpower a neighbor. In some cases, roving warrior bands threatened communities for no other purpose than plunder. Citizens who might have laid down their weapons after the fighting was over had to remain vigilant against anarchical units of soldiers who roamed the countryside. The most unsettling demographic feature of mainland Greece at the close of the century was this large and impoverished floating population that the Greek leaders were unable to anchor to the land.

Fortunately, the sudden availability of thousands of Greek mercenary soldiers was coincident with recognition abroad that Greeks were the best warriors in the world. It became a status symbol for foreign rulers to hire Greek troops as their personal bodyguards or as elite units of their armies. A few Greek despots or tyrants such as Dionysius of Syracuse, Jason of Pherae, and Clearchus of Heraclea could afford to hire mercenaries on a long-term basis, but these Greek rulers were unusually wealthy. More commonly, the wealth necessary to hire mercenaries, as well as the need for them, came from the Persian Empire. Purposely divided into autonomous provinces whose only connecting thread was fealty to the king, the empire was riven by internal competition between satraps as well as frequent revolts by subject peoples. And the Persians had by now gained a healthy respect for Greek fighting prowess.

To the Greeks, the wealth of Persia was the stuff of dreams. They saw the empire partly as multitudes of docile, lash-driven barbarians, among whom they would be culturally superior, and in part as a land of inexhaustible riches with high wages and opportunities for lucrative plunder. In either case, to the mercenaries, fortunes were to be made in the East, not in their own ruined homeland. When agents arrived from Persia seeking soldiers for hire, Greek society was happy to be rid of its "exportable proletariat." Foreign rulers, at the same time, gained valuable military resources to maintain or expand their power.

Xenophon, a citizen of Athens, was born into an aristocratic family, landowners with oligarchic sympathies. Born between 430 and 425 B.C., when the population of Athens had already been forced behind its walls by the Spartan invasions, he had been no less cut adrift by the end of the Peloponnesian War than the most coarse mercenary soldier wandering through Greece.

The Athenian wealthy class were generally dissatisfied with democracy as it developed in their city and their unrest found expression the brief but violent oligarchic revolutions in 411 and 404 B.C. Xenophon was young at the time, but he and his family then supported the Thirty Tyrants whom the Spartans imposed on the city after its defeat in 404 B.C. When, during the following year, the Thirty Tyrants were violently overthrown, the Spartans made sure a general pardon was extended to Athens's oligarchists. But Xenophon, perhaps prudently, developed a wanderlust. He had patriotically served Athens as a hoplite during the war, but like many upper-class Athenians he had gained a profound admiration for the Spartan constitution and that society's consequent stability. He did not envision an enjoyable future in Athens.

In the winter of 402-401 B.C. Xenophon was invited by a Boeotian friend, Proxenus, to join a contingent of mercenaries that was about to enter the service of Cyrus, the Persian satrap of western Asia Minor. They were needed, Proxenus said, to quell a revolt by the Pisidians, an indigenous people who had revolted against Persian rule.

In Athens, Xenophon, a student of the great philosopher Socrates, who had also associated with the Thirty Tyrants, asked his teacher for advice on whether he should join the expedition. Socrates was concerned for the welfare of his pupil and tried to discourage him. The Persian Cyrus had supported the Spartans during the late war and now ruled Athens's former allies along the Ionian coast. Feelings in Athens still ran high against both the Spartans and Persians. Socrates was afraid that once Xenophon departed Athens he would not be allowed to return. The philosopher recommended that his pupil consult the oracle at Delphi for guidance.

Xenophon went to Delphi but did not pose the question suggested by his teacher. Instead of asking the oracle whether he should join the mercenaries, he only asked in what manner he should sacrifice to the gods in order to ensure a safe and prosperous return. When Xenophon returned to Athens and reported to his teacher what he had asked the oracle, Socrates was displeased. Nevertheless, he counseled his pupil to make the appropriate sacrifices to the gods as the oracle had directed. After the sacrifices, Xenophon set sail with Proxenus to join the various contingents of mercenaries being assembled by Cyrus near the Persian city of Sardis.

Like many of the Greeks who joined this mercenary army in 401 B.C., Xenophon saw a chance to make his reputation and fortune in the East. He may also have been motivated by a sense of adventure or curiosity, and in any case he had begun to feel unwelcome in Athens. At the beginning of the expedition, he described himself as "neither a soldier nor commander." Since Proxenus was the general of the Boeotian mercenaries, Xenophon probably acted as an aide to his friend, or as what today we would call a staff officer.

At Sardis, Xenophon was introduced to Cyrus, his inner circle of advisers, and to other Greeks who had brought units of mercenaries from Thrace and throughout the mainland. Cyrus explained to the assembled Greek officers that they had been hired to supplement his main force of Persian infantry and cavalry. The Greeks were promised a generous per diem to be paid in Persian darics and the chance to amass a small fortune from the plunder that was sure to fall their way.

As the fifth century B.C. drew to a close, the Greek world that once had ascendancy over the Persian Empire within its grasp was in ruins. Athens, once the Greeks's most powerful city, was an impotent, surrendered husk. The Athenians's blood-rivals, the Spartans, were little better off, and had sold their souls to the devil, or Persians, for the final push in the war that gained them victory. The Persian Empire had looked on throughout the conflict, entirely satisfied that the prostration of Greece they had failed to force with their own troops had been achieved by the Greeks fighting each other. The Persians had only grown richer and more secure during the latter part of the fifth century, while the Greek world tore itself apart. To many Greeks, like Xenophon, the lure of adventure or employment in the East was far more promising than what they could expect from remaining in their own ravaged country.

Thus Xenophon was drawn, as were over ten thousand other Greeks, into Persian service. And it would not be until months later, once they were deep into the heart of the Persian Empire, that they would learn their mission was not to quell minor revolts, but to provide the cutting edge for conquering Artaxerxes II, Persia's "king of kings."

III
THE QUARREL OF THE
PERSIAN BROTHERS

The story of the Greek mercenaries in Persia is like a complicated fabric woven from many threads. Some threads are more dominant than others yet each plays a part in holding the fabric together and each gives to the cloth some element of its style and character. One of the most colorful threads in this story comes from the royal court of Persia, beginning with Parysatis, the wife of King Darius II.

Parysatis was born into the Achaemenid Palace as the result of a dalliance between Artaxerxes I and a royal concubine. She was raised in her father's court along with many siblings of similar status who were neither royalty nor commoners. From within this pampered, insulated world, however, Parysatis was determined to win favor and establish a higher place for herself in the hierarchy. She succeeded in marrying her half-brother, Darius, who was also the product of the king's lust for a royal concubine. Darius was equally as ambitious as the woman he had chosen to marry and was intent on one day becoming king of Persia. The marriage proved advantageous to both parties and over the years Parysatis proved a valuable resource to her husband as he maneuvered his way toward the throne.

When the old king Artaxerxes I died in 424 B.C., Darius had no more chance of taking the throne of Persia than any of his other seventeen illegitimate half-brothers. Only his eldest brother, who was the product of the king's marriage, had any legal claim to the throne. So it was he, Xerxes II, who became king; but he reigned for only forty-five days before he was murdered. Darius seized the throne shortly afterward, having almost certainly played a role in his brother's death. After Darius stabilized his regency, aided by Parysatis, he proceeded to rule Persia for nearly twenty years.

Parysatis was a strong-willed, capable woman who bore her husband thirteen children during their long marriage. Of that number only five lived, four sons and a daughter. The eldest son was named Artaxerxes, after his grandfather. The second child was a daughter, Amestris. Of all her children the royal mother came to love her third more than any of the others and she called this favorite son Cyrus, after the greatest king of Persia. The queen's maternal preference, however, set into motion a fatal rivalry between Cyrus and his elder brother, Artaxerxes. The competition that was subtly nurtured in childhood intensified as the years passed, and as the brothers matured it evolved into hatred. The issue that divided them was not simply a mother's favor; at stake was who would be the next king of Persia.

Artaxerxes, as the eldest son, claimed the right to the throne. He remained close by his father's side and endeavored to master the skills of statecraft. The aging Darius never clearly designated an heir even though Artaxerxes exercised his right to be called the crown prince. He also maintained his residence in Babylon, the city that had become the administrative center of the empire.

When it came time to marry, Artaxerxes took as his wife Stateira, a woman the equal of his mother in strength of will, ambition, and ruthlessness. The crown prince's new wife set about to do all she could to ensure that her husband would become the next king of Persia. The friction between these two women at court, each vying to advance her favorite to the throne, prompted Parysatis to plot even more aggressively in favor of Cyrus.

Parysatis referred to Cyrus as the one who had been born "into the purple." This meant that while Artaxerxes and his sister Amestris, had been born before Darius ascended the throne of Persia, Cyrus was born after Darius had been crowned king. He could thus be considered the eldest son of the king. When Cyrus turned seventeen, through the intervention of his mother he was placed in a position of considerable power and wealth within the empire. In 407 B.C., his father appointed him satrap of the rich provinces of Lydia, Greater Phrygia, and Cappadocia. In effect, Cyrus became the Persian civil and military authority for all of western Asia Minor—a region that included the Greek Ionian coast.

Appointing Cyrus to such a responsible and sensitive post also signaled a significant shift in Persian foreign policy toward the Greeks.

The satrapies of Asia Minor were the farthest west of all the Persian administrative provinces and thus closest to the Greeks. Prior to Cyrus's appointment these satrapies had been under the control of two senior governors, Tissaphernes and Pharnabazus.

Both these satraps, with the tacit consent of King Darius, had followed a policy of playing one Greek city-state against another. They used lavish gifts of money and considerable diplomatic meddling in an effort to keep the Greeks divided. The policy worked for a while and benefited the Persians, especially through the latter half of the fifth century B.C. while the Greeks were preoccupied fighting each other in the Peloponnesian Wars.

When Cyrus came to power in Asia Minor, things changed. He was an admirer of the Spartan state and inclined to favor the Lacedaemonians over the other Greeks. As governor of the westernmost satrapies of the empire he was in a position because of his wealth and influence to render the Spartans valuable aid, especially as the Peloponnesian Wars in Greece were entering their final and most crucial phase.

The Spartans were considered the best professional soldiers in the ancient world and as Cyrus cultivated their friendship he believed the time would come when they could be of considerable aid to him in his bid to seize the Persian throne. Parysatis, too, urged him to cultivate the friendship of the Spartans and she approved when he abandoned the policies of Tissaphernes and Pharnabazus.

Shortly after he became satrap, Cyrus established his capital at Sardis, about sixty-five miles east of the Aegean port city of Izmir. Sardis was an old city even at the dawn of the fifth century B.C. Today the Turkish town is named Salihli and, as in ancient times, it contains layer upon layer of some of the most spectacular Lydian, Persian, Greek, and Roman ruins to be found anywhere in the world. The site of the ancient city is located less than a mile outside of the town at the base of the Boz Mountains, where Mt. Timolus rises from the broad plain of the Gediz River.

While the town of Salihli is hardly worth a look, I found the site nearby beautiful and well worth a visit by anyone interested in ancient history. The Artemis temple at Sardis, for example, is one of the seven largest of all the Greek temples in the ancient world. The plain around Sardis remains, as it was in ancient times, a lush garden. The grapes, figs, dates, other varieties of fruit and cotton to be found recall for the visitor ancient descriptions of the gardens of the Lydian and Persian eras for which Sardis was famous.

In his palace Cyrus began to cultivate the friendship of the Spartans. He received the Spartan commander Lysander and gave him considerable aid for the Spartan war against Athens which was raging on the Greek mainland and on the Aegean Sea.

While Cyrus cultivated the Spartans, Tissaphernes, the former satrap of Asia Minor, attempted to continue his old policies of courting all the Greeks. He tried to play one group of Greeks off against the other but he lacked the influence to even introduce Athenian envoys at the royal court in Babylon. The effective maneuvering of the queen at Babylon kept Tissaphernes away from the king. The queen and her favorite son, even though separated by a thousand miles, skillfully coordinated their efforts and moved Tissaphernes away from King Darius and out of the royal circle.

The young Cyrus learned quickly in his new position as satrap of Asia Minor and he gained valuable experience both as an administrator within his own provinces and as a power broker among the Greeks in their wars. Cyrus and Lysander became good friends and Cyrus advanced the Spartan general even more funds over the next three years to carry on the war against the Athenians. Lysander and other Spartan leaders who visited the palace at Sardis came to regard the young prince as a worthy ally and were willing to overlook the fact that he was in Greek eyes a "barbarian." The Spartans thought well of Cyrus. The money kept coming and they encouraged him in his dream to one day take for himself the throne of Persia. According to the ancient sources the Spartans liked Cyrus not only because he gave them money but because he had many admirable qualities.

As a child, the Greek sources tell us that Cyrus had been regarded as the best among the sons of the nobility. It was customary that all the sons of the Persian nobility were raised at the court of Darius, especially while their fathers were posted in the provinces. This policy not only ensured the equality and consistency of their education but it also guaranteed their fidelity to the king. The presence of these young boys at court served to maintain the honesty and loyalty of their fathers who administered the various satrapies of the empire and oversaw the considerable wealth that flowed from them to the coffers of the king.

In his youth, Cyrus demonstrated a modest and obedient nature, no doubt the product of his mother's stern hand and interest. He proved diligent and eager to learn. Cyrus learned to value truth and even as a young boy gained a reputation for honesty. As the royal governor in the satrapies of Lydia, Phrygia, and Cappadocia that reputation served him well and earned him allies.

Both the Persians who lived in his satrapy and those among the Greeks who came into contact with Cyrus came to trust and admire him. In spite of his youth Cyrus proved a man willing to stand by his friends and allies in times of need. As a satrap he showed that he could be generous in rewarding those who were loyal and merciless in punishing those who betrayed him. Cyrus was often heard to say that he wished only to live long enough to see his friends rewarded and his enemies punished. That was not to be however, for in the end the gods determined it would be his enemies who would triumph over Cyrus and most of his friends would go to an early death as a result of their loyalty to him.

Cyrus was not loved by everyone. He incurred the enmity of many Persians, but most notably that of Tissaphernes, the former satrap and military commander of Western Asia Minor. Tissaphernes was compelled to return to Babylon when he lost his satrapy to Cyrus, and he moved into the circle of the crown prince Artaxerxes. There he became a close adviser to the older brother and would come to play a part in the defeat of Cyrus on the field of battle at Cunaxa. Tissaphernes would become the nemesis of Xenophon and the Greek mercenaries at the end of the war and he would dog them every step of their long journey home.

While he was satrap Cyrus began to demonstrate, often recklessly, that he intended to become king of Persia. One day two cousins came from Babylon to visit him at Sardis. Upon their arrival they entered his presence for an audience and apparently failed to hide their hands in the wide sleeves of their robes. This "hiding of the hands" was a sign of respect reserved for the "king of kings" and the crown prince Artaxerxes at Babylon. Cyrus, in a fit of rage, ordered the execution of the unfortunate pair for failing to show him the respect he demanded as the future king of Persia.

When word reached Babylon of what Cyrus had done it was interpreted as a sign that he was exercising royal prerogatives. It caused concern among the supporters of his brother and they speculated that Cyrus might attempt to seize the throne by force if Artaxerxes were to be designated heir to the throne. The matter came to a head at court when Darius fell seriously ill. Cyrus was summoned to his father's deathbed at Babylon, but before he left Sardis for the long journey east he called for the Spartan commander Lysander. As satrap Cyrus had cultivated strong ties of friendship with the Greek cities along the coast of Asia Minor and his influence among them eventually extended to the Greek mainland where he played a part in determining the outcome of the Peloponnesian War. Lysander and the Spartans now owed Cyrus a large debt that the young prince might have to count on.

The question of succession was always a factor in the life of the Persian court no matter what the dynasty or who was king. Both Cyrus and Artaxerxes were present at the deathbed with Parysatis. As they waited for Darius to die, each brother was confident that he would be designated heir to the throne. Cyrus was the favorite of his mother and she had told him so many times over the years that he alone had been "born to the purple" and was destined to be the king of Persia. Artaxerxes was the oldest and had stayed closer to his father's side.

Royal scholars, at the urging of Parysatis, had prepared briefs after finding precedent in Persian law for Cyrus to take the throne over the claims of his older brother. The scholars had discovered that eighty years before the Persian court had faced a similar problem. Xerxes I had been chosen king of Persia over the claims of his older brother in a dispute that involved the same issue. Xerxes had prevailed and ascended the throne of Persia because he had been "born into the purple" while his older brother had not.

The briefs of the scholars commissioned by Parysatis, however, were to be of no help to Cyrus. From the royal deathbed it was Artaxerxes who, at the very last moment, received the blessing of the dying king. Darius II died in 404 B.C. at Babylon after nearly twenty years of rule. Artaxerxes took the throne. Tissaphernes was now advisor to the new king and he used his position to further damage Cyrus by playing on the new king's suspicions and insecurities. Tissaphernes warned Artaxerxes that Cyrus was disloyal and could be plotting to assassinate him.

According to Persian custom, the coronation ceremonies for Artaxerxes II were to be held in the ancient capital of Pasargadae in the mountains of Iran. There in the temple of Cyrus the Great, the most famous of the Persian kings, Artaxerxes would be dressed in the robes of the first and greatest king of Persia. He would be crowned "king of kings" in elaborate ceremonies where he would be fed fig cakes, chew turpentine wood, and drink a cup of sour milk.

For the young and ambitious Cyrus this was too much to bear. The thought of his brother as king, and the coronation to be held in the temple of his namesake drove him to a desperate state of anger. Members of the royal bodyguard found the young prince lurking near the king's chambers, and upon searching him they found a dagger concealed beneath his robes.

Cyrus was brought before his brother where Tissaphernes charged him before the royal court with plotting to assassinate the new king. There is some controversy over the truth of this accusation in the manuscripts. Greek writers like Xenophon, obviously favorably inclined toward Cyrus, maintained that Tissaphernes made up the charges because he hated Cyrus. Modern historians of Persian history have expressed little doubt that given Cyrus's temperament and the competitive climate that prevailed at the Persian court, he may well have intended to kill his brother, if not at the urging of his mother, Parysatis, at least with her tacit consent. After all, his father Darius II, twenty years earlier, had taken the throne of Persia after murdering his brother. Cyrus was brought before Artaxerxes II, and condemned to death. Parysatis intervened on behalf of her younger son, however, and argued persuasively and passionately that her elder son should not begin his rule with the stain of fratricide upon his royal robes. There may also have been extenuating circumstances lost to history, such as Cyrus's being drunk or "not himself," that led Artaxerxes to believe his younger brother was not a long-term threat.

The mother's influence prevailed and Cyrus's life was spared. So persuasive was Parysatis in her pleadings that not only did Cyrus escape death, but Artaxerxes allowed him to return as satrap to his former province in Asia Minor. As he left the imperial city and traveled west, the young Cyrus was relieved to still have his royal head upon his shoulders. But now Cyrus hated Artaxerxes more than ever, not just for claiming the throne but for the humiliation and disgrace that he and Tissaphernes had forced him to endure in front of the Persian nobility.

By the summer of 403 B.C., Cyrus was actively plotting against his brother. His first step was to consolidate power throughout his satrapy. Then, in need of allies, he turned for support to the Greeks.

First he approached the Spartans who owed him a debt from their wars with Athens. Then Cyrus turned for help to the Greeks who inhabited the many towns and cities that dotted the western and northern coasts of Asia Minor along the borders of his satrapy.

The Greeks responded to his call with offers of soldiers. Cyrus sent orders to his garrison commanders throughout western Asia Minor to enlist as many Greek soldiers, especially those from the Peloponnese, as they could into their commands. So that he would not raise suspicions at Babylon or Persepolis, Cyrus ordered that the Greek mercenaries be disguised as garrison troops and placed under Persian commanders. Tissaphernes, however, had spies throughout the territory and they reported to him at Babylon on the build-up of troops in Asia Minor and the recruitment of Greek mercenaries.

While Tissaphernes had the left ear of the king at court, Parysatis, the plotting mother, had his right ear in the royal chambers. As Tissaphernes warned the king about his brother, the loving mother repeatedly assured her eldest that his younger brother was a loyal subject. She assured the king that Cyrus meant him no harm and was only raising these troops to defend his satrapy against rebellious elements in the province as well as against his enemy and accuser, Tissaphernes.

Artaxerxes, sitting confidently by this time upon the throne, was willing to accept the explanation offered by his mother. In the intrigues of the royal court it pleased the king to see his younger brother and Tissaphernes fighting. If they fought each other, Artaxerxes reasoned, it gave them less time and inclination to plot against him. As well, he must have been seduced in large part by the repeated assurances of his mother and thus lulled into a false sense of security. Artaxerxes was emotionally weak when it came to his mother and she used this weakness to the advantage of Cyrus.

Cyrus, at the urging of his mother, did everything he could to foster his elder brother's sense of well-being. When envoys from Artaxerxes arrived in Sardis they were received with exceptional courtesy and treated with great generosity. So well were they treated, and so lavishly entertained and rewarded while at the court of Cyrus, that when the envoys returned to Babylon they carried with them the most expensive and exquisite gifts. They reported to Artaxerxes that his younger brother was the most loyal of his subjects and they sang his praises while dressed in robes and jewelry given them by Cyrus.

Cyrus made sure that he paid the tribute due his brother regularly, and often he exceeded the amounts expected of him. The steady flow of gold and other precious commodities from the satrapy of Cyrus into the treasuries of Artaxerxes at Babylon and Persepolis only lulled the king into greater complacency and further strengthened his belief in the loyalty of his brother to the throne. The loving mother, Parysatis, was always close by to further reinforce this false sense of trust in her eldest son. As the years passed the king failed to perceive the threat that was rapidly developing against him in the far western part of his empire.

While Cyrus played the obsequious loyal subject to his royal brother in the east, he was raising an army in the west. Beyond the borders of the Persian Empire, across the Hellespont in Grecian Thrace, Cyrus cultivated the friendship of a renegade warrior. Here in the wilds of northern Greece, hidden from the "royal eyes and ears" of the king, he began to raise the nucleus of the mercenary army with which he intended to seize the crown at Persia.

Cyrus had hired a Spartan to recruit and train this army. The man that Cyrus had found was an ancient Patton, an outspoken soldier who followed no rules but his own and made no effort to disguise his disdain for politicians. Clearchus was a man born to war. He had gained his experience in long years of fighting the Athenians in the Peloponnesian War. As a soldier he was competent in every respect and men followed him willingly into battle. As a man he was self-possessed, confident, and secure to a fault. Clearchus was a man who loved war, any war.

When peace finally came to the Greek mainland in 403 B.C., Clearchus returned home to Sparta. He was middle-aged, restless and, with no war to fight, found himself without purpose. So he looked for another war, and found one against the Thracian tribes in northern Greece. Clearchus persuaded the ruling officials at Sparta, the ephors, that the Greek colonists in Thrace, a peninsula that forms the western landmass of the entrance to the Dardenelles (the Hellespont), were being persecuted by the Thracians. Sparta, he argued, had a duty as the primary military power on the mainland, to intervene on behalf of her fellow Greeks.

The ephors were apprehensive about Spartan involvement in another war so soon after the end of the long and costly conflict against Athens. Clearchus, however, had an intimidating presence in the assembly and extracted from them a hastily passed mandate approving his war in Thrace. Clearchus left Sparta quickly thereafter with his troops and marched them to Corinth. At Corinth he prepared his army to set sail on a flotilla of ships for Thrace.

As soon as Clearchus had left Sparta and his intimidating presence was no longer felt in the councils, the ephors reconsidered their decision to wage war in Thrace. They sent orders to Clearchus at Corinth to abandon the campaign and return to Sparta. When the envoys reached the fleet anchored at the Isthmus of Corinth and gave Clearchus his new orders he would not hear of it. He ignored the orders of the ephors and set sail with his army to wage his war in Thrace.

By refusing to return home as ordered, Clearchus had broken the supreme law of Sparta. Obedience to the state was a law that Spartans had followed for centuries without question and for which generations of them had laid down their lives. At Thermopylae, eighty years before, three hundred Spartans had died fighting against the forces of the Persian Empire rather than disobey the will of the state. The monument erected to their sacrifice reads: "Stranger, go tell the Spartans that here we lie, obedient to their laws." Obedience was the cornerstone of the Spartan society; it was the foundation upon which everything else rested, and Clearchus had broken that bond.

For his insubordination, Clearchus was tried in abstentia and condemned to death by the ephors. He was now a renegade, a man who could not return home, and no city in Greece would risk offending Sparta by opening its gates to welcome him. So he looked for service in the pay of a foreign ruler and Cyrus found in Clearchus just the man he needed to raise and train a mercenary force for the war against his brother.

Clearchus got his war in northern Greece against the Thracians and Cyrus paid the bill. Clearchus used the war to train his army and with the plunder taken from the looted and burned Thracian towns and villages he replenished the war chests of his Persian employer. The war in Thrace proved an excellent investment for Cyrus while Clearchus used the war almost as daily exercise for his army. The fighting against the Thracians kept the mercenaries fit until Cyrus would be ready for them to cross over into Asia Minor and begin the long journey to Babylon.

Clearchus, the man who had disobeyed the laws of Sparta, made discipline and obedience the core of his mercenary army. He accomplished both by being severe. He punished insubordination, the very thing Sparta had condemned him to death for, in the harshest manner. He had a temper when faced with disobedience by his subordinates and often he later regretted his impulsive and often violent responses to it.

Clearchus sometimes punished on principle but more often out of fits of rage. He believed that fear of punishment was what held an army together and that his soldiers needed to fear him more than they feared the enemy. While on the march he carried a stick and when he saw a man who was lagging behind or not throwing his back sufficiently into the work, Clearchus would hit him. Yet Clearchus was also a man who would readily get into the mud to help soldiers free a stuck wagon, and soldiers vied among themselves to match his energy and courage.

As a result, his troops obeyed him without question, especially in times of combat. His appearance and manner inspired fear and confidence among his men but never affection. He was nearly fifty when he entered the service of Cyrus and had become more gloomy and somber in appearance than he had ever been in his long military career. Cyrus paid Clearchus well to train the army, 10,000 gold Persian Darics, every last coin of which Clearchus invested in the army to better equip, reward, and train his men.

While Clearchus conducted his war in northern Greece against the Thracians, Cyrus began raising a second army of Greek mercenaries within the boundaries of his satrapy. This army he formed under the pretext of defending some of his territories against Tissaphernes, his rival in the east, as well as some dissident factions that had surfaced in Pisidia along the southern coast of Turkey.

When word of what Cyrus was doing eventually reached the royal court in Babylon, Artaxerxes became concerned. The queen mother assured her elder son that Cyrus was just taking defensive measures to protect his holdings against the aggressive Tissaphernes and other dissident factions within his satrapy. This was a pretext that the king was willing to accept since Cyrus paid him his royal tribute and it pleased him to keep his brother and Tissaphernes at odds with each other, reasoning still that with both men fighting each other they would be less inclined to plot against him and thus more controllable.

Cyrus set about to raise a third army under the command of another Greek exile and renegade, Aristippus. This army was main-

tained and trained in Thessaly, the northern part of the Greek mainland near Mt. Olympus. Aristippus kept this army in top fighting
shape by using them against his political opponents in Thessaly much
as Clearchus was using his army in Thrace. Finally Cyrus hired three
hundred heavily armed Spartan mercenaries that he designated as his
personal bodyguard.

Near his capital at Sardis, Cyrus ordered a general mustering of
his mercenaries and his regular Persian forces. The plain at Castolus is
where Cyrus first took a count of his troops. It was located outside the
small Turkish town of Alasehir about eight to ten miles southeast of
Sardis and near the Greek ruins of Philadelphia. It was the only place
large enough and flat enough in the area around Sardis where Cyrus
could have brought together all his forces to be assembled.

At Castolus, Cyrus assembled all his Greek mercenaries and their
commanders except for Clearchus and Aristippus. They were en route
from northern Greece to join him further east of Castolus at a place
called Celaenae. When the count was taken on the plain at Castolus it
was reported to Cyrus that the Greek generals already assembled there
were Xenias from Arcadia with four thousand hoplites; Proxenus
from Boeotia with fifteen hundren hoplites and five hundred light-
armed troops; Sophaenetus from Stymphalia with one thousand
hoplites; as well as the generals Socrates and Pasion from Achea.
Among the Persian troops Cyrus had assembled an army of nearly one
hundred thousand men most of whom had been recruited from his
satrapy and the rest from the surrounding provinces.

From the plain of Castolus, Cyrus marched his army of Greeks
and Persians southeast a distance of nearly one hundred miles to the
city of Colossae. The trip took four days for the army to complete as
they marched along a narrow plain and over relatively flat terrain. At
Colossae they rested seven days until another Greek mercenary commander, Menon from Thessaly, joined them with his contingent of one
thousand hoplites and five hundred peltasts.

Today that journey can be duplicated by following the small but
scenic secondary road that runs from Salihli southeast to Denizli. The
road follows the same narrow plain and the journey takes about two
hours to complete. The distance is just under a hundred miles, almost
exactly the distance specified in the manuscripts. The narrow road follows what would have been a portion of the ancient road from Sardis
leading to the Bey Mountains, and then to the Mediterranean coast

and the Turkish city of Antalya. Along the route one passes the abandoned site of the ancient city of Tripolis located near the small village of Yenicekent.

The ruins of Tripolis are located in a remote area not far from the main road and within the confines of the village. The problem is that while this site, like many others, is not far off the main road, it can be very difficult to find without a guide. It is necessary to rely on local people for direction. While there are small yellow signs placed along the main road pointing in the general direction of the site, these signs are confusing and essentially useless in helping to locate the ruins.

Today all that remains of many of these once magnificent cities like Tripolis and Colossae are large mounds, a few walls, and scattered remains of columns and foundation blocks. The sites along the route taken by Cyrus and the Greeks remain largely undisturbed and worth a visit. Broken relics can be found nearly everywhere around them and many of the local people who live nearby are only too willing to sell the unsuspecting tourist any number of artifacts, genuine or fake, for outrageous prices. It is amazing how these "simple village people" are capable of mentally calculating their prices for an interested tourist in German marks or American dollars. They will explain in a combination of the most excitable broken English and provincial Turkish that the artifacts were recently uncovered by farmers plowing their fields nearby. The fields are cultivated right up to the ruins and shepherds frequently graze their flocks on the sites. The villagers will barter the artifacts for just about anything, including worn jeans, t-shirts, and sweatpants.

The site of the ancient city of Colossae is located about ten miles south along a dirt road that leads from the modern Turkish city of Denizli. The site is a disappointment. It remains largely unexcavated but one can see the outline of what must have been a magnificent city. Across the valley from Colossae, just a few miles away, are the ruins of the cities of Laodicea and Hierapolis. While both of these cities postdate the time period of this story they are magnificent and worth a visit.

The area around the town of Denizli is as rich in archaeological sites as it is in agricultural produce. After visiting the area it is easy to understand why the ancient Greeks, Persians, and later Romans located their cities in these valleys. The ruins of the city of Hierapolis and the thermal baths of Pamukkale are magnificent. The thermal springs provided a spa for the wealthy Greeks, Persians, and Romans just as today they provide relaxing and therapeutic benefits for modern tourists. Hierapolis and Pamukkale are major tourist sites and easy to locate, although most of the ruins are from the Roman period.

From Colossae, Cyrus and his army marched sixty miles east to another city called Celaenae. Here Clearchus and several other Greek commanders arrived to join them. In ancient times Celaenae was a massive fortress and palace which had been built by Xerxes I after he returned from his infamous defeat by the Greeks in 480 B.C. From the distances described in the ancient Greek manuscripts Celaenae must have been located near the modern Turkish town of Dinar. There is no evidence of ruins there to support the description of the massive fortress given in the manuscripts, but the wide plain near Dinar is certainly suitable for Cyrus to have held a mustering of all his troops. The manuscripts describe a vast plain and the flat land near Dinar fits the description perfectly.

When Clearchus arrived at Celaenae he had with him a force of one thousand hoplites, eight hundred peltasts, and two hundred archers. The mercenary commander Sosis came from the Greek city-state of Syracuse on the island of Sicily, and the commander Agias came from Arched in central Greece. Both these commanders brought with them another thirteen hundred hoplites. Aristippus, the commander from Thessaly, failed to join Cyrus at Celaenae as he had promised with his four thousand hoplites. Instead, he sent his friend Menon to replace him with only one thousand soldiers.

When the last of the Greek commanders had arrived, Cyrus held a review of all his troops on the wide plain. As they passed in review the count of the Greeks was put at eleven thousand hoplites and two thousand peltasts. Cyrus had expected that the total number of Greeks in his service would have come to fifteen thousand at Celaenae, but since Aristippus had failed to report he had to content himself with a total of thirteen thousand soldiers.

The army left Celaenae after several days and marched about thirty-five miles northeast to the city of Peltae. This site corresponds by distance and direction to the modern Turkish town of Sandikli. From Peltae, Cyrus and his army marched another forty miles further north to a town called Ceramon-agora. This town is described in the ancient manuscripts as having been well-known throughout the ancient world as a tile and ceramic market. In ancient Greek, *ceramon* means ceramic and *agora* means market. Today that area of Turkey, from Afyon to Kutahya, is as famous for its tiles and ceramics as it was in ancient times and well worth a visit. From Ceramon the army marched one hundred miles further east along the wide plain to the city of Caystru-pedion. Again using distances from the manuscripts, this ancient site corresponds to the Turkish town of Aksehir where there are some interesting ruins.

When the army stopped to camp on the plain, trouble developed between the mercenaries and Cyrus over the issue of pay. The Greeks complained to their officers that for those of them who had been in the service of Cyrus the longest it had been nearly three months and they had still not been paid. They complained because they had to buy their own provisions daily from the markets of the villages and towns that they passed and because many of them from mainland Greece had paid the expenses of their passage to Persia out of their own pockets. This caused many of the newly arrived mercenaries to become anxious over their pay as well and tensions increased. Cyrus kept putting off the Greek demands for money with excuses and promises. Those among the Greek officers who were most loyal to Cyrus tried to calm their men and act as a buffer, but the situation continued to worsen. Then, just as matters over the pay issue were coming to a dangerous stage between Cyrus and the Greeks, the entire camp was distracted by the arrival of an elaborate caravan which had come from the Taurus mountains to the southeast.

Epyaxa, the wife of the aged King Syennesis of Cilicia, had arrived with her entourage to visit Cyrus. Shortly after her arrival Cyrus called together the Greeks and paid them four months wages instead of the three they had demanded. The Greeks were pleased and the beautiful, young queen stayed in the camp for two weeks thereafter. As the days passed it became evident that she was a woman who delighted in being in the midst of so many warriors.

One night, as the queen dined with Cyrus in the royal tent, she persuaded him to review all his troops for her. The next morning Cyrus ordered the entire army to assemble on the wide plain near a place called Tyriaeum. This wide plain is easily located and begins just a few miles east of the city of Aksehir. While the precise location where Cyrus reviewed his troops is impossible to determine, it must lie some-where on this plain between Aksehir and Konya. This plain is much wider than either of the ones at Celaenae or Castolus. As one moves further east into the center of Turkey the plains in general become much larger than those which exist nearer the Aegean coast.

The commanders, both Greek and Persian, were ordered to prepare their units in their finest battle dress for a grand parade to honor the Cilician queen. The review of the army quickly became a festive occasion for the entire region. The people from the surrounding villages and towns all came to watch. Soon a large crowd had gathered on the plain to await the start of the grand review. The local merchants, as well as those who accompanied the army, lost no time in setting up stands to hawk their wares.

By the time all the troops had assembled on the plain it was nearing midday. Cyrus drove his chariot around the troops to inspect them while the queen followed in her carriage. Then Cyrus ordered the Persian formations to march past the queen of Cilicia. In their finest military dress and in their best order they passed in review before the young queen. The infantry were followed by the horsemen and then at last came the chariots. At the end of the parade all the Persian forces stood down, stacked their arms, and prepared to watch the final procession.

It was now the Greeks's turn to pass in review. The Greeks were the most disciplined soldiers in the ancient world and they were well-drilled in maneuvers. In their polished armor and bronze plumed helmets they were proud to show this barbarian queen how superior they were to any other soldiers in the world. As they passed in review they executed their movements with precision and in perfect drill formation. Then they proceeded to march out onto the wide plain and re-form their ranks at a considerable distance away from the crowd.

This was the first time that the thirteen thousand Greek mercenaries had marched together in full battle dress. Wearing their red tunics, with their shields and weapons uncovered, an excitement, or esprit de corps, swept through their ranks. As this spirit gained momentum and the infantry reached the wide expanse of the plains, they broke their marching formations and spontaneously began to re-form themselves into the dreaded phalanx. Without orders from their commanders, and acting in perfect coordination under their own volition, they began to move into battle lines.

The Greek commanders, seeing what was happening within their ranks and sensing the mood that had built up among their troops, ordered them to turn and face the direction of the spectators. The

Greeks, under the control of their officers, turned, re-formed their lines, and the phalanx began a slow advance in the direction of the crowd as if preparing to engage an enemy.

The crowd that had assembled that day to watch the review was large and up to this point it had been jovial. Merchants were busy displaying and selling their goods while the crowd was generally enjoying the festive atmosphere that had been created by the review of troops. But as the Greeks began their maneuvers out on the plain the crowd suddenly became quiet. At first everyone was curious as to what the Greeks were doing so far out on the plain when the review had finished. Then as they could see the Greeks re-forming into the phalanx they became apprehensive. As the Greek phalanx advanced toward the crowd many of the spectators who had never seen the phalanx before became frightened. Their fear grew and spread as the Greeks marched closer. The Greeks moved in perfect formation with their weapons at the ready. As they advanced toward the crowd they began their rhythmic war chant, the panthion.

So fearful was the appearance of the advancing phalanx and so intent and menacing its manner that the mood among the crowd quickly turned from fear to panic. Members of the royal entourage as well as common people scattered to all parts of the plain and the nearby villages seeking cover. The merchants left their stands filled with goods and fled for safety. Food was left cooking over the fires and wine in the cups. Even Queen Epyaxa took flight in her carriage and returned to the safety of her camp. In her tent she reclined upon the royal couch for she had felt herself become weak and nearly faint from the excitement of being in the presence of so many men under arms.

On the plain Cyrus stood his ground as the Greeks approached. He remained at the reviewing stand and delighted in their antics. As he watched his mercenaries he became impatient for the day when they would scatter the army of his brother as easily as they had scattered his own. At the reviewing stand the phalanx came apart and the Greeks returned to their tents, laughing, to prepare their dinner.

As for Epyaxa, from that day until the day she left to return home, she took every opportunity to walk about the camp of the Greeks. As she moved among the mercenaries, the sense of so many hungry and violent men about her only inflamed her that much more. Each night, in the comfort and luxury of the royal tent, it was Cyrus who profited from her excitement.

From the plains of Tyriaeum the army marched about 66 miles to the last city on the borders of Phyrigia, Iconium. This site corresponds by name and distance to the Turkish city of Konya. Today, Konya is one of the great cultural centers of Turkey and home to the Sufi Order known to Westerners as the Whirling Dervishes. An ancient city even before Cyrus and the Greeks arrived, it has seen the passage of many historical epochs. It became the capital of the Seljuk Turks from the twelfth through the fourteenth centuries A.D. and is a city which, like so much of Turkey, has layer after layer of history within its walls.

Iconium was an important milestone for Cyrus. He had reached his Rubicon, as this city was the last on the eastern borders of his satrapy and marked the limit of his territorial authority.

Once Cyrus passed beyond Iconium and the territorial limits of Phyrigia he had exceeded his royal mandate as a satrap. He had no right to move beyond Iconium with an army without the permission of the king at Babylon. As he led his army out of Phyrigia and east into the territory of Lycaonia, the mood among his officers, both Greek and Persian became somber. The officers talked among themselves and Cyrus sensed their uneasiness. He sent the Cilician queen home to her cuckold husband.

The territory of Lycaonia is a large and fertile plain that stretches from Konya to the foot of the Taurus Mountains near the provincial Turkish town of Eregli. There Cyrus turned loose his Greek mercenaries on the unsuspecting and largely defenseless population. For three days, the Greeks plundered, raped, and murdered throughout the countryside. As they ravaged and burned villages, Cyrus and the main body of the army moved southeast to the city of Dana. Dana is probably the Turkish town of Eregli, since the distance from Konya to Eregli, about one hundred miles, is almost exactly that specified in the manuscripts. At Dana, Cyrus ordered the execution of two local men he accused of plotting against him. One of the men was a "wearer of the royal purple," meaning he was considered royalty at the court of Artaxerxes, while the second unfortunate man was only a minor functionary.

Queen Epyaxa took a different route home to Cilicia than the one which Cyrus followed. She had with her a sizable escort of Greeks under the command of Menon but the force was small enough and mobile enough to attempt a more difficult but shorter route through the mountains than the army of Cyrus. The first part of their journey was toward the southeast over the wide plains from which the queen had first come. The column made considerable progress until it entered the Taurus Mountains. While crossing the mountains, Menon lost two companies of soldiers, nearly one hundred men. These men had purposely remained behind the main column to provide a rear guard. Either they were ambushed and massacred by the Cilicians or they became lost in the mountains and perished while trying to rejoin the column. One rumor that ran among the Greeks was that these men had made the mistake of stopping to loot and burn a small mountain village. During the looting a large contingent of soldiers from the army of King Syennesis caught them and they were all killed. Equally plausible as an explanation is that they had become lost in the mountains, and without adequate shelter, provisions, or a guide, especially at that altitude, they would have died from exposure. The Taurus Mountains can be an unforgiving place when the elements of nature turn harsh.

When Queen Epyaxa and her escort finally reached Tarsus, Cyrus was still five days behind them and moving toward the city by way of two narrow mountain passes known as the Cilician Gates. When Menon and the queen reached Tarsus they found the city nearly deserted. Most of the citizens had fled to the hinterlands when word reached them that Cyrus was approaching. They had fled to escape the carnage they were sure would follow since word of what the Greeks had done in Lycaonia had already reached them. King Syennesis had left the city with a small force and taken to the mountains, ostensibly to block Cyrus at the Cilician Gates. Menon speculated that it might have been this force that ambushed and massacred his rear guard, so in retaliation he ordered his men to plunder the city and especially the palace of the king.

As Cyrus entered the mountains with the main contingent of his army he had his scouts probe the road ahead. If the king's army, or even a small group of them, held the crucial passes, Cyrus could not advance. Most of the army waited below on the wide plain while the scouts moved along the small road and up into the mountains. The road wound its way slowly over the two narrow and relatively high mountain passes (1,300 meters) that guard the entrance to Tarsus and the Mediterranean coastline. Those passes are not as well-known today as they were in ancient times when the Cilician Gates were the only way to travel from the plains of Cappadocia over the Taurus Mountains and into Cilicia. The Turkish government cut a channel through the mountains a few years ago and put in a superhighway. Now there is little traffic over the old road but it is well worth taking as it winds its way over the passes and through picturesque countryside.

The scouts returned after a few hours and reported to Cyrus that they had seen the soldiers of Syennesis in considerable numbers guarding the first pass. But when the king saw them he lost his taste for a fight with Cyrus and withdrew from his position. Perhaps the old king feared being caught in the mountains between Cyrus in front of him and the Greeks under Menon behind him. The king had also received word some days earlier that a large convoy of Spartan war triremes and supply ships were sailing toward Tarsus. The king speculated that these ships carried reinforcements as well as supplies for Cyrus and would compound his problems.

Syennesis abandoned his position at the passes and his troops faded into the higher elevations. Cyrus and his army climbed over the two passes without opposition and descended to the other side of the mountain range. They came down onto a beautiful plain that was described in the manuscripts as having been rich with crops of sesame, millet, panic grass, wheat, and barley. Today that same plain lies between the cities of Tarsus and Adana and is one of the most fertile places in all Turkey. The plain is surrounded on three sides by high mountains and on the fourth by the Mediterranean Sea. It produces an abundance of crops because of the uniquely temperate climatic conditions and the naturally fertile nature of the soil. The weather is always the right mixture of rain and sun, so the region enjoys three growing seasons per year.

When Cyrus and the army arrived at Tarsus they found that Menon's men had burned and looted many sections of the city, including the royal palace of Syennesis. Only a few innkeepers, prostitutes, and merchants had stayed behind in the deserted city, attracted by the prospect of selling wine, food, and sex to the invading army. Cyrus installed himself in a section of the king's palace and sent word to the old man in the mountains that he should come down. Syennesis had taken refuge with the remnants of his army and most of Tarsus's civilian population in the surrounding mountain villages, many of which can still be found throughout the Tarsus range. Syennesis sent back word that he would not enter Tarsus without pledges of safe conduct. Epyaxa prevailed on him to put aside his fears and return to the city.

Reluctantly the old king left the safety of the mountain villages and meekly returned to see what had happened to the city over which he had ruled for so many years.

When Cyrus and the king finally met in the palace, Cyrus demanded a large sum of money. The old king revealed where the last of his gold was hidden, as the queen reclined upon her royal couch next to her young Persian lover. When all the gold had been surrendered Cyrus bestowed upon the cuckold king gifts and honors. He promised Syennesis that his land would not be further plundered. All those present agreed among themselves that the deeper Cyrus moved into the Persian Empire the more he began to assume royal prerogatives. He had crossed the border into Lycaonia, executed two men at Dana, and now he had humbled the king of Cilicia, a vassal of Artaxerxes.

Cyrus remained at Tarsus for twenty days. During that time another revolt broke out among the Greeks. This time it was over something much more serious than money. Cyrus had never fully explained to the Greek soldiers why he had hired them and what their mission was to be. He had described in general terms that he needed them to put down some rebellious elements in his satrapy, but he had never revealed his intention to march to the very gates of Babylon to challenge his brother, Artaxerxes, for the throne of Persia. While many of the Greeks suspected his intent, only Clearchus had been taken into the confidence of Cyrus and knew the true purpose of the expedition. It had become obvious by now to all the Greeks that Cyrus intended to put himself upon the throne of Persia. This meant they would have to undertake a long and difficult march through Syria and deep into Mesopotamia. Then they would have to fight what was sure to be a major battle against Artaxerxes at Babylon.

The Greeks debated among themselves and many argued that they had only been hired to help Cyrus put down some regional conflicts with the Pisidians. For that they had agreed to be paid a daric a day and whatever they could loot. They had not agreed to march with him over a thousand miles to confront the great king of Persia in a major battle.

Tension between the Greeks and Cyrus increased each day. As the situation worsened, Cyrus turned to his friend Clearchus for support. The Greek commander called the mercenaries to assembly, and relying on the force of his presence and his reputation, he ordered the Greek army to move forward on his command. The soldiers stood their ground and simply stared at Clearchus. Not a hoplite or peltast would move forward on his command. The entire Greek army stood as one in defiance to its commander. The officers and men of the Persian army stood watching in amazement. They had never before seen ordinary soldiers defy their commander. Defiance and insubordination were virtually unheard of in the Persian army, and in those rare instances where it had occurred, perhaps within a small company, it was punished by immediate execution.

The Greeks, however, were not ordinary soldiers of the ancient world. Barbarians were driven into combat by the lash and out of fear of their commanders. The Greeks would obey only by their own consent. Clearchus ordered the troops to move again with all the force of his presence and reputation. This time the Greeks responded by pelting him with rocks and Clearchus was nearly killed. He was forced to retreat to his camp where he realized that he could not command these men by force alone. Perhaps he could command his own smaller army of two thousand through the force of his will, as he had done in Thrace, but the assembled presence of the entire force of thirteen thousand was too great to be moved by the fear of any one man. Clearchus would need to bend these Greeks to his will through persuasion.

The next morning, after the Greeks had eaten, Clearchus called for a general assembly. At the assembly he begged permission to address the army, not as their commander, but as a fellow Greek, a Spartan, and a soldier. He mounted a hastily constructed platform so that as many soldiers as possible could see him. Heralds were placed throughout the crowd to carry his words to those too far in the back to hear.

The once-feared Spartan commander stood before the Greek army and without saying a word he proceeded to weep. The mercenaries were stunned. Here was the proud, strong, and defiant Spartan leader standing before them weeping like a woman. He was so vulnerable as he wept that the army quickly fell to silence. The fearless Spartan, tears streaming down his face, recounted to the assembled Greeks the story of his friendship with Cyrus. He told them how he had accepted money from Cyrus and used it to equip and pay the army in Thrace and never taken even one daric for his own purse.

Clearchus spoke on through his tears about the bond he had forged with them fighting the Thracians. He recounted how he took pride in their victories together as Greeks and that now he found himself forced to make a difficult choice. Either he must honor his word to his friend Cyrus and desert the Greeks, or he must turn his back on a loyal and good Persian friend to remain with his Greek brothers. Then he lifted his sword to the heavens and cried out for all to hear, "I am a Greek, and I cannot betray Greeks to remain a friend to barbarians." He vowed to turn his back on Cyrus and follow the Greek army in whatever capacity they would have him. Without the army, Clearchus shouted to the heavens, he could not live. They were his life and his purpose. They were the same body and the same spirit. Where the army went, he concluded, so also would he follow as a general or as a common soldier.

With those words Clearchus finished his speech and his chin rested upon his chest. The army was silent. Then after several seconds of stunned silence many of the soldiers and officers on the front lines ran toward him and surrounded him. They pressed forward to touch him affectionately and they praised his words. They praised him for choosing to remain with his Greek brothers and for not siding with the Persians. Two of the senior commanders, Xenias and Pasion, along with their men, joined those already assembled around Clearchus and they moved closer to touch their leader. Soon it seemed like the entire army had closed around him and taken him within its embrace.

Cyrus had placed spies among the Greeks, and they reported to him what Clearchus had said and how the Greeks had reacted. Cyrus was distressed at the news and sent a messenger to Clearchus with orders that he should report to the royal tent immediately. When the messenger went to the camp of the Greeks and relayed the message from Cyrus, Clearchus publicly refused the summons. Then Cyrus sent a second messenger and Clearchus made another show before the army of refusing the summons. Each time Cyrus sent a messenger Clearchus made a public display of refusal, to the delight of the Greeks. By a secret messenger late that same night, however, Clearchus sent word to his Persian friend and benefactor to be patient and not to lose trust in him. Clearchus told Cyrus to continue to send for him each day but not to be angered by his public refusal to obey the summons. Clearchus assured Cyrus, by their bond of friendship, that the matter would eventually be resolved in his favor.

Several days passed and the tensions in the Greek camp diminished. Finally, Clearchus determined that the time was right for another general assembly. He sensed that the Greeks craved for him to take command once more and give them direction. When the army had assembled he told them that Cyrus considered himself wronged by the Greeks and that they were no longer in his pay. He recounted how each day Cyrus would send for him and how each day Clearchus would refuse to go. He was ashamed to face his old friend, and he also feared to go to him, for while Cyrus was a good and generous friend he was also a dangerous man when angered.

Clearchus went on to explain to the army how he feared not only for his own life at the hands of Cyrus but how he feared more for the well-being and safe return of the Greek army. They had to decide on the best course of action, and he warned that they had to decide quickly. Clearchus advised the Greeks it would be best to leave this place. At that point he stopped speaking and turned the podium over to any of the other Greeks, officers or enlisted men, who wished to speak on the subject. Many men rose to take their turn at the podium. Some spoke to express their own ideas and others spoke at the instigation of Clearchus, for he had planted among the soldiers men whom he counted on to speak in support of remaining with Cyrus.

One speaker suggested asking Cyrus for ships on which to sail home, while another suggested asking for guides to show them the way back over land. Another man rose and pointed out that Cyrus would not be inclined to give either ships or guides to the men who were dashing his aspirations to be king of Persia. Did the Greeks really believe they could trust a man to keep his word who felt betrayed by them?

The last speaker rose and outlined a solution that seemed to please all the factions among the Greeks. The speaker proposed sending a delegation of Greeks under Clearchus to visit Cyrus and hear in detail what he was planning. If in fact Cyrus confirmed to them his intention to march against his brother in Babylon, then the Greeks should demand more pay for their services. After all, a long march to Babylon and a war against Artaxerxes was not what they had signed on for.

However, the Greeks had come this far for money and if they could earn more they would continue. If Cyrus would not agree to more pay, the Greeks should demand that he release them from his service and proceed with his own army of Persians against his brother. The Greeks would ask that they should be allowed to depart in friendship. If an agreement to continue in his service could be made, then they would follow him to Babylon willingly, as free men in his pay.

Clearchus rose and accepted the proposal. He told the assembly that he was prepared to follow whomever they chose as their general and carry out their wishes. He would follow the Greek army as a common soldier if that was the will of the assembly, for he was a man who could follow as well as he had led. The Greeks approved the plan by unanimous vote and then went on to confirm Clearchus as their leader. Clearchus and the delegation of Greeks met that same night with Cyrus in his quarters. They made their proposition as he listened attentively. Then he replied to them that for the immediate future he wished only for them to march twelve more days with him to the banks of the Euphrates River. There he would confront an old enemy, Abrocomas, the satrap of Syria. Once Abrocomas was defeated, Cyrus assured the Greeks that they would all deliberate on the matter, Persians and Greeks alike.

In exchange for the Greek pledge to march against Abrocomas, Cyrus agreed to an increase in pay for each mercenary. The pay of each Greek would be increased from a daric to a daric and a half. They agreed to march with him as far as the banks of the Euphrates River in Syria. As the Greeks left the royal tent that day they were sure to a man that Cyrus was intent on moving against his brother. Though Cyrus had never told them directly, not a Greek among them that day thought differently.

With the Greek revolt temporarily resolved, Cyrus ordered that camp be broken the next day. The army left Tarsus and marched one hundred miles east for five days to Issus, the last city in the territory of Cilicia. Issus was a large and prosperous city in ancient times, situated on the sea. The army had been resting there for three days when a convoy of Spartan supply ships sailed into port. Then, after another convoy of supply ships belonging to Cyrus arrived escorted by several Spartan warships, the army was provisioned.

On board one of the warships was a commander named Cheirisophus. Along with nearly a thousand hoplites he had been sent by the Spartan ephors to aid Cyrus. The ephors had sent them to Cyrus as an expression of Spartan friendship and appreciation for his help in ending the Peloponnesian Wars. These Spartans were the only group in the army of Cyrus that had any official connection with a Greek city-state, as all the rest of the Greeks were mercenaries who acted as independent agents without ties to any political entity.

IV
BATTLE FOR THE EMPIRE

The army left Issus and began to move south along the coast of the Mediterranean Sea toward the border with Syria. After less than a full day's march they encountered a group of some four hundred Greek mercenaries who had deserted from the army of the Persian general Abrocomas. These Greeks offered to join Cyrus to fight against their former employer. Cyrus accepted their offer and they fell in among the ranks of the other Greek mercenaries.

Cyrus and the army continued to move along the coast until they came to a place referred to in the manuscripts as the "Gates between Cilicia and Syria." These were two parallel walls, each with its own fortresses that divided Cilicia from Syria. Each wall had a gate, hence the name, and between the two parallel walls flowed the river Carsus. The walls of these "gates" began in the cliffs of the Nur Mountains where the river has its source and they paralleled the river, like so many sentries, as it made its way to the sea. The northern or Cilician wall and fortress were garrisoned by soldiers from the army of King Syennesis while the southern wall and fortress across the river were under the control of the satrap Abrocomas and a contingent of Persian soldiers.

Cyrus sent for his navy in order to ferry his troops by sea around the southern wall. From there he intended to launch an attack on the southern wall and fortress from behind. When Abrocomas learned that Cyrus was advancing he withdrew his forces and moved them over the mountains and through the Beilan Pass into Syria. Artaxerxes had instructed Abrocomas to raise this army months before with the intent of using it against the Egyptians. Now the king ordered Abrocomas to retreat to Babylon and join the royal army to meet the new threat posed by Cyrus.

83

With the southern wall deserted of defenders, Cyrus and his army moved around it and then marched farther south to the Phoenician coastal city of Myriandus, now called Iskenderun. This was another thriving port and many merchant ships lay at anchor within its harbor. Cyrus and the army remained at Myriandus for seven days, provisioning themselves for the next and most dangerous stage of their march. Henceforth, the army would head inland through Syria along the banks of the Euphrates River. Cyrus wished to get within striking distance of Babylon, and his army would be vulnerable to surprise attack along the route by advanced Persian forces or even, for that matter, the entire army of the king. Cyrus was unsure of what or how much his brother knew about his expedition.

While the army was at Myriandus, two of the senior Greek commanders, Xenias and Pasion, deserted. Earlier, their troops had gone over to the Spartan, Clearchus, and they no longer held commands. The two generals paid a ship's captain to take them and their valuables aboard and sail them back to Asia Minor. When Cyrus found out what they had done he could have had the slower merchant vessel overtaken by some of his faster warships as it left the harbor. Instead he chose to allow the two Greeks to escape.

Cyrus held the wives and children of these two commanders on the southwestern coast of Turkey, yet he sent orders to his garrison commander to release them. Both Xenias and Pasion had given Cyrus loyal service to that point so he chose to allow them to escape without retaliation. What is not clear from the ancient manuscripts is why Cyrus held their families hostage. Was it normal for Cyrus to hold hostage the families of his Greek commanders as insurance, or had he made an exception for Xenias and Pasion? The fact that the two commanders deserted knowing that Cyrus held their families may indicate they had privately received permission to leave while Cyrus publicly turned their departure into a display of his magnanimity. The Greeks were favorably impressed by the charity Cyrus showed the two generals and their families. As a result, many of the common soldiers among the Greeks became more favorably inclined toward him.

At Myriandus, Cyrus turned his army east and followed the same route as Abrocomas over the 2,400-foot-high Beilan Pass. It took four days and a distance of sixty-six miles, for the army to finally cross the mountains and reach the banks of the river Chalus. In the ancient sources the Beilan Pass is referred to as another "Syrian Gate," so-called because it offers an easy passage over the Mt. Amanus range (Nur Mountains) and leads into eastern Syria. This route functioned as the primary land-link between the Mediterranean coast and deeper Asia for centuries. No other road in the ancient world has a longer record for the passage of armies and caravans than this route which Cyrus followed from upper Syria to Mesopotamia.

Cyrus marched the army along this relatively easy route five more days for one hundred miles until they came to the Dardas River. From there they marched east three more days for fifty miles, until they arrived at the banks of the Euphrates River where sat a large and prosperous city called Thapsacus. Given the distances described in the manuscripts and the proximity of the city to the Euphrates River, Thapsacus is probably the Syrian town of Ar Raqqah or the nearby village of Meskene.

At Thapsacus the army rested for five days until, on the last night in camp, Cyrus called the Greek officers to his tent. He finally revealed to them his plan to march against his brother in Babylon and seize the throne of Persia. The Greek officers were not surprised and they returned to their camp to explain the plan to the soldiers. When the Greeks assembled and heard what Cyrus was planning to do they became angry. Waging a limited campaign in the vicinity of Asia Minor was one thing; marching into the heart of the Persian Empire to risk battle with the king's main armies was another. Many of the soldiers believed their officers knew all along that Cyrus had intended to march against his brother and had kept the plan secret from the army until they were well within Persian territory, too late to turn back. The soldiers accused some of their officers of having tricked them and of being in collusion with the pretender Cyrus. Then the mercenaries voted to demand a substantial increase in pay or they would refuse to continue forward.

When Cyrus heard the demands he offered each Greek soldier five minas in silver when the army reached Babylon and full pay when they returned to Ionia. This was an unusual and generous arrangement. Cyrus was willing to pay the surviving Greek mercenaries for their homeward journey to the western coast of Turkey. Usually mercenaries in the ancient world were paid on the spot after a campaign ended and then quickly discharged to make their way home at their own expense. Given how far the Greeks had penetrated into Asia, it seems reasonable, though expensive, for Cyrus to have agreed to pay them for their long journey home. The Greeks agreed to the terms and the army prepared to cross over to the left bank of the Euphrates River.

As Cyrus and his army prepared to cross the river the local people lined the banks to watch. They were amazed to see the first contingents of soldiers enter the river and cross the usually deep waters of the Euphrates at only chest height. Nobody could remember having seen the river so low before and the Persian seers in the army proclaimed to all who were assembled by the river bank that the waters had receded to allow Cyrus to cross. Likewise, the superstitious Greeks interpreted the shallow level of the river as an auspicious omen. They commented to each other that it proved Cyrus was destined to be the next king of Persia and that their campaign would be successful.

As Cyrus and the army marched along the banks of the Euphrates they passed through Syria, a distance of 165 miles, in nine days. Then the army took another five days and traveled 115 miles through a plain that is described in the manuscripts as having been "as flat as the sea" and a virtual paradise of wild game. There were fragrant shrubs and reeds all around the plain but not a tree to be seen. The landscape abounded with exotic animals, some of which the Greeks had never before encountered. As they passed through this plain they marveled at the ostriches, gazelle, and wild birds. When they killed and roasted some of the birds they were reminded of the taste of partridges they were familiar with in Greece.

After a brief rest, Cyrus was anxious to continue the march because he had become uneasy about remaining too long in any one place. He believed that the quicker his army arrived upon the field of battle at Babylon the less prepared his brother would be.

The more observant among the Greek officers had noticed on their long journey into Persia that while the empire was vast and contained many resources, it was also weak. The great size of Persia made it difficult to defend against a quick thrust from its periphery. The Greeks remarked among themselves how easily they had been able to penetrate almost a thousand miles into the empire without serious resistance. They were now within striking distance of Babylon and had yet to see any sign of the king or his vaunted army. The only royal army the Greeks had come even close to encountering was that of Abrocomas, and he had run from them rather than fight. Armies of the king had to be brought together from great distances and the Greeks observed that an invading army, even a small one, that was well-organized and moved decisively, had a marked advantage. These observations would not be lost on Alexander of Macedon sixty years later when he would invade and conquer Persia.

Cyrus and the Greeks continued their march along the Euphrates River and eventually came to the city of Charmande. This city was a prosperous trading center where the army was able to reprovision. Greek troops normally bought their provisions on a daily basis from merchants who followed the army. When the army stopped at a town or city, the soldiers bought their provisions from local inhabitants who set up a market, usually in the shadow of the town walls. The main market tended to be in the center of the town or village. Today, throughout modern Turkey, and in fact the entire Middle East and much of Mediterranean Europe, the same system prevails. Each town and village has a central marketplace, a *markezi* in Turkish, which, as in ancient times, is near the center of the town and is often the hub of all commercial and considerable social activity.

While the army was resting at Charmande, one of Menon's men got into a dispute with a soldier serving under Clearchus. It began as a simple argument between two common soldiers but it escalated and almost destroyed Cyrus's plans. The men involved were from different mercenary units and apparently they began arguing over possession of some items that had been bought in the marketplace. The dispute was brought to Clearchus to resolve since the argument had broken out in his camp. Clearchus settled the dispute quickly in favor of his own man; then, as might be expected from the stern Spartan commander, he ordered the other Greek soldier stripped, tied to a post, and flogged for good measure. The man took the flogging and after his release returned to his own camp where he showed his bleeding back to his mates.

Menon's soldiers were angered over the incident and the next day Clearchus made the mistake of riding through their camp on his way home from the market after shopping for provisions. A group of soldiers were chopping wood when one of them saw Clearchus and threw his hand ax at him, barely missing his head. Other soldiers surrounded Clearchus and held his horse by the bridle. Clearchus struggled to free his horse from their hold and the incident quickly gained momentum. A general outcry was raised throughout Menon's camp and soldiers descended from everywhere to see what the commotion was about. When Clearchus finally managed to free himself he was driven out of Menon's camp in a hail of stones.

Clearchus returned to his own camp in a fury and called his men to arms. They advanced fully armed against Menon's camp intent on taking revenge for this outrage to the honor of their commander. As Clearchus led his men toward the camp, Menon and his men armed themselves as well and came out to meet them. The two groups faced off and were about to come to blows when Proxenus arrived with a battalion of his hoplites. He placed his men between the two hostile parties and pleaded with both sides not to fight. Clearchus was still so angry that he would not be dissuaded. The situation became so tense that Cyrus was called from his tent and he too stood between the two opposing forces.

Cyrus invoked his long friendship with Clearchus and convinced him not to fight with Menon and the other Greeks. Then Cyrus lectured all the Greeks that if they began fighting among themselves over trivial matters, all would quickly be lost and the army would fall apart. Clearchus at last calmed down and the quarrel between the two commanders was resolved.

As the army began to move southeast again in the direction of Babylon, scouts reported to Cyrus that they had seen the tracks of large numbers of horses on the plain ahead. The scouts estimated about two thousand cavalry who were retreating and burning everything in their wake to deny Cyrus and his army provisions. The army marched for three more days, about forty miles, and entered the satrap of Babylonia. On the third day they arrived on a wide plain and Cyrus ordered his troops to assemble. They were now so close to Babylon that Cyrus expected the king and his army to appear as early as dawn the next day.

Cyrus and his officers met in his tent and discussed plans for the coming battle. It was agreed that Clearchus would take command of the right wing of the army while Menon would take the left. Cyrus would place his Persian forces in the center where he would be in direct command. In this way the stronger and more disciplined Greeks would protect both vulnerable flanks while being available to support the less reliable Persian soldiers in the center.

Following their meeting, Cyrus ordered a count of his forces. When the results were reported on the eve of battle he found he had

100,000 Persian troops, 10,400 Greek hoplites, and 2,500 Greek peltasts. The advancing army of Artaxerxes, according to the reports Cyrus was receiving, numbered 1,200,000 men with 200 scythe-bearing chariots. Six thousand horsemen under the commander of the king's bodyguard, Artagerses, were allegedly stationed in front of the king for his protection. The king's army was divided into four parts of 300,000 men each, under subsidiary commanders Tissaphernes, Gobryas, Arbaces, and Abrocomas, though the latter was not yet on the field after his retreat from Cyrus in Syria.

The numbers given for the Persian host are clearly cited in the ancient Greek and Latin manuscripts; however, they should not be taken seriously. The Greeks accepted the enormous size of the Persian Empire almost as a matter of political faith, and to them everything in Persia, from land area to population and wealth, was considered gigantic. Earlier, Herodotus had painstakingly cited 2,641,610 fighting men as the strength of the Persian army that descended on the three hundred Spartans at Thermopylae. There was also a self-serving tendency—common in all conflicts, up to and including the Persian Gulf War fought in the same region—to exaggerate an opponent's numbers to enhance the heroic aspect of one's own side. In truth, a million-man infantry army would have been incapable of maneuver, as well as incapable of staying in one place, for it would have immediately exhausted the sustenance from any ground on which it paused.

Even the figures given for Cyrus's army, including its suspiciously round number of 100,000 Asian troops, are viewed skeptically by modern historians. The roll call of Greeks is minutely specified by region or city of origin, and divided between hoplite and peltast, but the total of 12,900 is identical to the sum of troops counted at the beginning of the march (before the Greeks stopped to demand more pay). After a twelve-hundred-mile advance, some attrition in manpower or numbers "fit for duty" would be expected.

Nevertheless, there is no reason to believe that Artaxerxes was incapable of defending his empire with a far larger army than Cyrus commanded while invading it. The king, even if given less time to prepare, could call on numerous provinces and cities for men, while Cyrus drew his forces from his single satrapy in Asia Minor and from Greece. The more important comparison is qualitative, and here Cyrus may have held the advantage. The Persians were characterized by the Greeks as unwilling fighters, not unlike armies of coerced slaves.

Behind the king's regular troops and cavalry were masses of untrained, ill-equipped subjects that had to be forced into battle, though they could hardly be forced to fight. These unfortunate crowds would have had an especially difficult time against the Greeks, who had been trained since boyhood to fight for their independent communities, owned the best metal weapons and armor available, employed the most effective tactics, and most important of all, had acquired their discipline and skill at arms by fighting other Greeks.

The actual numbers involved in the battle between the brothers for the throne of Persia cannot at this point be accurately determined, but it's reasonable to assume that the king commanded a far larger army— though largely composed of ineffective conscripts—than his brother. As the battle unfolded, small unit actions and sudden maneuvers determined the outcome, lending further credence to the belief that the opposing armies were not as multitudinous as the ancient sources claim.

In his tent Cyrus listened nearly all that night to reports from the deserters, the advice of his own officers, and to tactical assessments from the Greek commanders. After the Greeks had finished their discussions, Cyrus addressed them. He explained why he had hired the Greeks and how he believed they were the best and most disciplined fighters in the world. They would give him not only a tactical and psychological advantage over his brother on the battlefield, but they would also serve to inspire and discipline the less reliable oriental soldiers that Cyrus had recruited from his satrapy to make up the bulk of his army. Cyrus praised the Greeks because they valued their freedom and he added the comment that of all things in life freedom was the most valuable. These were unusual words to hear from the Persian who expected to become the "king of kings" and rule an empire of conquered subjects. Perhaps exposure to the Greeks and their methods of thinking and acting over the past several months had begun to affect the young prince.

Then Cyrus explained to the Greeks what they might expect the next day when they engaged the Persian army in battle. The king's army would advance in a huge human wave. They would come against the Greek phalanx shouting and brandishing their weapons; however, this was only a show for the opening of the battle. The Persians, his own people, Cyrus sadly commented, were not brave fighters and he was sure that they would turn and run when confronted by the disciplined Greeks. History, they all agreed that night, had shown this to be the case in the two prior wars between Persia and Greece that century.

Cyrus promised every Greek soldier who fought bravely and survived that he would return home a rich man. Those Greeks who wished could remain with him in Persia and be assured a place of honor and wealth. A Samian officer, Gaulites, spoke up and criticized Cyrus for making grandiose and inflated promises only because he needed the Greeks. It remained to be seen, Gaulites commented, if Cyrus would keep his word after the battle and could deliver all that he had promised to so many.

Cyrus turned to Gaulites and told him how his father, Darius II, had built an empire that extended so far south that men cannot live there because of the heat, and so far north that men cannot live there because of the cold. That empire needed to be ruled and Cyrus needed loyal satraps to administer all the territory that lay between the two extremes. Those satraps, Cyrus promised, would be chosen from among his friends and loyal allies, and they would become rich and powerful men in the empire. The only fear Cyrus had, he told the Greeks that night, was that he would not have enough friends to give so many rewards to. Then, in a gesture of generosity and to show his confidence in the outcome of the battle, he promised the officers that each Greek soldier in his service would receive a crown of gold in addition to his pay.

When Cyrus had finished, many of the Greek officers pressed forward, crowding around him, each one demanding to know what his reward would be if he remained in Persia after the battle. Cyrus made lavish promises of a satrapy and unlimited treasure to each officer. As most of the Greeks left the royal tent that night they were content with their lot and hopeful for their futures if they survived the carnage of the battle which would soon be raging around them.

A few of the Greeks, those officers and generals closest to Cyrus, remained behind after the rest had left. They warned the young prince that on the morrow he would be well advised to remain behind the fighting lines, protected by his bodyguard and out of harm's way. This would be his first major engagement and it would be best if he acted prudently and not foolishly. Cyrus replied that he could not remain behind the lines but would venture forth to do battle with anyone who stood between him and the crown of Persia. There was no other choice for him, he explained, if he were to rule the Persian Empire.

Shortly after dawn the next day, Cyrus and his army moved forward about ten miles along the plain. They were dressed in full armor, with weapons at the ready and prepared to fight. About noon they came to a trench, about eighteen feet deep and thirty feet wide. The trench extended through the plain where it eventually reached a wall. The wall in turn extended from the Euphrates River northeast to the Tigris River. It was the Median Wall, built by the Babylonians two centuries earlier, but now the southern part of the wall was in ruins. Artaxerxes had constructed the trench as an additional obstacle. Cyrus and his army crossed the undefended trench, and when they reached the other side they saw tracks of both men and horses, evidently in retreat. Since Artaxerxes had abandoned the defense of the trench and it appeared his army was retreating, Cyrus and the Greeks concluded that the "king of kings" had lost his taste for battle.

The next day, Cyrus and his army marched forward in a much less disciplined manner than they had the day before. Their spirits were high and Cyrus had become overconfident. He was seated in his chariot with only a small bodyguard about him while his troops on the line of march were moving along the road strung-out and in disorder. Many of their weapons and armor had been loaded onto carts and pack animals for transport instead of being carried at the ready. By noon the army had come close to the place the scouts had chosen for the camp that night. From indications in the sources and modern map references, Cyrus's army had positioned itself on the eastern bank of the Euphrates River at the foot of a long plain that stretches east as far as the Tigris River.

As the army was preparing to pitch camp, a rider came toward them, his horse at full gallop. It was Pategyas, a scout and member of Cyrus's staff. He rode through the ranks of the soldiers shouting that the king was approaching with a large army ready for battle. There ensued a mad scramble among the invading forces. Men scattered to retrieve their weapons and armor from the carts and pack animals, and then to rejoin their battalions. Everything was in disorder. Cyrus leaped down from his chariot and began to put on his armor. He took his shield and spears and mounted his horse. Under the direction of their officers the army units quickly formed into battle lines.

Clearchus moved to the right flank close to the Euphrates River and Proxenus took position next to him. Menon and his army manned

the left flank of the Greek wing so that the Greek mercenaries constituted the entire right of Cyrus's army. A thousand Paphlagonian cavalry supported the Greeks's far right flank. Persian troops quickly
made up the center and left wing of the battle line. The position which
the army found itself in that afternoon was contrary to the order of
battle that Cyrus had issued the day before in his tent. Under the original battle plan the Greeks were to have covered both flanks of the
army. The change of plans was probably due to two factors. First,
there was so much disorder, confusion, and perhaps even panic when
the scout rode through the column with news of the king's advance
that everyone forgot the battle plan that had been issued the day
before. Second, and perhaps most important, the Greeks instinctively
formed their own battle line and would not separate in the face of danger by placing the unreliable soldiers of Cyrus between them. This
move may have cost Cyrus not only the battle of Cunaxa, but his life.

About six hundred heavily armored horsemen were assigned to
protect Cyrus. He insisted on remaining in the center and to the front
of the battle line, ignoring the advice of the Greeks to remain well
behind it. "Would you have me, who aspire to empire," Cyrus asked
Clearchus, "show myself unworthy of it?" While the horsemen who
protected him all wore helmets, Cyrus insisted on going into battle
with his head unprotected in a show of costly bravado. It was now
well past noon and the sun was high in the sky. It was hot and dusty
as the invaders awaited the king's appearance.

Cyrus's soldiers stood in battle formation and watched across the
wide, flat plain for any sign of the king and his army. Hour after hour
passed as they stood in the hot September sun, in full armor, and still
the enemy had not come into sight. Then far off in the distance a low,
white cloud began to appear on the horizon. It grew in size and
beneath it a broad, dark stain appeared on the ground and gradually
began to spread across the plain. Soon the Greeks could see flashes of
bronze and iron, reflections on the swords and spearpoints of the
approaching multitude of soldiers. As it came closer, the ranks of
advancing men became discernible and for the next hour the Greeks
watched in silence as the massive army of the Persian king methodically advanced. The army stretched from one end of the horizon to the
other, the ranks of the approaching soldiers seemingly without limit.
It was the 3rd of September 401 B.C., and one of the great battles in
ancient history was about to begin.

The site of the battlefield of Cunaxa is in Iraq about twenty-five miles due west of modern-day Baghdad. The same broad plain is there today where the armies clashed twenty-four hundred years ago. It is located in the area where the Tigris and Euphrates Rivers come closest together as they flow south from the mountains of Turkey to the Persian Gulf. The site of the great battle today is a depressed and run-down area of a few industrial structures, some deserted mines, water towers and scattered buildings, about fifteen miles west of Saddam Airport.

As the Persian troops advanced, the Greeks could see that they had been drawn up according to their national divisions within the empire and that they were marching forward in solid squares. Then the Greeks spotted the Persians's dreaded chariots as they came into view. Each chariot was drawn by four horses and carried scythes that extended out from the sides of its wheels. Some chariots had blades attached to their undercarriages that protruded downward so as to inflict the maximum amount of injury and mutilation possible upon any soldiers who fell beneath them. The chariots had been deployed so that they could be driven into the ranks of the Greeks to cut as many of them as possible to pieces before the king's infantry closed for combat.

As the army of the king came closer the Greeks began to make out more details in their ranks. Wooden or wicker shields, and formations of spearmen or bowmen became distinct. At the far left of the Persian line, by the river, were cavalry with white cuirasses, led by Tissaphernes. As they watched the advancing army, the Greek officers began to talk among themselves about how Cyrus had been mistaken about his brother's army. These Persians were not advancing as the Greeks had expected, in a disorganized mass, shouting and brandishing their weapons. Artaxerxes' soldiers were advancing in disciplined formations, in silence, with measured steps under the control of their officers and emotions. Their endless numbers caused the Greeks concern.

Cyrus rode laterally between the two armies, his long black hair unconcealed by a helmet, alternately eyeing his brother's forces and his own. On reaching the Greeks he shouted to Clearchus to abandon his position by the river and lead his troops against the enemy center, toward the king. Clearchus was a seasoned tactician, and he noted that the king's army extended too far beyond his left. He was unwilling to draw his right wing away from the protection of the Euphrates to send them against the Persian center for fear that the enemy would turn his flank. He may have been especially concerned about the Persian horsemen facing his far right. Clearchus shouted back to Cyrus that it would be best to leave tactical matters to him and in turn he would take care to make sure all went well. Cyrus seemed content with the answer and turned his horse to ride away from the Greek lines.

As Cyrus was riding away he heard a noise running through the Greek ranks. He encountered Xenophon and stopped to ask what the commotion was. Xenophon explained that the watchwords "Zeus, savior and victory" were being passed through the Greek line. Cyrus was pleased with this choice and rode away to take his position as commander at the center of his army.

When the king's soldiers had closed to within a mile of the Greek lines, Clearchus gave the order to begin the advance to meet them. The Greeks, formed into their phalanx, struck up the paean, their dreaded war chant, and began to march directly toward the Persian line in their front. First the phalanx moved forward at a steady walk and then, at a signal from the officers, began to advance at a faster pace. At the same moment the soldiers increased their pace, they changed their chant from the paean to the war cry for which they were feared throughout the ancient world.

As the Greeks closed for battle, their sound and appearance unnerved the Persian soldiers who opposed them. Some Greeks clashed their shields against their spears to increase the frightening clamor, and before the phalanx could make contact the Persians broke and ran. The panic spread across the left wing of the Persian line and literally thousands of men dropped their weapons and began to run. The exception was the contingent of Persian cavalry along the river, which charged into the peltasts on the far right of the Greek phalanx. The light troops couldn't hold the horsemen, but stabbed and hacked at them as they raced through.

On the main battle line, the Persian formations in front of the Greeks had come apart and the king's soldiers were in all-out flight from the battlefield. The Greeks pursued the Persians, keeping their ranks intact as they advanced. In the confusion of the ensuing panic some of the Persian chariots, those that had been deployed to support the advancing infantry line, ran over their own men. The small num-

ber of chariots that charged the Greek line passed harmlessly through
their ranks. When the Greeks saw the Persian chariots coming they
simply opened their ranks at a signal from their officers and let the
chariots pass through. Many of the drivers were thrown from their
chariots. The driverless horses, rather than plunge headlong into the
mass of soldiers before them, chose the path of least resistance and ran
through the files opened by the Greeks. For some reason or oversight,
the king had failed to order the greater number of his chariots against
the Greek phalanx at the start of the battle. Instead, those chariots had
been deployed at the center of the king's line and most of them were
well away from the Greeks.

The Greeks suffered only one casualty during this action, a man
on their left wounded by an arrow. Another man was run over by a
chariot but escaped unharmed. From his command post in the center
of his army Cyrus was pleased to see that the Greeks were routing the
enemy so quickly. Many in his bodyguard were already hailing him as
the new king of Persia. Cyrus kept his six hundred horsemen in tight
formation and set out toward the center of the opposing Persian line,
intent on finding his brother, Artaxerxes. Cyrus knew that his brother
would be in the center of the Persian formation since this was the
king's traditional position. It was also the safest place on the battlefield for a commander to be. From this position, center and slightly
behind the main battle line, the king could issue commands to both his
left and right flanks quickly.

When the two armies closed, the king's battle line was said to be
so long that Artaxerxes, in the center of his formation, was well
beyond Cyrus's left. This evokes a powerful image of the magnitude of
the king's forces, but in tactical terms makes little sense. It would
mean that Artaxerxes, either through accident or ignorance, was willing to let his left wing face the entire invading army on its own while
his center and right marched against empty space. Or it indicates not
so much the immense size of the king's army as its intent to execute a
flanking maneuver. In fact, when the king's left collapsed and fled
before the Greeks, his center and right wing began to wheel around
the left flank of Cyrus's army. The armies, once joined, were executing
a pirouette, the Persian left retreating and its right advancing, with the
effect that the two brothers, both positioned in the center of their
respective hosts, had now come within each other's range. At the head
of his 600-man heavy cavalry, Cyrus charged directly into the

approaching center of the Persian line. So fierce was his assault that the king's cavalry bodyguard of horsemen broke and began to scatter.

As the enemy line came apart and men began to panic and run, Cyrus's cavalry, in pursuit, began to lose its cohesion. Flushed with the taste of victory, they abandoned their formation and began to chase individual groups of fleeing enemy soldiers. Cyrus's mounted body-guard became just as scattered as the king's, and Cyrus suddenly found himself with only a few of his men around him. The next moments would decide the fate of the empire.

Cyrus was challenged by Artagerses, commander of the king's cav-alry, whose thrown javelin bounced off Cyrus's breastplate. Cyrus hurled a weapon of his own and caught Artagerses in a vulnerable spot between his armor—through the neck. Then Cyrus caught sight of his brother and rushed at him in a fury. He struck Artaxerxes in the chest, his javelin penetrating two inches through the royal armor. But before he could finish off the wounded king, Cyrus himself was struck just beneath the eye by a javelin and he fell from his horse. Accounts differ whether this was the killing blow, but he had at least been crip-pled, and as the king's men converged he had but moments to live. His only men nearby were "table companions," who may or may not have been proficient warriors, but eight of them died defending their prince. One was said to have thrown his body atop Cyrus's prostrate form and committed suicide with a dagger before the king's men could close. By the time the charge against the king had ended, Cyrus was dead, killed in the thick of combat. He had assaulted the center of the king's lines with too few troops.

Xenophon later commented that the willingness of Cyrus's com-panions to die in his defense was proof of the prince's virtues. Their sacrifice also indicated that Cyrus had not been felled by a lucky shot but had rashly charged into a part of the enemy line where the king held greater strength. The Greek physician Ctesias, who was in Persian service and who ministered to the king's wound, opined that if the Greek mercenaries had followed Cyrus's advice to attack toward the center instead of keeping to the safety of the Euphrates River on their right flank, the outcome of the battle would have been different.

So strong had the hatred between the royal brothers grown, that even with Cyrus dead and the battle raging all about him, Artaxerxes took time to participate in the mutilation of his brother's body. Cyrus's head and right hand were cut off by the king's men. The "offending hand" that had dared to strike a blow against the royal personage of the king, and the head that had dared to plot against him, were placed in a basket. Artaxerxes ordered them sent to Babylon so that after the battle he might preserve them as trophies and display them in celebration of his victory.

Later that day when Parysatis received word from her spies about the death of Cyrus, she hurried to Babylon. After the battle had ended and Artaxerxes had returned to Babylon in triumph, she convinced him to give over what was left of the body, and a part of Cyrus, at least, was given royal burial at Susa. The lamenting queen mother grieved for a short time and then devoted herself to the pursuit of revenge. The queen mother sought out those in the royal bodyguard who had killed and mutilated her beloved Cyrus on the battlefield. The commander of the king's bodyguard, Bagapates, who had decapitated Cyrus on orders from Artaxerxes, was the first to suffer the wrath of the queen. Parysatis won him from a drunken Artaxerxes one evening in a game of dice at the royal palace. She had Bagapates flayed alive and then crucified. All the others who participated in the killing and mutilation of her Cyrus were hunted down one by one. Each was imprisoned in the dungeons below the imperial palace at Babylon and then tortured to death in the slowest and most sadistic manner imaginable.

Artaxerxes' army, emboldened by the death of Cyrus, found their courage once more and regrouped. The soldiers who had been positioned on the left flank of Cyrus's army were demoralized and no longer stood their ground. They began to desert the field of battle in large numbers, allowing Artaxerxes' men to charge into their camp. There the king met Tissaphernes, whose cavalry had fought through the Greek light troops and Paphlagonian cavalry. The Persians plundered the invaders' wagons and baggage, murdering guards, slaves, and camp followers. Some Greeks had been left behind to guard their own camp and a number were killed in its defense. The king's soldiers captured Cyrus's two favorite concubines, a Phocaean woman of exceptional beauty and a younger Milesian woman. The Milesian concubine managed to escape from the soldiers and make her way, nearly naked, to the Greek camp and temporary safety.

At this point in the battle, the Persian king and the main body of Greeks were about three or four miles from one another. The Greeks were continuing to pursue the disintegrating left wing of Artaxerxes' army, totally unaware of what was occurring elsewhere. As the day drew to a close the Greeks believed the battle had been won, while Artaxerxes and his army several miles away contented themselves with plundering Cyrus's camp. Artaxerxes made a huge tactical mistake at this point by not cutting the Greeks off from their supply; but then the Greeks remained the most orderly, as well as dangerous, large formation of troops on the battlefield. And they would soon be returning from their pursuit of the Persian left. Tissaphernes finally prevailed on his king to stop looting the camp and re-form his troops to focus on the Greeks.

It was very late in the day and some of the Greek commanders, most notably Clearchus and Proxenus, began receiving vague reports that the Persians had gotten into the camp of Cyrus. They were unaware that Cyrus had been killed or the extent of the destruction of his army. When the battle began the Greeks had advanced straight ahead from their position on the right wing of Cyrus's army, while Artaxerxes had moved forward from his center a considerable distance away. Thus the two forces had passed one another at so great a distance that neither side even made visual contact. When the king was prevailed upon to withdraw from the burning camp of Cyrus, he faced the prospect that the Greek attack he had avoided earlier was now about to commence as the Greeks returned from their pursuit.

Artaxerxes, advised by Tissaphernes, re-formed his battle line and began to bring it into position against the rear of the Greek phalanx. The king moved until his flank was nearly marching in the Euphrates River. The two armies were facing one another, although this time their positions were reversed from earlier in the day. The Greeks had turned and under orders from their officers re-formed themselves to face the Persian threat that had developed behind them. They struck up the paean and proceeded to advance. Flushed with their earlier success against the left wing of the king's army, and having no respect for the military capability of the Persians, they were eager to engage this new threat in combat.

As the Greeks closed, ready to fight, the battle line of Artaxerxes began to come apart. The Persians broke and ran before the Greeks for the second time that day. Artaxerxes and his bodyguard retreated to a hill behind some villages and watched the rout of the imperial army. When the Greeks spotted the king they advanced toward him but the king and his entourage quickly left. Clearchus sent a mounted scout to the top of the hill to survey the plain and he reported that the entire Persian army of Artaxerxes was in headlong flight.

It was now nearly sunset and the Greeks, victorious and exhausted after the long afternoon of fighting, took a much-needed rest. They debated whether to remain in the villages for the night and send for their supplies, or begin the march back to their camp in the dark. As they debated their next move they began to wonder why they had not received any word from Cyrus. Some of the more optimistic Greeks speculated that Cyrus was in pursuit of the retreating Persian army. Cyrus, however, was dead and his head and hand were on the way to Babylon as trophies. His army was in disarray all over the battlefield and some of his close friends who had survived had deserted to the king while others had simply left the field.

The Greeks were unaware just how alone they were on the plain at Cunaxa as night settled upon them. Surrounded by Persians, they were almost twelve hundred long and dangerous miles from home. The Greek commanders decided it would be safer to return to their own camp so the army set out. When the Greeks reached their camp an hour or so later they found it burned and pillaged. The soldiers of Artaxerxes had quickly overrun the small number of guards who had been left behind to protect the camp, and they had pillaged what food and wine Cyrus had provided. The camp followers, prostitutes, merchants, and slaves were gone, either carried off by the triumphant army of Artaxerxes or killed.

The Greeks settled for the night among the ruins as best they could. There was no dinner that night and few men slept, even though most were tired. When the dawn came there was nothing for breakfast either. As the sun rose over Cunaxa that morning, the Greeks pondered their fate, not in assembly as was their custom but each man in a silent state of despond.

V
THE GREEKS ALONE

Just before the harsh summer sun began to rise in the sky, the Greek generals assembled outside Clearchus's tent to discuss their situation. They came together in the cool air before dawn and worried among themselves because they had still not received any word from Cyrus. The generals agreed to assemble their troops under arms just after sunrise and push forward until they found him. Then two horsemen rode into the camp from the west and reported to the Greeks that Cyrus was dead. They had been sent from Ariaeus, a close friend of Cyrus and his former second in command. Now Ariaeus was the commander of what was left of the army. After the carnage at Cunaxa he had retreated west onto a plain where the soldiers who remained with him had made a makeshift camp. He sent word with these two messengers that the Greeks should join him there before noon because he intended to return to Asia Minor. The messengers warned the Greek commanders that if they did not join Ariaeus before noon that day he would begin the long march home without them.

The news that Cyrus had been killed spread quickly through the Greek camp just as the soldiers were awakening. A great silence settled over the Greeks as the danger of their situation became evident. Clearchus told the messengers to return to Ariaeus and tell him the Greeks had upheld their end of the agreement with Cyrus. They had defeated the forces of the king and if Ariaeus had held his ground and not run, with Cyrus dead he could have become king of Persia. The Greeks wanted Ariaeus to return to the field of battle with his troops and they offered to make him king. The messengers returned to Ariaeus along with two Greek commanders, Cheirisophus the Laconian, and Menon the Thessalian. Menon had become a close friend of Ariaeus on the journey to Cunaxa and he believed that he could prevail upon his Persian friend to accept the Greek offer.

101

While the Greeks awaited Ariaeus's reply they slaughtered and butchered the last of their surviving oxen and baggage animals for food. Some of the soldiers returned to the nearby battlefield where they gathered arrows, broken wicker shields of the Persians, wooden shields of the Egyptians, and broken spears. With this kindling they made fires, boiled their meat, and resolved to live for another day.

Just before noon, Persian heralds sent by Artaxerxes arrived at the perimeter of the Greek camp. With them was a Greek, Phalinus, who had entered the service of the Persian kings years before as an advisor in battlefield tactics and the use of heavy infantry. The heralds called for the leaders of the Greeks to come forward and hear a message from Artaxerxes II, Persian king of kings. When the Greek generals assembled at the edge of the camp the heralds announced that Artaxerxes was victorious and had slain his brother Cyrus on the field of battle. The Persian king ordered the Greeks to surrender their arms and prostrate themselves before his royal person. Only then would he entertain their pleas for mercy.

Clearchus had been in the midst of a sacrifice when the heralds arrived. The other generals summoned him to come but he took his time at the altar and examined the organs that had been removed from the sacrificial victim. Clearchus reflected on the sacrifice and then slowly made his way through the camp to where the heralds of the king and his generals awaited him. He turned to the Greek, Phalinus, who accompanied the Persian heralds and told him to return to his master and tell him that these Greeks would die before they would surrender their arms or fall to their knees to beg mercy from any man, much less a barbarian.

Phalinus reminded Clearchus and the other Greeks that they were in the middle of the Persian Empire. They were alone, enclosed in a hostile land, and blocked from leaving by impassable rivers and high mountains. The Persian king could bring against them so many men that the Greeks could not slay all of them even if they were to offer their necks without resistance. The Greek generals replied that they supported Clearchus and were all of a similar mind. They would keep their arms. Phalinus laughed at them and called them fools. He asked mockingly if they were so stupid as to believe their bravery could prove superior to the might of the Persian king. Then Clearchus turned to Phalinus and asked for his advice, not as a servant of the king but as a Greek among fellow Greeks. Phalinus replied that the

Greeks had not a chance of saving themselves if they retained their arms. Their only hope was to comply with the demands of the king and then throw themselves upon his mercy.

Clearchus considered the advice for a moment and then replied that the Greeks could either be friends to the king or wage war against him. In either case they would need their arms. As Phalinus prepared to leave he offered the Greeks a truce on behalf of the king. The conditions of the truce required that the Greeks remain where they were. In return, the king promised to make no aggressive moves against them. Were the Greeks to move from their present position, either forward or in retreat, the forces of the king would attack. The Greeks agreed to the conditions and Phalinus returned to the camp of Artaxerxes.

Shortly after Phalinus and the heralds had departed, messengers from Ariaeus arrived. Ariaeus thanked the Greeks for their offer to make him king of Persia, but declined on the grounds that the Persians would never accept him on the throne. He was going home to the coast of Asia Minor and if the Greeks wished to join him they must come to his camp under cover of darkness. Menon had remained behind with Ariaeus and awaited the arrival of his comrades.

As the sun set on the Greek camp Clearchus called the generals and captains together and explained to them that the sacrifice he had conducted that morning had not been auspicious for waging war against Artaxerxes. It was evident that they could not remain where they were for they had neither provisions nor a secure defensive position. It was best that they join Ariaeus and return home to Greece. The journey would be long and difficult, for the Greeks had followed Cyrus nearly twelve hundred miles into the heart of the Persian Empire.

The generals and captains agreed and Clearchus was asked to take command. This time there was no vote by the soldiers in assembly or open debate; he simply assumed command because in this time of crisis the Greeks believed that he alone among them possessed the experience and resolve they would need if they were to return home safely. Shortly thereafter, Miltocythes, a Thracian commander and one of Clearchus's captains, left the Greek camp with forty horsemen and about three hundred infantry to desert to the king. Clearchus and the rest of the Greeks left the camp after darkness and marched most of the night to the camp of Ariaeus. The mercenaries arrived about midnight and Clearchus and the other generals met with Ariaeus in his tent.

That night the Greek generals and Ariaeus swore an oath that they would not betray each other and that they would be allies on the long march home. They sealed their oath by sacrificing a bull. The Greeks each dipped their swords in the blood of the victim and Ariaeus a lance tip. Then the men ate and drank and the talk turned to the route home.

Ariaeus was of the opinion that they should not attempt to return home by the same route they had used to come to Cunaxa. They would be sure to perish from starvation, for on their approach march both they and the Persian cavalry had stripped the country by burning and looting. The only choice open to them was to take a route that was longer but where they could obtain sufficient provisions along the way and be safe from attack by the forces of the king.

The Greeks suggested that even though they were short on provisions they would have to put as much distance between themselves and the king as quickly as they could. If they could put just three days between themselves and the king they would have a safe margin and be able to march in greater leisure. The Persian king would not dare follow them with a small and highly mobile army for he feared the Greeks in combat. If he attempted to follow with his full army it would move too slowly to present any threat to them on their retreat.

When daybreak came the Greeks and those who were left from Cyrus's army broke camp. The scouts started out first, moving northwest along the Euphrates River and keeping the rising sun to their right. They calculated that by sunset that day they would reach villages in the northern part of the province of Babylonia. The area had been untouched by the recent fighting and they were confident they would find provisions there.

By late afternoon the scouts sent a report back to the column that they had spotted large numbers of horsemen on the plain ahead. A general alarm was sounded throughout the column and the Greeks took up their arms. Ariaeus, who was making the journey in a cart since he had been wounded in the battle, put on his armor to prepare for a fight. Then the scouts returned to the column and reported that there was no need for alarm as they had mistaken animals grazing on the plains for horsemen. The soldiers stood down. A short time later the scouts reported that they could see smoke rising from villages nearby and they suspected that the king was probably encamping nearby.

Clearchus was leading the vanguard of the army and he knew he could not risk advancing against the king in combat. The Greeks were tired, many among the Persians were wounded, and the entire column was weak because few had eaten that day. But in spite of his weakness Clearchus knew that if the king were nearby the Greeks could not give the appearance of running from him. So he took his chances on confronting the king and led the column straight to the nearest villages in search of provisions and shelter. The army arrived at the villages by sunset but these villages had already been plundered and burned by the soldiers of the king. There was no firewood or food to be found.

As the night descended on the village, the encamped Greeks became frightened. There was little or no food and the confusion in the camp bordered on panic. Clearchus walked the camp all that night holding his baton, and his presence calmed the Greeks. As the situation stabilized and the men settled down he ordered the heralds to spread word throughout the camp that he was offering a reward for the identity of the man who had let an ass loose among the supplies. The soldiers laughed at his joke and many were able to sleep secure in the knowledge that Clearchus was keeping watch over them and all would turn out well.

In the Persian camp not far away, the king and his advisors learned from their scouts that the Greeks were camped in the villages nearby. The king became wary and ordered his camp to be broken at once and the army moved out in retreat. By dawn not a pack animal was to be seen grazing near the deserted Persian camp, nor a wisp of smoke rising from a campfire. The Persians had retreated to a more secure site several miles away from the Greeks. That morning Artaxerxes sent heralds to the Greeks to discuss another truce.

Just the day before, the Persian king had warned the Greeks that any movement by them would be cause for him to attack. His heralds had spoken harsh words about how the Persian king would annihilate the Greeks, but today he was unwilling to confront them in battle. The heralds arrived at the edge of the Greek camp but were kept waiting on the picket line until Clearchus had assembled the army in their battle dress and formed them for parade review. The heralds of Artaxerxes were then brought into the center of the camp to deliver their message before all the Greek soldiers. Clearchus and the other

generals stood by somberly and the heralds, in considerable fear for
their lives, spoke to the Greeks.

The heralds began by reminding the Greeks that Persians surrounded them. They had no provisions and no hope of escape. Yet the
king of kings, a benevolent and merciful ruler, had sent them, his heralds, to negotiate a truce with the Greeks on his behalf. Clearchus,
armed for battle and surrounded by the best-armed and most formi-
dable-looking of his troops, stared at the heralds for several minutes
after they had finished speaking. Then he walked directly to their
leader and spoke to him so that all the Greeks could hear.

"Go tell your king that we must fight first; for we have had no
breakfast and there is no man alive who will dare to talk to Greeks
about a truce unless he provides them first with a breakfast."

The heralds were stunned, unable to contain their amazement
when they heard these words. They mounted their horses and rode to
report to the king what they had been told. A short time later they
returned with word that a breakfast worthy of the Greeks was being
prepared for them in some nearby villages. The heralds had been commanded by the king to lead the Greeks to their breakfast. The Greeks
followed the heralds, keeping themselves in tight marching order, prepared at a moments notice to form their line of battle. Clearchus took
command of the rear guard.

The heralds led the Greeks to where abundant provisions had been
made ready. There was grain for bread, palm wine, and a sour drink
made from boiling palms. There were dates the likes of which the
Greeks had never tasted before. They found them remarkable for their
size, taste, and beauty. The soldiers feasted on hearts of palm which,
when they ate them to excess, caused headaches. The army remained
in these villages and feasted for three days. On the third day, messengers from the king arrived. Among them was Tissaphernes, as well as
the brother of the king's wife, and several other Persian nobles.

They were received in Clearchus's tent where Tissaphernes spoke
first to the assembled Greek officers through an interpreter. He por-
trayed himself as a friend of the Greeks and recounted to them how in
the last few days he had lobbied the great king to show mercy toward
them. Tissaphernes had even asked the king to allow him to lead the
Greeks home since he wished to return to his former satrapy of Asia
Minor. The king agreed to consider the request but he had ordered
Tissaphernes first to ask the Greeks why they had taken up arms and

joined Cyrus to fight against him. Tissaphernes counseled the Greeks to think well before they spoke for their answer would determine to a large degree their fate within Persia.

The Greeks withdrew and took counsel among themselves. Finally they emerged and Clearchus spoke for them. He explained that the Greeks had not joined Cyrus with the intention of making war upon Artaxerxes. They had come into his service as mercenaries who Cyrus had hired to help suppress some rebellious factions in the far reaches of his satrapy. They had been kept in the dark about the true purpose of his expedition until they were in Syria. Clearchus explained how Cyrus had used pretext after pretext to hide from them his true intention of making war upon his brother. When the Greeks finally found out his true purpose they were deep within Persian territory and it was too late for them to turn back.

They had no choice but to stand by Cyrus, since to desert in time of danger a man who had paid for their service generously and who had been a friend in prior times would have been against their nature. So they marched with Cyrus to fight against his brother the king. Now Cyrus was dead and the Greeks had no quarrel with Artaxerxes. They wished nothing more than to be allowed to return home to Greece. The king should know, Clearchus warned, that if the Greeks were attacked they would fight back, but if they were shown kindness they would return the same. Tissaphernes agreed to carry their message back to Artaxerxes. Until his return he assured the Greeks that the truce would continue to hold and that a market would be established for them where they would be able to purchase provisions from the royal stores.

The Greeks awaited Tissaphernes's return for three days, during which time they became anxious about their future. Every man in the camp watched for him to return. Finally on the third day when Tissaphernes did return he announced to the Greeks that he had good news for them. He had been able to prevail upon the merciful and generous nature of the king to spare them. It had not been easy, he told the Greeks, since many advisors around the king had argued that the Greeks should not be allowed to escape from Persia. They argued that the Greeks had to be destroyed as a lesson to others who might consider undertaking a similar campaign against the king.

Tissaphernes told the Greeks how using every skill he possessed he had prevailed upon the king to spare them. The Persian king finally

agreed to allow the Greeks to pass through his lands on their way
home. They would be allowed to purchase their provisions as they
went and in those areas where it was impossible to set up a market the
Greeks could forage from the countryside. The Greeks were required
to swear an oath that they would not harm any of the inhabitants of
the areas through which they passed, and that they would forage only
when a market was not available in which to purchase their provisions.

The matter was agreed and Tissaphernes and the Greeks made an
oath to each other before their gods. The Persian gave his right hand
in pledge to the Greek officers and in return the Greeks did the same.
Tissaphernes promised the Greeks he would return a few days later
and lead them home. The Greeks were grateful to Tissaphernes but little did they realize that "the ablest and most unscrupulous diplomat
that Persia ever produced" had taken them in.

The Greeks and Ariaeus camped close by one another and awaited
the return of Tissaphernes. Twenty days went by without word from
the king nor a sign from Tissaphernes. All during that time
Tissaphernes was working behind the scenes to change the balance of
power against the Greeks. The Greeks noticed that almost daily during this period close relatives and friends of Ariaeus came to visit him
in his camp. They came to assure him that the king bore him no further ill will now that Cyrus was dead, and wished him to return to his
former place as a loyal subject. The constant visits by relatives, including Ariaeus's brothers and other Persians from the court, began to concern the Greeks. They perceived that as the days passed Ariaeus grew
more and more distant from them.

Among both Greek officers and soldiers there was mounting concern about the long delay. Many of the officers feared the king might
be massing his troops for a surprise attack while others suggested that
the Persians were digging deep trenches or building high walls to seal
in the Greeks. Some expressed their belief that the king would never
let them return to Greece to tell the world that a small band of Greeks
had come to the very gates of Babylon and had been victorious in battle over the forces of the Persians. All the while they were supplied
with ample amounts of provisions from the king's stores. They ate and
drank well as they awaited Tissaphernes return, and some worried
that the army was becoming complacent.

Clearchus listened to the concerns of his men and was deeply troubled. Yet he tried to play down their concerns by rationalizing that the passage of so many days without word was causing the men to think foolish thoughts. He knew it would be a mistake for the Greeks to break camp and move. They had no guides to lead them home and little food to sustain them beyond the first few days' march. The Euphrates River blocked them and they could not risk crossing it and being attacked. The Persians outnumbered the Greeks, yet Clearchus calmed his soldiers and assured them each day that the king would have attacked them much earlier if that had been his intent. The king would not have taken the time and effort to arrange a truce and provide them with provisions. Finally, Clearchus argued, the Greeks had given their oath and their word was sacred even when given to a barbarian. Secretly, Clearchus feared that Ariaeus, their only ally, was preparing to desert them and he knew that they could not remain here indefinitely waiting for word from Tissaphernes. The morale of the Greek soldiers was becoming worse each day while the commitment of Ariaeus to remain with the Greeks weakened. All this is what the skilled Tissaphernes had intended to bring about.

When Tissaphernes finally returned to the Greek camp he was at the head of his own army. He gave the Greeks the impression that he intended to return home to his satrapy and thus would accompany them most of the way. Orontas, satrap of Armenia, was with him, as was his wife, the daughter of the king. He explained to the Greeks that they would not be following the route west by which they had entered Babylonia with Cyrus but would move east toward the Tigris River a few miles away and then north. The manuscripts do not offer any explanation as to why the Greeks accepted this route but perhaps they headed north toward the border with Armenia to accommodate Orontas. Tissaphernes must have told them he then intended to move west through the wide Anatolian Plateau.

When the Greeks were ready, Tissaphernes took the lead with his forces and led them east away from the Euphrates River. Ariaeus followed Tissaphernes and the Greeks were last in the long column. Late that afternoon when the column stopped for the night, Ariaeus and his men camped with Tissaphernes and Orontas while the Greeks established their own camp a mile or so from the Persians. The Greeks mounted a night guard and put into place security procedures as if they were in enemy territory. As dusk settled some of the Greeks went foraging for firewood, while others collected fodder for their animals.

A few of the Greeks on one of the foraging parties came across some Persian soldiers. Arguments erupted after one group hurled insults at the other. Some of the soldiers came to blows, though no one was killed or seriously injured. There were no further incidents that night and the next day the column moved out. Tensions between the Greeks and the Persians continued to increase as each long day on the march passed.

Within a few days, the slowly moving column came to the Median Wall that measured twenty feet thick and nearly a hundred feet high. This, the Greeks were told, was sixty miles in length and ended close to the city of Babylon. From this wall the column marched another two days northeast, crossing on its way numerous canals that issued forth from the Tigris River. Irrigation ditches branched off from these canals to water the fields, and marching over them proved difficult and slow. Finally the column reached the western bank of the Tigris River and halted outside the walls of a large city named Sittace. The Greeks camped beside the city in a beautiful park while Tissaphernes crossed the river and pitched his camp out of sight of the Greeks.

That night a Persian entered the camp and warned the Greeks to be vigilant. He told Clearchus that Tissaphernes intended to destroy the bridge over the Tigris River and thus trap the Greeks between the river and the labyrinth of canals behind them. The Persian warning was dismissed as a hoax, but the Greeks posted guards at the bridge anyway and passed a tense night. No attack came and at dawn the Greeks crossed the Tigris by the bridge without incident.

The Greeks caught up with Tissaphernes and the column and marched north with them along the Tigris River some sixty-six miles. They came at last to another large city named Opis, the site of a great Persian victory over the Babylonians. As they passed Opis and continued north the column encountered the bastard brother of Cyrus and Artaxerxes. He was in command of a large army of Persians and he halted to watch the Greeks pass without saying a word. Clearchus led his men and they marched almost in review in front of the Persian soldiers who watched the well-disciplined Greeks in amazement.

From there the Greeks followed Tissaphernes some one hundred miles through the province of Media, to the villages of Parysatis. There, Tissaphernes, by way of insulting the memory of Cyrus "through the mother who bore him" turned the villages over to the Greeks and let them rape, murder, and pillage. When the Greeks were done the column took up the march again, keeping the Tigris River on their left as they continued to move north. Then they came to a prosperous city named Caenae where the people came out from behind the walls to greet the Greeks with loaves of bread, cheeses, and wine. The Greeks and the Persians camped near the city and remained there three days to rest and provision themselves.

The tension between the Greeks and the Persians continued to increase and Clearchus resolved to have a meeting with Tissaphernes before it reached the point of all-out fighting. He sent a messenger to Tissaphernes, and the reply came back that Clearchus could come to the Persian camp. At their meeting in Tissaphernes's tent, Clearchus related the mutual pledges the two leaders had given to cooperate with one another and to refrain from injury. Yet he pointed out that both men were distrustful of the other and that tensions were high between their soldiers. All this mistrust, Clearchus warned, threatened to disrupt the truce.

Clearchus urged that they dispel this mutual distrust, most of which he maintained was caused by dissident factions in both camps who spread rumors and sought to drive a wedge between them. The Greek commander expressed his fear that one of the two sides might make a preemptive strike against the other out of fear. Clearchus believed that through a conference they could settle any misunderstandings and strengthen their bonds of trust. The Greeks, he went on, desired to be faithful to Tissaphernes because they valued as sacred the oaths of friendship they had taken with him before the gods. Any man who broke his oath to the gods, the Greeks believed, would not find refuge from their wrath. Then Clearchus was remarkably candid with Tissaphernes. He confessed that the Greeks needed him to lead them home and to furnish them with supplies along the way.

Clearchus also admitted that the Greeks had stood beside Cyrus because they believed he would make an able ruler over Persia and remain their good friend. Now Cyrus was dead and they would be fools to turn against the man who held all the power. In addition, the Greeks could be as useful to Tissaphernes as they had been to Cyrus because, Clearchus pointed out, they were mercenary soldiers and the best in the world. The Greeks could be used effectively to fight against the enemies of Tissaphernes, such as the Pisidians, the Mysians, and even the Egyptians. Clearchus pledged that the Greeks could serve Tissaphernes as they had Cyrus, not for pay alone but as a friend. The

Greeks would fight for him out of gratitude for saving them from the wrath of the king. Clearchus swore his allegiance and advised Tissaphernes not to be swayed by the words of others. Clearchus suggested that Tissaphernes bring forth those in his company who had sought to drive a wedge between them so that the Greeks could confront them, face to face.

Tissaphernes listened intently to Clearchus's words. When at last he began to speak it was in warm tones of friendship and praise for the Greeks. He praised Clearchus for his "sensible" and "honest" manner in seeking to resolve their differences. For his part, Tissaphernes pointed out that if the king sought to destroy the Greeks he could have done so by sheer force of numbers. The route home for the Greeks was long and full of places where the Persian forces could use their numbers to advantage. There were wide plains where Persian cavalry and chariots in great numbers could overwhelm the Greek infantry, and there were countless mountain passes, narrow gorges, and deep rivers, where the Greeks could be ambushed. The route home could be stripped of provisions. Crops could be burned well in advance of the Greeks, wells poisoned, and animals slaughtered. And when hunger and thirst had exhausted the Greeks, the Persians could simply allow them to starve alone in the deserts or mountains. With all these factors in their favor, why, Tissaphernes asked, should the Persians resort to deception? Why feign a truce with the Greeks and then ambush them? For the Persians as well regarded their oaths to the gods as sacred and their word to be upheld. The Persians would not resort to breaking their oaths to the gods or to the Greeks. They were not barbarians, Tissaphernes reminded Clearchus, but cultured men.

Then Tissaphernes went into a long explanation of how the Persian king had chosen to spare the Greeks because he, Tissaphernes, had prevailed upon him to spare their lives. Just as they had been loyal allies to Cyrus, so Tissaphernes wished the Greeks to be his brothers, not just for wages paid and service rendered. Then Tissaphernes confided in Clearchus, "the king alone may wear the tiara upon his head, but another, with the help of the Greeks, might easily wear that same crown." The message was clear; Tissaphernes aspired to the Persian throne. Clearchus thought that for that reason alone Tissaphernes desired the friendship and help of the Greeks.

Clearchus was taken in by the words of Tissaphernes. He replied that the Persian noble should not allow others to drive a wedge

between them with false accusations and suspicions. Tissaphernes suggested that Clearchus should return the next day with all his captains
and generals so that the Persians could point out those among them
who were disloyal. In return the Persians would give up those men in
their own camp who had made accusations and spread false rumors
about the Greeks.

Clearchus fell into the Persian trap. He pledged his word to return
the next day with his officers and to give up those Greeks who had
spoken out against the Persians. The conversation ended on a harmonious note and Tissaphernes invited Clearchus to a lavish dinner. In
the Persian camp that night all manner of kindness and honor was
bestowed upon Clearchus. As the Greek commander dined and drank
at Tissaphernes's table he became more and more entangled in the
silken web spun by the most venomous spider in the Persian Empire.

The next morning Clearchus returned to the Greek camp and
recounted his conversation with Tissaphernes. Clearchus believed he
was on the best of terms with Tissaphernes and that the breach had
been closed between them. It only remained to denounce those disloyal officers who had brought the Greeks so close to disaster.
Clearchus ordered that all the officers must go with him to
Tissaphernes the next day and those among the Greeks who had made
false accusations against the Persians would be punished as traitors.

Clearchus had already marked another commander, Menon, as a
traitor. For he suspected that the Greek general had already had secret
meetings with Tissaphernes and Ariaeus, and that he was actively plotting against him with the intention of taking command of the army.
Many of the soldiers in the assembly objected to the proposal, warning that the Greek captains and generals should not go into the Persian
camp all at once unescorted. Many argued that Tissaphernes could not
be trusted. Clearchus replied that to enter the Persian camp with a
bodyguard would show a lack of trust and undo all that he had
accomplished the night before. Finally after much discussion and arguing, it was agreed that five generals and twenty captains should go
with a bodyguard of two hundred soldiers. The bodyguard would go
into the Persian camp on the pretext of needing to buy supplies from
the many merchants who accompanied the army.

That afternoon the Greeks arrived at the tent of Tissaphernes. The
generals were Proxenus, a close friend of Xenophon; Menon, the suspected traitor; Agias from Arcadia; Socrates from Achaea; and

Clearchus. The captains were ordered to wait outside the tent until their presence would be required. Shortly after the generals walked into the tent, they were seized by Persian soldiers. The captains were murdered where they waited outside, and the unsuspecting Greek bodyguards in the Persian camp were hunted down in small groups and murdered as they shopped in the market.

The Persian cavalry then rode out onto the plains and killed any Greeks they found who had strayed from the safety of their camp. A badly wounded captain, Nicarchus, escaped the carnage on the plain and made it back to the Greek camp. Holding his bowels in his hands, he was surrounded by anxious Greeks and with his dying breaths he warned them what was happening. A panic swept through the Greek camp. The Greeks feared they would be attacked at any moment and many ran to take up their arms.

Soon a contingent of Persians approached the Greeks led by Ariaeus, Artaozus, and Mithradates, once the most faithful friends of Cyrus and now men in the pay of Tissaphernes. Ariaeus had played his role in the seizure of the Greek generals and was thus forgiven his transgressions against the king and was to be rewarded with the satrapy of Greater Phrygia. When they approached the Greek camp as close as they dared, Ariaeus called out for those officers who were left to approach so that they might receive a message from the king. Two generals, Cleanor and Sophaenetus, went forward under heavy guard to hear what Ariaeus had to say. Xenophon went along with them because he was worried about his friend Proxenus and anxious for any news of him.

When the Greeks were within hearing distance, Ariaeus told them that Clearchus, perjurer and violator of his oaths, was dead, but that Proxenus and Menon, because they had denounced Clearchus, had been spared. The king demanded the surrender of all Greek arms. Cleanor spoke for the Greeks and replied that Ariaeus and the other emissaries were the most deceptive of all men. Once they had been loyal friends of Cyrus and had given oaths of friendship to the Greeks. They had sworn to the gods, and now they had betrayed the Greeks and joined Tissaphernes, the enemy of Cyrus.

Ariaeus replied that Clearchus had been plotting against Tissaphernes and all the Persians. Xenophon spoke up and declared that if in fact Clearchus had been plotting to violate the truce he had received his just desserts but that Proxenus and Menon should be returned to the Greek camp forthwith. The Persians briefly conferred among themselves and then departed.

But the Greek generals were no longer in the camp of Tissaphernes. They were in chains and on their way to Babylon where they would be taken before the king, paraded as trophies and then beheaded. Clearchus went to his death as he had led his life, proud and upright. He was fifty years old. Proxenus had been a student of Gorgias of Leontini, the most expensive teacher of philosophy in Greece. He valued honesty, was a good friend of Xenophon, and had hoped that in joining the service of Cyrus he would gain fame, riches, and great power in the east. As a general he was more frightened of his men then they were of him and because of his scholarly manner he could command gentlemen, but not soldiers. At the time of his death he was thirty.

Menon had been a man eager for wealth, and he used military command as a means toward that end. He would be a friend to anyone who possessed power and he would use any means at his disposal to accomplish what he wanted. He saw honesty as a folly. Affection and loyalty he felt toward no man and the property of his friends he saw as an easy mark to take because they trusted him. He regarded honest and principled men like Proxenus as weak. Menon was a man who prided himself upon his ability to deceive those who trusted him. He fabricated lies and mocked those men who were weaker and less powerful than he was. His status as a general was earned partly because he had had intimate relations with Ariaeus. In the end, the Persians seemed to recognize his character. While the other generals were beheaded, a quick death, Menon was tortured for nearly a year in the Babylonian dungeons underneath the royal palace. Agias and Socrates were good generals and honest men. Both were about thirty-five when they died.

From the ancient sources it appears that only Clearchus was given a proper burial. Parysatis was able to obtain his body from Artaxerxes and she had some of her slaves bury him in an unmarked grave outside of Babylon. The location of the grave was designated by the planting of a ring of simple palm trees, and thus was sent to his eternal rest the once-feared Spartan commander.

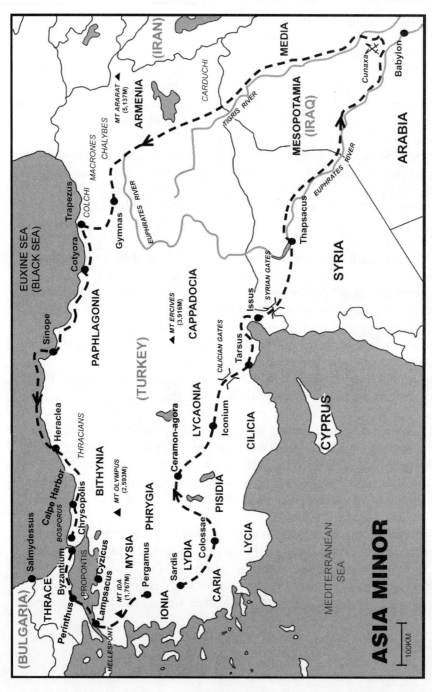

The Route of the Greek Mercenaries

VI
THE PERSIAN GAUNTLET

The Greeks were frightened and confused. Poor judgment had sent their senior officers to their deaths at the hands of the Persians. While Clearchus had been a good soldier he was no match for Tissaphernes in deception and intrigue. The Greeks had been psychologically out-maneuvered by a master and now they found themselves in desperate straits. Most of their officers had been killed or captured, including Clearchus, their most senior general and the source of their self-confidence. The mercenaries were full of anxiety. They were sur-rounded by the forces of the king in a hostile land where they could expect no help from the local people in the form of supplies or guides. The Greeks were nearly twelve hundred miles inland from the Turkish coast of the Aegean Sea and a thousand miles from the nearest Greek cities. The mercenaries could not move west because they were cut off by impassable rivers, canals, and a massive series of irrigation ditches. Tissaphernes had led them exactly where he wanted them to go. Even if they were able to move west and cross the canals and rivers, they had no cavalry left to support them if they tried to cross the wide plains. On the plains, the king's swarms of cavalry and chariots would have the advantage in battle.

That night few men in the Greek camp had an appetite. A mood of despondency settled upon them, a worse depression than they had ever known. Many men just lay down wherever they happened to be but few were able to sleep. Most of the soldiers were not frightened of dying but they longed for their homes. Some thought of their wives and children while others of their parents and friends. In every mind that night was the thought that soon they would all be captured, tor-tured to death, and then buried in some unmarked mass grave in the Persian desert. If they were lucky they would all be killed fighting and their bodies left to become carrion for scavengers. The Greeks were superstitious and they worried about their souls if they were not given proper burial after death. In either case they would be forgotten by their world and no one would ever know what had happened to them, a prospect that troubled them most of all.

When the army was in its darkest hour and hope of survival was slim, Xenophon came forward. He was not an officer and to this point in the campaign he had played a minor role. As he lay in his tent that night he wondered why the Greeks, those brave men he had campaigned with these past months, were now sinking to such depths of despair. They had given up and were resolved to let fate do with them what she wanted. This was not their nature. Why should they lie there on the cold, hard ground and wait for the dawn and their deaths? Xenophon had no doubt that Tissaphernes would attack shortly after first light. Why should the Greeks wait to be slaughtered like sheep? Why should they pray and hope that some god might intervene at the last minute to save them? The Greeks must save themselves, taking command of their own destiny. Then he arose and called together those captains who had served under his friend Proxenus.

When the captains had gathered around his tent Xenophon recounted his thoughts to them. The Greeks had been outsmarted by Tissaphernes. He had dealt them a severe blow with the murder of their senior officers, but now the Greeks must take the initiative against the Persians. They could not wait for a Persian attack. They must make preparations for the best fight possible against the army of the king when the time came. The only other choice was to passively await their deaths at Persian hands. Artaxerxes would show them no mercy. He had slaughtered his own brother Cyrus on the field of battle and Xenophon had no desire to have his own head impaled on a stake and taken to Babylon as a trophy. There was no doubt that those of them captured by the king would be subject to the most barbaric tortures as an example to other Greeks who might consider a similar expedition against the empire. Why should the Greeks passively accept death at Persian hands?

The Greeks were professional soldiers, the best in the world. They were better conditioned to endure hardships than the Persians, and they were also blessed by the gods. Xenophon urged the officers to set an example of courage for the common soldiers. There were few generals left so captains would have to be elected generals and all the ranks of the officers filled. In spite of his youth and lack of experience Xenophon offered to become a general if the Greeks would have him.

A captain named Apollonides rose and spoke to the assembled captains against Xenophon. Apollonides argued that the Greeks were fools if they thought they could stand against the forces of Artaxerxes. He went on to recite all the disadvantages facing them and he urged that they try and win the king's mercy through persuasion, and if need be, surrender.

Xenophon challenged the arguments of Apollonides and reminded the captains of the Persian treachery they had just witnessed. Was Apollonides really fool enough to believe the king would honor any promises he made to the Greeks? What the king understood was strength and Xenophon reminded the captains how each time the Greeks were armed and stood ready to fight, the king had retreated and proposed a truce. The Persian king was treacherous and cunning but he would never stand up to the Greeks—disciplined soldiers who were ready to fight and die for their freedom.

Xenophon denounced Apollonides before the officers and branded him a disgrace to Greece. Another captain, Agasias the Stymphalian, rose to speak and accused Apollonides of not really being a Greek at all. He pointed to his pierced ears and accused him of being a Lydian. The Lydians were considered effeminate by the Greeks and as a result of his ears Apollonides was driven from the tent.

The captains supported Xenophon and they went out into the Greek camp and assembled every officer they could find. Where a division had lost its general they assembled the captains who remained. Where a division had no officers they selected the most senior men from among the soldiers. It was near midnight when all the officers were finally assembled outside Xenophon's tent and their number was taken to be about a hundred.

Hieronymus the Elean brought the assembled officers to order and explained why they had been summoned. Then he asked Xenophon to describe his plan. Xenophon rose and began by recounting the treachery of the king. He told how their generals and many of the captains had been captured and murdered when they had been invited to the tent of Tissaphernes during a truce. He assured the assembled officers that a similar fate awaited them all if they did nothing more but await the next move of the king.

The only salvation for the Greek army now lay in the courage and leadership of its officers who were still alive. These officers, Xenophon went on, must inspire the soldiers with confidence and show them leadership. For if the soldiers saw in their captains fear and indecision they would weaken even more and there would be no chance to save the army. The officers had to provide the example when it came to courage and prove to the soldiers that they were capable of leading. Discipline and resolve, Xenophon emphasized, would see the army through this dark time, just as they had always maintained the Greeks through difficulty.

Xenophon proposed that new generals be chosen to replace those who had been captured and murdered by Tissaphernes. Then the soldiers had to be roused from their lethargy so that the army could once again become the formidable fighting machine that had struck such fear into the hearts of the Persians at Cunaxa. It was the skill, resolve, and courage of the fighting men that win battles, he said, not numbers. Even if they lost, Xenophon went on, death is the common end for all men. The Greeks should prepare to meet it bravely, for those men who fear dying and try to save themselves in any possible way invariably die cruel and shameful deaths. Men who fight bravely die quickly and honorably. Their chances of returning to their native Greece and enjoying old age were better if they fought bravely than if they did nothing but await the slaughter that was sure to come at the hands of Artaxerxes and Tissaphernes.

Cheirisophus the Spartan, one of the few generals who had escaped the massacre because he did not accompany the others to the Persian camp, rose to speak next. He praised Xenophon for his words and urged the other officers to follow his example, even though, he said, Xenophon was "only an Athenian." He praised his deeds and said what the army needed was more officers like Xenophon. He concluded by urging the officers to return to their respective units and elect new commanders. Following the elections the new commanders would meet in the center of the camp to plan a new strategy and then there would be a general meeting of the army.

The assembled captains agreed and returned to their units to begin the elections. By the time all the elections had been completed and all the commanders and junior officers chosen it was nearly dawn. Xenophon was elected as a general to replace his friend Proxenus while Timasion, a Dardanian, had been chosen to replace Clearchus. Xanthicles an Achaean replaced Socrates, while Cleanor the Arcadian replaced Agias and Philesius the Achaean took the place of Menon. Now the army once more had a full complement of generals.

At the assembly of the soldiers, Cheirisophus the Lacedaemonian, who was now the most senior general, rose to speak first. He recounted the treachery of their ally Ariaeus in deserting them, the treachery of the Persians, and the odds that the army now faced. He urged the assembled Greeks to choose a glorious death in battle to slaughter in their tents. Cleanor the Arcadian rose and spoke. He also recounted the treachery of the king, of Tissaphernes, and of Ariaeus. Persians, he went on, were men who could not be trusted and who broke their vows to the gods and turned on the men whom they had invited into their tents as guests. So the Greeks must not make any more treaties with the Persians and they must place their faith in their own valor and in the will of the gods.

Dressed in his finest armor, Xenophon rose to address the assembly. If it were to be his fate to die in Persia and this was what the gods had intended for him, then he would meet his death on the field of battle dressed in his finest attire. As he said this, a soldier in the crowd sneezed and the army fell silent. The Greeks were highly superstitious and this was interpreted by all as a favorable sign from Zeus. Every man fell to his knees. A ritual sacrifice was held to thank the god for this auspicious sign. After the sacrifice Xenophon proposed that when the Greeks reached a safe haven they make full sacrifice to Zeus, and all agreed.

Then Xenophon listed all the army's strengths. First, they were morally in the right because they had stood by their oath and upheld their word to the Persians. It was the Persians who had violated the oath to the gods and who had no respect for the truce. Then he recounted the famous battles in which their forefathers had defeated the Persian armies that had come to conquer Greece. He recounted how the Persian king Darius I and later his son Xerxes had tried to conquer their native land and how both had been defeated by the bravery of the Greeks.

The Greeks were free men, he continued, and they paid homage only to the gods. Greeks were born free, they had a tradition of freedom and they would remain free until they died. At Cunaxa the Greeks had defeated the Persian king and sent him running. They had fought bravely for Cyrus and now they were fighting for their own lives. They could fight their way home if need be, they could swim across the deepest and widest rivers, they could march across deserts, and they could live off the land. When they finally returned home they would assemble the largest army of Greeks that the world had ever seen and they would invade Persia. They would take vast areas of the Persian empire and live in luxury. The riches of this land belonged to whoever was strong enough to take them. The army cheered Xenophon, and his words lifted their spirits.

At the conclusion of the assembly, Xenophon advised the Greeks that they should prepare to move out into the countryside as soon as possible. They could not wait for Tissaphernes and his army to attack. First they must burn their wagons and tents so that they could move quickly. The army would need to have the maximum number of men under arms. All excess baggage would be abandoned and each Greek would carry only his weapons and what he needed to eat and drink for that day.

During the course of their march, Xenophon warned, the soldiers must show the greatest respect and obedience to the officers they had elected. The Persian king had captured their generals and many of their captains, thinking that by executing them there would be disorder in the Greek camp and all discipline would be destroyed. The new commanders had an equal obligation to inspire confidence in their soldiers and to show that they were better able to lead than the old generals had been. The soldiers agreed that if one of them were disobedient to an officer, the soldiers themselves would punish that man. In that way the Persian king would have before him fourteen thousand men with the resolve and character of Clearchus.

Xenophon then offered to relinquish the podium to any among the Greeks, officer or common soldier, who might have a better plan to offer. No one came forward and Xenophon suggested they move quickly, for dawn was well upon them and there was little time to spare. The Greeks settled the matter with a show of hands and then went to rejoin their units under their new commanders.

The first order was to break camp and then march to the nearest villages where the Greeks could get provisions. There were some villages about two miles away from them and for the march Xenophon proposed that the hoplites form a hollow square with the essential baggage and the camp followers in the middle for safety. Cheirisophus took the lead, and then the two generals with the most experience took each flank. The youngest commanders, of whom Xenophon was one, took the rear to cover their retreat. As the army moved through the countryside the generals decided they could make adjustments as needed in the command structure if the marching arrangement did not prove suitable.

The wagons and tents were put to the torch and any articles of excess baggage were thrown into the fires that raged everywhere throughout the Greek camp. The Greeks prepared their breakfast but before they had finished their meals the Persian Mithradates with about thirty horsemen approached the Greek camp. From a safe distance he summoned the leaders of the Greeks to approach within earshot for he wished to speak to them. The Greek leaders walked forward with a heavily armed bodyguard ready for any sign of treachery. Mithradates began by recounting how he had been a faithful friend to Cyrus and now he assured them he was their friend as well. He had come to their camp to learn the Greeks's intentions. The Greek generals took counsel with each other and then asked Cheirisophus to speak for them. Cheirisophus explained to Mithradates how the Greeks only wished to return home and as long as no one stood in their way they would do no harm. He warned Mithradates that if anyone tried to block their route home they were prepared to fight to the last man.

Mithradates laughed. He told the Greeks that they were powerless to go anywhere in this vast land without the permission of the king. It then became clear that he had been sent to undertake further treachery so the Greeks warned him to leave while he could still ride. The Greek generals decided that from now on there should be no more negotiations with the Persians. That night a Greek captain, Nicarchus the Arcadian, deserted the camp with about twenty men. The army marched all the next day without seeing the Persians. Toward the end of the day Mithradates appeared again, this time with about four hundred men. He approached the Greek column under the guise of friendship and used his flag of truce to get his men as close to the Greek rear guard as they could. Then without warning the Persians drew their bows and began to shoot their arrows at the Greeks. They wounded a number of soldiers, but because the Greeks had no cavalry they were unable to drive Mithradates and his men out of range. In spite of their disadvantage, Xenophon and some of his soldiers who made up the rear guard set out on foot after the archers and succeeded in driving them out of range.

By the end of that day the first elements of the column had reached the villages. It had taken most of the day for the entire Greek column to cover about three miles and arrive at these villages. Many of the soldiers were depressed because the column had made so little progress. Some of the officers, most notably Cheirisophus and the older generals, were frustrated and they criticized Xenophon and his rear guard for slowing down the column to engage in a worthless and ineffectual pursuit of the Persian cavalry. Xenophon admitted he had made an error and agreed that the senior officers were right to find fault with him. What the skirmish had shown was the superiority of the Persian longbowmen over the Greeks. These skilled archers could reach the Greek ranks with their arrows while staying out of range of the Greek bowmen and javelin throwers. The Greeks used a short bow that had only half the range of the Persian longbow.

The generals decided to take whatever horses the Greeks had in the baggage train and form a cavalry of their own, no matter how small, to keep the Persians at bay. A detachment of fifty horsemen was formed and outfitted to provide protection against another attack by the mounted Persian bowmen. The next day the Greek army was on the move again. While they were crossing a gorge, all the time fearing the Persians might attack, Mithradates appeared again. This time he had brought with him a thousand horsemen and four thousand bowmen and slingers on foot. He had become overconfident as a result of his success the day before, and had convinced Tissaphernes that with a larger force he could defeat these Greeks. Mithradates was cautious and did not attack immediately. He waited until they had passed about a mile beyond the gorge and then he followed them in. This was a tactical mistake. Once his troops had entered the gorge the fifty Greek horsemen turned away from the column and charged straight for the Persians. The Greek foot soldiers in the rear guard followed their horsemen as quickly as they could to support them.

The soldiers of Mithradates were taken by surprise when the Greeks turned on them and charged. They became confused and a congested melee took place within the gorge. The Greek cavalry were able to hold the Persians until their infantry came up. Most of the Persian force was caught in the gorge and the Greek infantry slaughtered them there. After the fight the Greeks disfigured the Persian dead so that the sight of their mutilated bodies would demoralize their comrades.

The Greeks continued their march all the rest of that day without seeing any Persians. By nightfall they had reached the banks of the Tigris River again and encamped by a deserted city named Larisa. Larisa had once been a great city of the Assyrians. Even deserted it was still an imposing structure with walls twenty-five feet in width and a hundred feet high. The walls were built of clay bricks and rested upon a stone foundation. Cyrus the Great, it was said, had laid siege to this city but the walls were so thick and high he was never able to take it. The next day the Greeks marched about twenty miles and came to another deserted city, Mespila, the famous capital of the Assyrian Empire. From there the Greeks marched forward about another twenty miles.

While the Greeks were completing this stage of the march, Tissaphernes appeared behind them with a large army. He drew his army up on the rear and flanks of the Greeks but held his soldiers back. He would not risk a decisive battle with the Greeks even though he greatly outnumbered them. He ordered his bowmen to discharge their arrows. The Greek slingers and bowmen responded against the Persians, and Tissaphernes withdrew his army out of range. All that day and into the next the Persians followed the Greeks at a safe distance. As the Greeks moved forward they began to realize that the square was a poor marching formation in this terrain. When the Greeks had to pass through a narrow gorge or cross a bridge the entire formation had to squeeze together and this threw the troops into confusion. Once they had crossed the gorge or bridge it took some time for the army to regroup and begin the march again.

The generals decided it would be best to reorganize the army, so they formed six companies of a hundred men each placed under the command of a captain. When the army had to draw together because of an obstruction in its path these companies would drop back to provide protection. In that way the main body of the army could take its time passing an obstacle and there was less confusion when they regrouped afterward.

As the Greeks proceeded through the countryside, the scouts caught sight of a large palace with many villages around it. The villages and the palace lay at the base of a large mountain, but to reach them the Greeks had to pass over several smaller hills first. The officers were relieved to see the hills since they were always apprehensive about the Persian cavalry when they had to cross any expanse of flat land. The Persian cavalry was much larger and better equipped than the Greek horsemen and the Greek infantry was always vulnerable to attack on flat terrain. The hills would protect them from the Persian horsemen and they would regain the tactical advantage as they advanced toward the villages.

When the Greeks reached the villages they found abundant provisions of flour, wine, and barley for their horses. The army remained in these villages for three days to provision and tend to their wounded. On the fourth day the Greeks left the safety of the villages and moved once more onto the broad, flat terrain that was so dangerous for them. They moved slowly as many of their men were wounded and being carried, while other soldiers had to carry extra weapons and supplies. Tissaphernes and his army continued to shadow the Greeks at a safe distance.

After a few days the Greeks noticed that the Persians followed a pattern. As soon as it became late afternoon they stopped to pitch their camp for the night well away from the Greeks. The Greek scouts sent out to spy on the Persians reported that they were poorly disciplined and their camp a bordello of disorganization. Each night the Persians tied their horses together in large numbers and then hobbled them. They did this to prevent the horses from running away if they got loose from the tether. The Greeks considered an attack during the night since the Persians would have to untie their horses from the tether, untie the legs of their horses where they had been hobbled, and put on saddlecloths and bridles. Then the horsemen would have to put on their own armor and mount. All of this was time-consuming under normal circumstances, but at night, roused from sleep during an attack and among so much confusion the Persians were vulnerable. This was why the Persian commanders always made sure they camped a good six to eight miles away from the Greeks every night. Since the Greeks lacked sufficient cavalry to make the attack they abandoned the idea and maintained their defensive posture.

For the next three days the Greeks saw no sign of Tissaphernes and his army. By this time the Greeks had followed the main road to the base of a great mountain. The scouts reported that the high ground all along their route at the base of the mountain had been occupied by an advanced detachment of Tissaphernes army. Cheirisophus summoned Xenophon from the rear so he could take counsel with him. The danger was evident to both commanders. The Persians commanding the heights would prevent the Greeks from passing along the road. In the meantime the rest of Tissaphernes army would catch up with the Greeks and they would be trapped at the base of the mountain.

Xenophon observed that if the Greeks could capture the summit of the mountain they could come down behind the Persians. With the Greeks above and below them, the Persian contingent would never be able to hold its position above the roadway and would probably abandon it. Xenophon and Cheirisophus discussed taking the summit. Xenophon joked that in view of Cheirisophus's age it would be better if he, Xenophon, led the climb up the mountain. He was given a detachment of peltasts from the front ranks and a handpicked group of three hundred infantry. Under Xenophon's command they set out at a jog for the summit.

As soon as the Persians guarding the heights saw what the Greeks were trying to do they dispatched soldiers to try and capture the summit as well. It was now a race between the Greeks and the Persians to see who would take the commanding heights and thus gain the advantage. There was shouting and encouragement from both sides as their men raced along different routes to reach the top of the mountain.

Xenophon was riding his horse and urging on his men when one of the peltasts, Soteridas the Sicyonian, yelled at him that he had an unfair advantage because he was riding. At that, Xenophon dismounted, pushed Soteridas out of his place in the formation and took his shield from him. The horse by this time had to be abandoned because the ground had become too steep. Xenophon carried the Sicyonian's shield even though he was burdened with his own armor and ran alongside keeping up with the other foot soldiers. Even though the shield was an extra burden, Xenophon kept up with the lighter armed troops in the race for the top. The rest of the soldiers in the line pelted Soteridas with stones as they ran until they shamed him into taking back his shield from Xenophon. The Greeks reached the summit before the Persians.

When the Persians holding the heights above the road saw that the Greeks had reached the summit first they knew they could not hold their positions. They abandoned the mountainside. Tissaphernes and Ariaeus saw what had happened and halted their column. The two Persian commanders sat upon their horses for several minutes and just watched the Greeks. Then they turned off by another road and with their army disappeared from view.

The main body of the Greeks was able to pass along this section of the road safely and descend onto another plain. Here the army encamped in a village with abundant supplies. The Greeks found that there were many villages in this plain along the banks of the Tigris River and they were able to gather a large quantity of provisions and captives. Tissaphernes and his army appeared on the plain and began to burn all the villages around them in order to deny the Greeks provisions. Some of the Greeks became despondent when they saw what was happening but Xenophon pointed out to them that the king, by burning his own villages, was forced to acknowledge that the Greeks controlled the countryside. The Persians were burning their own villages rather than confront the Greeks in combat.

The Greek officers gathered in council that night to discuss their next course of action. Many were concerned as the army was moving between high mountains to the east of them and a very deep river to their west. The Greeks had no boats to cross the river, and even if they could get across there were considerable numbers of Persian cavalry waiting to attack them on the other side. It was decided in counsel that the army would retreat back to the villages that had not been burned and reassess the situation. The next morning the Greeks began an orderly march back to the villages and Tissaphernes gazed in amazement to see them returning to the plain. Still he would not risk an attack.

That evening, in the safety of the villages, the Greek officers held another council. A number of Persians had been captured in the past few days and these were brought to the council for interrogation about the route ahead. The prisoners told the Greeks that the road they had been traveling stemmed from Babylon in the south. By this time the Greeks had come about two hundred miles north along the Tigris River from the battlefield of Cunaxa. The road east of them led to the Persian city of Susa and the summer palace of the king. The road west, across the Tigris River, led to Lydia and Ionia, the most direct way home for the Greeks. The road north led through the mountains to Armenia and the satrapy of Orontas, son-in-law of Artaxerxes.

The Greek officers debated among themselves about the best way to return home, and came to the consensus that the only two routes available to the army were those which led west or north. The westerly route was the most dangerous and would require them to cross the Tigris River, then march over a broad plain and finally to cross the Euphrates River. Both rivers were wide and deep, and even if they succeeded in crossing the Tigris, the plain that lay between the two rivers was a dangerous place for the Greeks to be caught. It was wide and flat and Tissaphernes would have the advantage over them in both instances. Furthermore, the villages that lay between the two rivers would be burned by the Persians in order to deny the Greeks provision. Even should they make it across the plain and over the Euphrates River, much of the land to the west had already been stripped of food, burned and looted by the army of Cyrus as it had moved east toward Cunaxa months before.

The only safe alternative, the Greeks concluded, was for them to march north through the mountains to Armenia. From there they could cross the two great rivers nearer their source where they would be narrow and more fordable. The headwaters of the Tigris and Euphrates Rivers at that location are very close together and the Greeks reasoned they would even be able to go around them easily. Furthermore, the remote villages to the north were beyond the reach of Tissaphernes. These villages would provide the Greeks with needed provisions as they moved through the mountains. The terrain would give the Greeks the advantage if Tissaphernes tried to follow them and it would be impossible for him to move ahead of them to cut off their route. So that night the Greeks decided that their route home would be north along the Tigris River until they reached the Armenian mountains. Then they would enter Armenia, and move further north until they could make their turn to the west and proceed through the center of Turkey along the great Anatolian Plateau, through Cappadocia and Lydia to the Aegean Sea.

The northern route to Armenia was not without problems. The mountains were home to a fiercely independent people called the Carduchi. Over the years these mountain people had withstood repeated attempts by the king to bring them under his control. The Persian prisoners recounted to the Greeks how the great king had once sent an army of over a hundred thousand men into those mountains to subdue the Carduchi. Not a Persian soldier among them returned home.

Today those same mountains are home to the Kurds, the descendants of the Carduchi. The area remains politically unsettled and the most dangerous place to travel in Turkey.

It was now almost October and winter would soon be descending on the mountains and holding their route home in its icy grip. The Greek officers debated among themselves all that night, and just before dawn of the next day the assembly of the Greeks voted that the route home would be north to Armenia and from there due west. Then the Greeks offered their sacrifices to the gods for a safe journey. At dawn the column would turn north to begin the first phase of the long march home.

VII
NORTH TO THE SEA

Shortly before the last watch of the night had ended, while it was still dark, the Greeks quietly began to pack their few possessions. Then they assembled in their ranks for the first leg of their long march. They were headed north toward Armenia and the generals were anxious that they pass a particular stretch of the plain that lay between their camp and the safety of the mountains. The officers wanted the army to cross the plain as quickly and quietly as possible before the sun rose and the Persian scouts could see what they were doing. Cheirisophus, with a vanguard of lightly armed troops, moved out ahead of the main body of the army while Xenophon followed behind at a slower pace with heavily armed hoplites acting as the rear guard.

Cheirisophus was anxious that the vanguard should secure the summit of the first pass into the mountains to ensure the safe passage of the army that followed. When the vanguard reached the first of the mountains they discovered numerous villages in the hollows and valleys but found that most had been deserted. The Greeks were entering the land of the Carduchi, a particularly fierce mountain people whose modern descendents are known as the Kurds. The Carduchi had watched the approach of the Greek army and then abandoned their villages, taking their wives and children to safety in the higher reaches of the mountains.

When the main force reached these villages, Cheirisophus ordered the soldiers not to loot or burn any of the houses or other buildings. They were to take only the provisions they needed and nothing more. Nor did the Greeks molest any of the elderly villagers who had remained near their homes. Cheirisophus hoped the Carduchi might view the Greek actions favorably and allow the army to pass peacefully through their territory. Just as darkness was falling and Xenophon and the last of the rear guard were descending from the mountain pass into these villages, the Carduchi attacked some Greek stragglers. Several of the Greeks were killed and many wounded in a hail of rocks, stones, and arrows.

All through that night the Carduchi lit fires in the mountains and the Greeks below could hear them calling to each other. The next morning the officers met and agreed that because the next stage of the march through the mountains would be difficult, the army should keep only its most indispensable items and the strongest of the baggage animals. Everything else had to be left behind if the soldiers were to survive the next several weeks in this difficult mountainous terrain. Most of the loot the Greeks had accumulated and all of the captives and slaves would have to be left behind. The captives at this point consisted mostly of young women and children who had been taken from villages as the Greeks passed through. Among the captives were a few Persian soldiers who had been taken prisoner during the recent fighting with Mithradates and held for questioning. While the captive women provided comfort for the soldiers each night, they and the children only slowed the army down during the day. All the captives, but especially the Persian soldiers, had to be guarded on the march and this took a number of Greeks out of the battle line. The captives also had to be fed and this required carrying extra provisions.

Once the officers made the decision to leave the loot and captives behind the order was passed through the ranks. Many of the soldiers were angry and unwilling to leave behind their valuables. In their loneliness some of the Greek soldiers had formed emotional attachments with captive women. After breakfast the next morning, as the troops broke camp and began to form their line of march, Xenophon stationed some of his officers along both sides of the route. As the troops began to move forward those officers inspected the soldiers who passed. Many tried to smuggle their possessions past the officers while others tried to disguise some of the women or young boys as soldiers. The women and boys were taken from the column and herded together by the side of the road. The group became bigger and soon the captives and the Persian prisoners began pleading with the Greek officers not to leave them behind in the mountains. They would be slaughtered by the Carduchi or die from cold and hunger. There was no chance for them to survive if the Greeks left them behind. The Persian prisoners begged the Greeks to at least leave them some weapons for their protection. None of the captives had adequate clothing to survive in the cold mountain climate and only a few had a little food given them by soldiers who had taken pity. Leaving them behind under these conditions was a sentence of death.

Urged on by their officers stationed on either side, the Greeks moved forward, deaf to the pleas and cries of the condemned captives they were leaving behind. Some of the captives tried in vain to follow the column, only to be driven back in a hail of stones thrown by the rear guard. The Greeks could only think of themselves that day. The column moved into the higher elevations and the cries of those left behind became fainter with each passing step. Finally the captives were no longer in sight and the only sound the Greeks could hear was the movement of their boots on the hard ground.

The next day the Greeks encountered a severe storm, the kind that comes often in the mountains. It was violent and frightening, especially for those among the Greeks who had never experienced high-altitude weather. The column continued forward, climbing farther into the mountains even as their provisions were running low and the rain pelted them mercilessly. The officers worried among themselves and knew they had to find another village before long for provisions and shelter. As the column continued to move along the narrow mountain trails, the Carduchi attacked by ambush. Anywhere the mountain track became narrow and treacherous, or where they could lie concealed from view, the Carduchi struck at the Greeks. The Greeks had to drive them back into hiding and this slowed the progress of the column even more. Without letting up, the Carduchi continued to press the Greeks with ferocious hit and run attacks from both sides of the narrow track and often from the ledges above the column.

Cheirisophus, in spite of the attacks against the column, kept up a relentless pace. With the vanguard he kept pushing forward and climbing higher no matter how badly the Greek column came under attack and how many Greeks were being killed or wounded. The brunt of the fighting that day fell upon Xenophon who was in the rear with the heavier-armed and slower soldiers. The rear guard was forced to sustain assault after assault and casualties mounted quickly. Xenophon repeatedly sent word forward for Cheirisophus to slow the pace as his men fighting the rear action were falling behind and risked being cut off from the main column. Cheirisophus sent back the same message each time—Xenophon and the rear guard would have to keep up, there would be no slowing of the pace.

Finally the column reached a spot where they could regroup and rest in safety. The Carduchi, for the moment at least, could not reach them. As the soldiers dropped by the side of the path to rest, Xenophon pushed his way to the front of the column to find Cheirisophus. When he reached the Spartan commander Xenophon was in a fury. He reproached Cheirisophus for not slowing the column and for causing the deaths of so many Greeks. Xenophon was angry that they had been forced to leave behind the bodies of their fallen comrades. The Greek dead were sure to be mutilated by the Carduchi rather than given the burial they deserved as brave soldiers and loyal comrades.

Cheirisophus said nothing and allowed Xenophon to vent his anger. He then raised his hand and pointed to higher mountains still ahead of them. The narrow path that led to them climbed so high it seemed to disappear in the clouds. Xenophon could see that Cheirisophus had posted soldiers along the path and had secured the heights. Cheirisophus explained that he had pushed the column hard at the cost of so many Greek lives to seize these heights before the enemy could fortify them. Without the heights in their control even more Greeks would have been lost when the column attempted to move forward.

That night, as the Greeks camped, Xenophon brought forward two prisoners his men had captured during one of the attacks by the Carduchi. The men were brought into the tent of Cheirisophus to be questioned through an interpreter. Neither man would speak and after several tries Cheirisophus lost his patience. He ordered the throat of one of the men cut. The order was quickly carried out and the blood of the dying man pooled before the feet of his companion. The second man lost his nerve and offered to lead the Greeks through the mountains in return for his life. The prisoner explained that there was one particularly difficult and dangerous pass ahead that the Greeks must secure before his kinsmen or they would never be able to get through the mountains.

The officers called for a volunteer group to move ahead of the main column and secure the pass. Over two thousand men came forward. This group took a light dinner and set out with the guide under cover of darkness. All that night they climbed silently through a steady rain which had begun as they left camp. It continued to rain on them, often heavily, throughout that night. As the group moved toward the pass, Xenophon and the rear guard kept the Carduchi at bay. The soldiers of the main column tried to rest as best they could among the rocks while the rain soaked them, the wind chilled them, and the Carduchi harassed them. All through the night and even during the periods of heaviest rain the Carduchi launched attacks from ambush. They rolled rocks down upon the Greeks and made attacks in small groups against the sleeping soldiers.

Just before dawn the rain finally stopped and the party with the guide finally reached the heights just above the pass. They found the pass below guarded by only a small number of the Carduchi, most of whom were asleep while the rest were sitting around a fire. They were not expecting an attack by the Greeks so were caught unprepared. All of them were slaughtered and the main column of the Greeks was able to move up to the pass. Resistance by the Carduchi along the route from this point on was very light with only a few brief and scattered attacks.

Xenophon and the rear guard had become cut off from the main column as they had stayed behind to hold off the Carduchi. Then, unexpectedly, the Carduchi approached Xenophon and asked for a talk. Through an interpreter, Xenophon listened as their chiefs asked the Greeks for a truce. As a condition of the truce Xenophon demanded that the Carduchi return the bodies of his men who had been killed in the fighting over the last several days. The Carduchi agreed to return the dead if the Greeks would not burn their villages as they passed through the mountains. Xenophon agreed and a truce was put into place. But as Xenophon and the rear guard were moving along the road to join the main column, the Carduchi again attacked. After some difficulty the rear guard were able to break contact and join once more with the main column.

By this time the main body had come upon and secured a large mountain village with abundant supplies, especially wine. While the Greeks awaited the arrival of Xenophon and the rear guard they had consumed most of the wine. Representatives of the Carduchi approached the village and offered to give back the bodies of the Greek dead in return for the guide. The Greeks made the exchange and spent the next day giving proper burial to their dead while the Carduchi tortured and then executed the guide. The following day the Greeks continued their march following the narrow mountain road north.

Wherever the road ahead became narrow and dangerous the Carduchi were waiting to attack. In each instance Xenophon and the rear guard would circle around and above the Carduchi and drive them from their positions blocking the advance of the main column. The Carduchi were lightly armed with bows and spears, and proved an agile and difficult foe. They were excellent bowmen and their arrows were shot with such force that they often pierced the shields and breastplates of the Greeks. The next day the Greeks came upon some villages above the plain bordering the Centrites River. The river was about a mile from these villages and served as the border between the mountains of the Carduchi and Armenia. The Greeks were glad to be out of these mountains, away from the Carduchi, and on a level marching plain once more. For seven days they had done nothing but march and fight their way through the mountains, so they took their leisure in these villages and recovered their strength. They took particular pleasure in recounting to each other over warm meals what they had suffered in the mountains and how they had triumphed over nature and the Carduchi.

After several days resting in these villages the Greek column prepared to move out to the plain and into the territory of the Armenians. As the column moved onto the plain the vanguard saw horsemen across the river, fully armed and supported by infantry on the bluffs above. The troops facing the Greeks were garrison soldiers of Orontas, satrap of Armenia and son-in-law of Artaxerxes. These troops were commanded by a Persian general, Artuchas, and had been sent to stop the Greeks from entering Armenia. Fortunately for the Greeks, Orontas and his main force, accompanied by Tissaphernes, were still miles away. The Greeks tried to ford the river but the current was swift and the footing too difficult. They retreated back to the villages where they saw the Carduchi massing in large numbers in the mountains. The Carduchi were heavily armed and preparing for a major battle.

The Greeks became despondent over their situation. They had the Carduchi behind them, a deep, cold, and swiftly flowing river in front of them, and an army of Persians waiting on the other side of the river. For a day and a night the Greeks stayed in the villages and their depression increased. The next morning the Greeks offered sacrifices to the gods and their officers conferred. The omens from the sacrifices were reported to be favorable and the mood of the Greeks improved. The officers ordered their men to eat a hearty breakfast.

While Xenophon was having his breakfast two soldiers came to him with information. The two had been gathering wood downstream when they came upon some rocks. There they found an old man, a woman, and some little girls putting what looked liked bags of clothes into some caves. The place was not accessible to the Persian cavalry because of rocks on both sides of the river. The two soldiers proceeded to cross the river and to their surprise discovered the water was only waist deep and the current weak. They reached the other side with little effort. Then they recrossed the river undetected and came immediately to Xenophon to report what they had found.

When Xenophon heard of their discovery he poured a libation of wine for all to celebrate. He led the two soldiers to Cheirisophus and they again described what they had found. Cheirisophus was elated and he too ordered a libation. Then he gave orders for the column to prepare to cross at the rocky site downstream. The officers agreed that Cheirisophus would cross the river with half the army while Xenophon protected them from attack by the Carduchi. The baggage train, with the animals and camp followers, would cross once Cheirisophus had secured the opposite bank—by this time the number of camp followers had swelled again with women and children captured from the villages. Xenophon and his section of the column would cross the river last while keeping the Carduchi at bay.

As the Greeks under Cheirisophus moved along the southern riverbank, the Persian cavalry on the opposite bank paralleled them. When the Greeks reached the rocky ford the column split into three sections and began to cross. The priests offered sacrifices to the river gods, while Cheirisophus threw off his cloak, took up his arms, and plunged into the river. While the priests prayed, the women in the baggage train screamed and wailed, and arrows from the Persian archers across the river rained down on them. But Cheirisophus and the advanced detachment of the Greeks made it to the other side.

Xenophon and the rear guard moved downstream from the crossing point. The Persian cavalry, fearing he meant to cross the river there and come up behind them, deserted their positions and followed him downstream on the opposite bank. Cheirisophus and his men pushed toward the Persian infantry who waited on the bluffs. When the Persian infantry saw their cavalry in confusion and the large numbers of Greeks coming toward them, they abandoned their positions and fled. The Greeks took possession of the bluffs above the river and even captured the Persian baggage train and a large amount of booty.

Xenophon turned his men and headed back up river to the crossing point. At that moment the Carduchi began descending onto the plain to attack the Greek rear guard. The baggage train and the camp followers had not completed the crossings. Xenophon moved his troops into position at the crossing and turned them to face the Carduchi. Cheirisophus, having secured his position, sent reinforcements to aid Xenophon. Xenophon countermanded the order as the reinforcements began to cross the river. He ordered them to stay on the opposite bank and provide cover for his own troops as they came across. Xenophon and his men formed into the phalanx and charged the Carduchi.

The Greeks struck up the paean and advanced against the tribesmen. While the Carduchi were skilled mountain fighters and dangerous from ambush, they lacked the skill or equipment to meet seasoned Greek infantry in confrontational combat on flat ground. The Carduchi ran from the plain back to the mountains and the Greeks gave chase. Upon a prearranged signal, the Greeks broke off the attack, dissolved their phalanx and ran back to the river to cross. Some of the Carduchi turned and chased the Greeks. From the river's edge they managed to wound many of the Greeks with their arrows as they crossed. The majority of the Carduchi, however, returned to their villages in the mountains.

When the crossing had been completed the Greeks regrouped and formed into line of battle. It was now beyond midday and they began the march into Armenia. Their spirits were high and the going was easy. For nearly twenty miles there was neither a village nor an enemy soldier to be seen. The Greeks concluded that because of the nearly constant wars between the Carduchi and the Armenians over the years the area was unsafe for settlement and had remained barren.

It was now late in November and the Greeks finally reached the first town in Armenia. It was of considerable size and contained a palace for the satrap Orontas. The houses were unusual in that they were surrounded by turrets. Provisions were plentiful in the town and the Greeks ate and drank well that night. From this town the column marched to the headwaters of the Tigris River and then north another fifty miles to the Teleboas River and the limits of western Armenia. At the river they encountered a troop of horsemen dispatched by the satrap of Armenia, Tiribazus. The Persian commander indicated through his interpreter that he wished to parley and the Greek officers agreed to listen to what he had to say.

Tiribazus offered the Greeks a truce. They could move through his territory unhampered, free to take whatever provisions they needed, but they were not to loot or burn the villages and towns they passed. The Greeks agreed to his terms and a truce was made. The Greeks marched another fifty miles through level country with the cavalry of Tiribazus following about a mile behind them. They finally reached a large palace surrounded by many villages and camped there. That night there was a heavy snowfall and at first the Greek commanders thought to divide their troops and quarter them in the various villages where there were abundant supplies of wine and food. However, some of the officers feared dividing the army with Tiribazus so close behind. They had not forgotten the treachery of Tissaphernes and Artaxerxes and were distrustful of the Persians. It was agreed among the officers to keep the troops together, and the necessary precautions were taken to secure the Greek camp.

The cold and snow that night proved too much for the soldiers in their tents. The officers reversed their earlier decision and let the soldiers divide into groups and take refuge in the villages. There were some Greeks who had violated the terms of the truce with Tiribazus by burning and looting homes that they passed on the march. Those soldiers were forced to remain outside in the snow that night as punishment. The Greeks remained in the villages all that next day. The next night they became apprehensive so they sent out a party to spy on Tiribazus and the Persians. The reconnaissance party captured a sentry and brought him back to camp for questioning. He told the Greeks that Tiribazus planned to ambush the Greeks on a mountain pass a few miles ahead.

The Greeks sent ahead a detachment of soldiers that night to secure the pass. Then the main Greek column marched to the pass the next day without incident, but the going was slow because of the deep snow. Before the day ended, the entire column had crossed over the pass where Tiribazus had intended to ambush them and descended onto a level plain. Over the next several days the Greeks struggled through the snow but managed to cover nearly a hundred miles marching north over the plain. This stage of the march was made even more difficult because a strong north wind blew directly into their faces and froze everything it touched, both men and animals.

The wind blew at the Greeks so hard day and night that at times it made marching nearly impossible. One of the priests suggested they had angered one of the gods and perhaps a sacrifice to the north wind might appease him. A sacrifice was held and following that ritual it seemed to the Greeks that the wind abated, at least to an extent that allowed them to resume the march. The snow along the route became deeper the further north they marched and nearly thirty of the Greeks, as well as many of the slaves and camp followers, died from exposure. Most of the Greeks managed to survive the cold nights by building fires and sleeping close to them. By morning the hot coals and embers had melted holes in the snow all the way down to the ground. Some of the soldiers measured the depth of the holes and determined that the snow was six feet in depth. As the march continued, hunger, cold, and fatigue began to take a heavy toll. Men began to drop all along the column. Xenophon ordered that those who had fallen should be given extra rations and once many of these men had eaten they were able to join the column and resume the slow march north.

Cheirisophus and the vanguard reached a town surrounded by a large wall. When they stopped outside the wall the local people called down to ask who they were and where they were headed. The Greeks had an interpreter with them and under orders from Cheirisophus and fearful for his life, he replied that they had come from the Persian king and were searching his satrap. The townsmen accepted the explanation and invited the Greeks inside the walls. Cheirisophus and the vanguard quartered themselves and awaited the arrival of the column. Those in the column who could not reach the village because of exhaustion spent that night in the open and many died from the cold.

All the while, Tiribazus and his army shadowed the Greeks at a safe distance. The Persians also suffered from the cold and many of their soldiers, like the Greeks, became blind from the glare of the snow or lost fingers and toes from frostbite. But both the Greeks and the Persians following them had to keep moving because of the cold. Many of the Greeks had worn out their boots and now wore freshly flayed ox-hides on their feet. Soldiers continued to fall behind, and Xenophon with the rear guard urged them to continue the march, for the army of Tiribazus was following close behind. When some of these men would not obey him because they were too sick or tired, Xenophon became angry. Many of the exhausted soldiers fell by the wayside and when he came upon them they told him to simply kill them for they could not walk another step. As the number of stragglers increased, Xenophon and the rear guard were forced to mount an attack against the pursuing Persians to gain more time for the column. The Persians themselves were so miserable from the elements that they ran from Xenophon and his men rather than put up a fight.

As Xenophon and the rear guard moved forward toward the town they found their soldiers all along the route lying in the snow, wrapped in their blankets. Xenophon and his men, exhausted and despondent, bivouacked where they were, without food or shelter, too tired to move forward to the comfort and warmth of the town. The next morning Cheirisophus sent out some of his men to help the sick and lame back to the town. The distance from the town to where many of the Greeks had spent the night in the snow was less than two miles, yet not a man among those who had fallen that night had the strength to walk the distance alone and without help.

In the town, the Greek officers decided to risk dividing the soldiers and quartering some of them in nearby villages, even though the column of Tiribazus following them posed a danger. Cheirisophus stayed in the town where he had become comfortable in the home of one of the more prosperous citizens. Xenophon was assigned a village farther away. When Xenophon and his men arrived at the village they found that a young captain and some of his men had already seized the best homes for themselves. They had made slaves of many of the villagers and the captain had taken for himself the daughter of the village chief, a young girl who had been married only eight days before.

When Xenophon and his men arrived, the young captain relinquished his hold on the village. The houses in these villages were unusual, according to the manuscripts, in that they had been dug beneath the ground. The entrances were like the mouths of wells and the inhabitants descended by a ladder into the main living quarters. In their houses the villagers kept their goats, sheep, cattle, and fowl. The animals entered and exited by tunnels dug for them below the living quarters. In these homes Xenophon and the Greeks found comfortable lodging, warmth, and abundant food. In the center of nearly every communal living area was a large bowl filled with barley wine. When the villagers were thirsty they took a straw and drew the mixture into their mouths until they had their fill. The Greeks found the wine was so strong that many of them had to dilute it with water in order to drink it.

Xenophon moved into the home of the village chief. He treated the man with respect and promised him that his wife and children would not be harmed. Xenophon nevertheless kept them under close guard. That night the Greeks ate and drank their fill and slept well in warm quarters. The next day Xenophon took the village chief and set out to visit Cheirisophus. As he passed the various villages he stopped to visit the Greeks quartered there and he found the soldiers in good spirits. They were eating, drinking, and generally abusing the local residents at will. Every time he stopped, the soldiers insisted he luncheon with them and they served him abundant portions of lamb, veal, and poultry. In addition there was bread and plenty of barley wine to drink. Xenophon encouraged the village chief to eat but the chief quietly declined each time.

When Xenophon reached Cheirisophus in the town he found him reclining on a couch in a great room being served by a number of Armenian boys. He showed the boys what he wanted done by signs, treating them as if they were deaf and dumb as they responded to his every command. Xenophon and Cheirisophus exchanged greetings and through an interpreter they undertook to question the chief. The chief told them the neighboring country was inhabited by the Chalybians and he explained to the Greeks where the road to their territory lay. Xenophon returned to his village with the chief and sacrificed a horse since he understood it was sacred to the sun god of the Persians. The Greeks took most of the villagers' horses, which they found were smaller than the Persian variety but more spirited. The village chief advised the Greeks to wrap the feet of the horses in burlap bags when riding them through the deeper snow or the horses would sink to their bellies and no longer be able to move.

The Greeks remained in these villages for seven days and there was never a sign of Tiribazus. On the day of departure they took the village chief as guide and his only son, a boy just coming into the prime of his youth, as hostage. The boy was given over to the care of Pleisthenes of Amphipolis with the agreement that if the father fulfilled his promise to guide the Greeks through the land of the Chalybians he could return home with the boy. If not, both would be killed. The Greeks set out the next morning and moved north through the snow. For three days they moved through the mountains without seeing a village. Cheirisophus became impatient and accused the chief of purposely avoiding the villages to deny the Greeks provisions and

XENOPHON When the original Greek generals were murdered by the Persian Tissaphernes, Xenophon emerged as general of the "Ten Thousand" and led the Greek survivors through Mesopotamia and Asia Minor on their way home to Greece.

GREEK HOPLITES Greek soldiers, or hoplites, wore distinctively shaped
helmets, breast and back plates to protect the upper body, and greaves
over their lower forelegs. The Greek warrior depicted on the opposite
page, top, is protected with leather straps that hang from his breastplate. He holds a long spear commonly used in phalanx formations.
The hoplite depicted opposite page, bottom, holding his shield while
grasping a short sword is wearing a Doric-style helmet. The Athenian
hoplite shown carved in marble, above, is carrying a long spear and
shield and is protected with typical Greek armor on his torso and legs.

Greek shield.

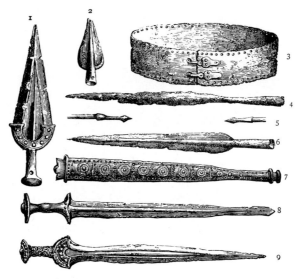

1. Dagger 2. Javelin head 3. Bronze belt 4. Spear head 5. Arrow heads
6. Spear head 7. Sword scabbard 8. Sword 9. Sword

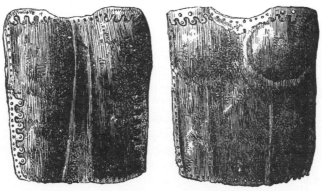

Breast and back plates.

PERSIANS

A century before Xenophon's march, Darius I (right) expanded the Persian empire west to the Ionian coastline and east to the Indus valley. He built two large palace cities at Susa and Persepolis. At the time, his armed bodyguards, the Immortals (depicted below), were an elite military unit.

SARDIS The city of Sardis, to the right of the mountain above, was the ancient capital of the Persian satrap Cyrus. It was from Sardis that the ill-fated expedition of Cyrus and the Greek mercenaries began in the spring of 401 B.C.

PALACE OF CYRUS These Persian ruins still show glimpses of the splendor of this once great royal palace that belonged to Cyrus, satrap of Asia Minor.

PALACE OF CYRUS The richness of the Persian empire and the influence of the Greeks is evident in the richly carved façade over this palace doorway (above), and the mosaic-floored courtyard (below).

GREEK TEMPLE Situated close to Greece, the western areas of the satrapy of Asia Minor were influenced by Greek culture. Just two kilometers outside of Cyrus's palace, a Greek temple (above and below) was built.

SARDIS TO COLOSSAE
The route from Sardis to
Colossae (Denizli) is today as it
was in ancient times—a virtual
cornucopia of produce (right).
Cyrus and the Greeks passed
by the ancient city of Tripolis,
where today only small
remains are visible (below).

LAODICEA Near the city of Colossae can be seen the ruins of Laodicea, a city that thrived in the Roman period.

HIERAPOLIS Looking from the heights above the ruins of the ancient city of Hierapolis, you can see the valley through which Cyrus led his Greek mercenaries as they traveled to Colossae where they rested seven days before turning east.

HIERAPOLIS Although most of the ruins visible today (above and below) date from the Roman period, Hierapolis was once a thriving city for many people from different cultures including Persians, Greeks, and Romans.

COLOSSAE Near Colossae and Hierapolis lie the warm thermal springs of Pamukkale (above) where wealthy Greeks, Persians, and Romans came for the baths and spas located there. All that remains of the ancient city of Colossae today (below) is a mound of dirt and remnants of columns.

CILICIAN GATES These narrow mountain passes through the Taurus Mountains lead by a treacherous mountain road to the city of the Cilician Queen Epyaxa, mistress of Cyrus.

TAURUS MOUNTAINS These mountains rise high above the plains of Cappodocia near the city of Tarsus.

MOUNTAINS NEAR ARMENIA With winter coming on, the Greek mercenaries under the command of Xenophon and Cheirisophus crossed over these desolate mountains as they marched north toward the Black Sea.

ZIGANA PASS The mountain pass shown here is very likely the same pass over the last mountain barrier the Greeks encountered on their way to the sea.

COTYORA At this Greek city and colony of the Sinopians located on the Black Sea, the mercenaries menaced the inhabitants and forced the Sinopians to negotiate a settlement with Xenophon.

CALPE HARBOR A small and peaceful ancient town was located on the Black Sea on this harbor. The Greek mercenaries under Xenophon stayed here for a long period of time recuperating from their march.

CALPE HARBOR Xenophon wanted to settle the mercenaries here and build a city. Today, the remains of ancient walls—perhaps built by Xenophon's men—can still be seen.

shelter. The chief argued that there were no villages in these mountains and Cheirisophus struck him in front of his son. That night the chief escaped from the Greeks leaving his young son behind.

When Xenophon and Cheirisophus discovered the chief had left they argued with each other. Xenophon felt it was wrong for Cheirisophus to have struck the chief and then stupid of him not to have posted a guard on him that night. The two argued over the matter while Pleisthenes, who had fallen in love with the young Armenian boy, refused to kill him. Xenophon and Cheirisophus resolved their differences and Pleisthenes eventually took the boy home to Greece with him.

The Greeks continued their march for ten more days without incident or any sign of Tiribazus. Then they came to another pass leading over a mountain and down onto a plain. The Greek vanguard found the pass guarded by a combined force of Chalybians, Taochians, and Phasians. Cheirisophus halted the column about three miles from the pass and had the soldiers form into a modified line of battle while the officers went into counsel on how to take the pass. Some of the officers argued in favor of a direct frontal assault as quickly as possible to force a way through the pass before the enemy was reinforced. Xenophon however, wished to minimize Greek casualties and take the pass in the easiest way possible. He favored finding another way over the mountain or else sending a detachment of Greeks to come down behind the enemy. A detachment could take the high ground above the enemy that night and launch a surprise attack on them just before dawn. Stealing the position seemed to Xenophon the best solution. It was a tactic the Greeks had used before when fighting in the mountains and it seemed appropriate to use it again.

Xenophon proposed that Cheirisophus lead the party since the Spartans, he had heard, were experts at stealing. Cheirisophus bantered in return that he had heard the Athenians were experts at stealing the public funds. In fact, he commented, the best Athenians, the politicians, steal all the time in spite of the risk. He suggested Xenophon display his Athenian training at stealing. The banter went back and forth until Xenophon volunteered to take the heights from the enemy but only after he had had his dinner. Cheirisophus agreed and ordered that the army be moved closer to the pass to make it appear that on the next day they would try and force their way through.

That night, Xenophon set out from the camp with a detachment of soldiers under cover of darkness. At dawn, Cheirisophus moved the main Greek body forward and the enemy moved down from the pass to meet them. Just then Xenophon and his men made their appearance in the heights above. The enemy, seeing that they were caught between Xenophon and Cheirisophus, decided to run rather than fight. The Greeks secured the pass, and when the last member of the column had gotten safely through they sacrificed to the gods and erected a monument of rocks there. The column then descended onto a plain and reached a number of nearby villages that were well-provisioned.

From these villages the Greeks continued to march north for five days through the country of the Taochians, a distance of nearly one hundred miles. Provisions began to run low but the Taochians in their towns kept behind strong walls that the Greeks could not breach. These walls were built into the sides of cliffs and often impossible to storm from below or above. The Greeks became desperate for supplies and decided to force an entry into one of the larger strongholds. Time and again they were repulsed in their efforts as the Taochians rolled huge rocks down on them, crushing many of the Greeks.

Then the Greeks sallied forth in mock attacks, and when the rocks began to come, quickly moved out of range. In this way they hoped the Taochians would run out of rocks. Finally, after several attempts, the Greeks were able to rush one of the walls and gain an entry.

What the Greeks witnessed next was a dreadful spectacle that shocked even the most callous among them. The Taochian women and children had assembled at the farthest end of the main wall that had been built at the edge of a large cliff. There they were protected by the last of their men. As the first of the Greeks approached, the women pushed or threw their children over the cliff. When all the children had been killed the women jumped to their deaths. Then the Taochian men who had survived the fighting assembled and together plunged over the side of the precipice.

Aeneas the Stymphalian ran after one old man who was dressed in particularly fine clothes and grabbed him just as he was about to jump. The old man struggled violently and dragged Aeneas with him over the edge to their deaths. The Greeks were stunned. Never had they witnessed a mass suicide like this and the experience left even the most hardened of the mercenaries shaken. Yet it took only a few minutes for the Greeks to recover from what they had seen and quickly set about searching the stronghold for survivors and valuables. They found only a few old people hiding but the Greeks secured large numbers of cattle, mules, sheep, and other provisions.

From this town the Greeks continued north into the land of the Chalybians, seven days march, or about 150 miles. They were to prove the bravest of all the tribes the Greeks had encountered in the mountains. The Chalybians wore thick corselets of linen that reached to the groin, greaves, and helmets. About their waists they carried a knife which they would use to cut the throats of any enemy soldiers they might capture or wound in battle. Then they would cut off the heads of the vanquished and carry them along on their march as trophies. Before they began a battle they would sing and dance to reinforce their own spirits and demoralize their enemy.

The Chalybians remained in their village strongholds as the Greeks passed and refused to give them provisions or shelter. The strongholds were well-fortified and the Greeks preferred to keep on the march and pass through this land as quickly as possible. The Greeks finally came to the Harpasus River and marched through the territory of the Scythinians, a distance of about seventy miles over a level plain. There they came to some villages where they stayed for three days, resting and collecting food.

From these villages the Greeks marched four more days and seventy more miles to a large and prosperous city called Gymnias. The ruler of the city sent ambassadors who extended friendship to the Greeks and offered provisions and a guide. When the guide was introduced to the Greeks he told them they would have to march through a hostile land but that after five days they would come to a place where they would be able to view the sea. The Greek column moved on as their guide urged them to burn and pillage every village along their route. The Greeks realized that the ruler of Gymnias had befriended them out of expectation that the Greeks would pillage and devastate the homes of his enemy—and the Greeks complied.

On the fifth day, the guide brought the column to the base of a great mountain called in the ancient manuscripts "Theches." This mountain is located in the Dogu Karandeniz Dagliar range of northwestern Turkey, and from all indications is probably Mt. Zigana. The entire range of these mountains stretches from a point where they touch the coast of the Black Sea several miles east of Trabzon to where they end in Russian Georgia behind the city of Batumi. These mountains were the last high barrier between the Greeks and the Black Sea.

The Greeks had spent a number of weeks fighting their way north through the mountains of Armenia and now they turned northwest toward the sea. The wind, snow, and hunger had all taken their toll on the long column. Most of the men at this stage were barely able to walk. They were cold and hungry and they moved ahead slowly in silent despond. Suddenly, as the vanguard climbed to a vantage point near the top of the mountain, a great shout went up. When Xenophon heard the commotion he was at the back of the column and he thought that the vanguard was under attack. He feared that the local people, angered because the Greeks had burned and looted their villages, had set an ambush. But the shout that came along the column that day was not one Xenophon was accustomed to hearing when his men were under attack. This was a different cry. It was a shout that grew louder as it passed down the line and it filled the column first with anxiety and then with joy.

Xenophon mounted his horse and pushed through the column toward the front to see what the commotion was about. Men all around him began breaking ranks, pushing and running forward to learn the cause of the furor. In a few moments Xenophon could make out the cry sweeping the column. Men were shouting to one another "The sea! The sea!" The scouts had spotted a vast body of water and the Greeks knew that they had finally arrived at the Euxine (Black) Sea. Mayhem spread through the ranks. Soldiers pushed forward; officers and men alike broke into a run toward the summit. Believing their ordeal was finally coming to an end the generals, captains, and common soldiers, joyful tears streaming down their faces, embraced each other without regard for rank. Without being told, they began to assemble rocks into a great cairn. Upon this crude altar they placed as offerings to the gods raw ox hides, walking sticks, and captured shields and weapons. The Greeks made sacrifice and thanked the gods for their safe passage. They released the guide to return to his home.

He was given a Persian horse to make his journey swifter, a silver cup, and ten darics as a reward. The Greeks surrounded the guide as he prepared to leave, wished him a safe journey and thanked him for his service. When they inquired what else he might want from them, he asked for one thing more—some rings from their fingers. He received hundreds, and placed them in a sack which he tied to his horse. Before he left, the guide showed the Greek scouts the road to the country of the Macronians and the sea beyond. Then he took his leave from their camp, anxious to begin his journey home. He would have to return alone through the land that the Greeks had just looted and burned. Burdened with his rewards, he set out on his long journey home through the land of his enemies.

The mountain pass that Xenophon and the Greeks crossed over is most likely the Zigana Pass. Mt. Zigana is one of several high mountains in that range and reaches a height of 3,082 meters. The pass is well-known and frequently traveled all year round because it is at 2,010 meters. Upon climbing this pass, I could find no place along the route that offered a view of the Black Sea because there was a heavy cloud cover over the mountains at the time and periods of rain. Views of the sea are rare in these mountains because of the frequent overcast, but I was assured by the locals that one can see the Black Sea from sections of the pass on clear days. Although I was unable to personally confirm a view of the sea from the Zigana Pass, it remains the most likely route for the Greeks to have taken. It is the only pass over the mountains that leads directly to Trabzon. In addition, the distance from the pass to Trabzon is nearly identical to that recorded in the ancient manuscripts.

Another possible, but much less likely, pass is the Salmenkas at 2,300 meters. This pass is over the Polut Mountain (2,856 meters) another high mountain in the same range, but farther east. This pass also leads to the Black Sea but some miles east of Trabzon and it does not fit the distance requirements specified in the manuscripts.

The Greeks spent that night on the pass and broke camp early the next morning. They were anxious to come down off the mountain and reach the sea. They believed to a man that all their troubles had finally come to an end not knowing how much more suffering lay ahead and how few of them would ever reach their homes. As the Greeks marched down from the mountain they entered into the land of the Macronians. These were another warlike people and they assembled in line of battle on the banks of a river to watch the Greek column pass on the other side. The Macronians taunted the Greeks as they passed, challenging them to cross over the river and fight. One of the peltasts came to Xenophon and explained that he had been a slave at Athens before he won his freedom and he recognized the language of these people. He had been taken into slavery at an early age but remembered parts of his native language. He believed that these Macronians were his own people. The peltast crossed to the other side under a flag of truce and conferred with the Macronians. As he spoke bits and pieces of their language, they welcomed him into their ranks and he in turn was able to assure them that the Greeks meant them no harm. A conference between the Greek officers and the Macronian chiefs was arranged and he explained to them that the Greeks only wanted to pass peacefully through their lands on their way to the sea.

The Macronians and Greeks made a truce and sealed the agreement by exchanging lances. Then the Macronians helped the Greeks get across the river, and provided them with a market to buy provisions. The Greeks exchanged what they had plundered in the mountains for food and other supplies. The Macronians mingled freely with the Greeks for three days and then conducted them to the land of the Colchians and another smaller mountain to cross.

The Colchians, however, proved less agreeable than the Macronians and blocked their way. Xenophon looked at these savage people and then turned to Cheirisophus. "These Colchians stand between us and the sea we have marched so far and fought so hard to reach. We will eat them raw." The Greeks assembled for battle and a count was made of the troops for the first time since they had left Cunaxa. The number of Greeks who had survived the winter came to 8,000 from the original group of 14,000. The Greeks prayed to their gods and then upon orders from the officers moved into their companies and forward for combat. As was their manner they first struck up their war chant and then their battle cry.

Cheirisophus and Xenophon each commanded a wing of the battle line and in the fight that ensued outflanked the enemy on both sides. When the Colchians saw what was happening they made the mistake of dividing their forces to confront the Greek flank attacks. This pulled the center of their force apart and the Greek heavy infantry went through their middle. The Colchians no longer stood their ground but broke and ran. Advanced detachments of the Greeks pushed through the chaotic center of the Colchians and cleared the road ahead.

Following the battle, the exhausted and hungry Greeks encamped in several mountain villages. There was nothing remarkable about these villages but the Greeks noticed that in the meadows around them were swarms of bees, for it was now early spring. In the villages the Greeks found vast quantities of honey which had been stored in jars. Most of the soldiers ate the honey, some of then in great quantities, and in a few minutes "went off their heads."

The soldiers who had eaten the greatest quantities of the honey soon began to suffer from diarrhea and vomiting. They went "crazy" or lay upon the ground almost like dead men. Those who had eaten only small quantities either became like men who were drunk or they became depressed. Not a man among them was able to stand on his own. The next day the Greeks were amazed to discover that no one had died. Then at about the same hour as they had eaten the honey the day before, the afflicted men began to rise out of their stupor. All over the village, men came to their senses and rose up as from the dead. By the fourth day, all those who had been stricken recovered as if from a drugging.

In the old section of Istanbul I made inquiries at the spice bazaar of the Yeni Cami near the Galata Bridge. A number of the spice merchants there who specialize in the selling of honey agreed that the best honey in Turkey comes from the area of Trapzon. All of the merchants interviewed said that there is a honey from that region that can only be purchased by special government permit or on the black market. That honey contains opium and is used by cancer patients seeking relief from pain. The merchants stated that the honey was produced from bees that had fed off the poppy plants in the mountain pastures and fields behind Trabzon. When I reached Trapzon and continued my inquiries, I learned that there are several types of honey produced in the area. The first is called *anzer bali* in Turkish and is used for medicinal purposes. The second honey is called *deli bali* or "crazy" honey and can prove fatal if ingested in large quantities. The "crazy" honey is made from the flower of the rhododendron bush.

From the land of the Colchians the army marched two days and some twenty-five miles to reach the sea at the Greek city of Trapezus. Trapezus was at that time a city colonized and inhabited by Greeks from Sinope, another larger city farther east along the Black Sea. When the mercenaries reached Trapezus it was late in the spring of 400 B.C. Xenophon and the army had crossed several difficult mountain ranges during the coldest months of winter, and most of the Greeks had survived.

The people of Trapezus welcomed their Greek brothers and orga-

nized a sacrifice to the gods and games of the Olympic style. The
Greeks gave thanks to Zeus for their safe deliverance, and sacrificed
to Heracles for his guidance through their long and difficult journey.
When the praying was over the games began. There were foot races
and horse races. When the racing was finished there were wrestling
and boxing contests, followed by a competition called the pancratium
that involved a combination of both wrestling and boxing. In spite of
months of marching and fighting in the mountains, a large number of
the mercenaries entered the games to compete in various contests.

There was a great deal of rivalry between the mercenaries and the
Greeks of Trapezus. There was shouting, laughter, and cheering during the games followed by prodigious amounts of drinking and feasting that lasted for many nights and days. The Greeks remained at
Trapezus for nearly a month. When what little money they had ran
out and the people of Trapezus indicated they would not provide supplies for free, the Greek mercenaries returned to the nearby mountains
and pillaged the villages of the Colchians.

VIII
BARBARIANS AND DISSENSION

When the "Ten Thousand" reached the Black Sea and the companionship of fellow Greeks along the coast, they believed that the worst part of their journey was behind them. After the mercenaries had completed the necessary sacrifices to thank the gods for their safe deliverance, they began to debate what to do next. Among the officers who spoke first was Leon of Thurii. He told the assembly that he was tired of marching up and down mountains, carrying his weapons and provisions, making camp each night, breaking camp each dawn, and fighting enemy after enemy nearly every step of the way. He was tired of being cold, tired, and hungry. What he wanted was to relax aboard a ship and sail home to Greece "stretched out on my back upon the deck like Odysseus."

The soldiers shouted approval of his idea and it carried the day. Cheirisophus volunteered to set sail on the first available ship and search out a friend of his, Anaxibius, who was a Spartan admiral. He promised to return with warships and transports enough to bring the Greeks home in style and comfort. He proposed that the army remain in the city of Trapezus, among fellow Greeks, until he returned. The soldiers were excited about the plan and voted for Cheirisophus to set sail as soon as possible.

Then Xenophon rose to speak. He supported Cheirisophus and reminded the army that much remained to be done before they would be ready to sail home. They would have to obtain their provisions from the territory surrounding the city of Trapezus, for the citizens could not support them until Cheirisophus returned with the ships. That territory was hostile and he reminded the Greeks of the dangers they had encountered while passing through there. Xenophon proposed that the officers organize foraging parties rather than permit

151

the men to go off on their own in small groups as they had been doing, at great risk of capture or death. It was agreed that foraging parties would be formed under the officers and each would register with a central command post as to where and when it was going out. The Greek camp would have to be located outside the city gates and then well-fortified against counterattacks by the enemy. Then Xenophon proposed that the soldiers should secure some ships of their own rather than wait for Cheirisophus to return with a fleet. He had observed that many merchant ships passed this part of the coastline. Some of those ships could be captured with the help from the Greeks of Trapezus. The captured ships could then be moored in the harbor until the Greeks had a sufficient quantity of them to transport the entire army, or until Cheirisophus returned with his fleet. The proposal was adopted by the assembly with the provision that the captured sailors would be well-paid to make them more amenable to staying and, when the time came, transporting the army back to Greece.

If this plan failed, Xenophon warned the assembly, they would need to have a contingency. He proposed that if all else failed they should once more take to the roads and walk home. This was a prospect most of the army bemoaned in one large voice. Xenophon did not put this last proposal to a vote but on his own sent envoys to urge the other Greek cities along the Black Sea coast to repair their roads so that the army could pass quickly through their territories.

The Greeks obtained a fifty-oared warship from the people of Trapezus and put it under the command of a Spartan *perioecus* named Dexippus. He was supposed to put out to sea and capture merchant vessels; instead, Dexippus and his crew deserted the army and disappeared into the Black Sea. It was speculated among the soldiers that he sailed the ship through the Dardenelles and back to Greece.

Then the mercenaries obtained a smaller, thirty-oared warship from the city and this time put it under the command of an Athenian, Polycrates. Polycrates proved reliable and went out to sea daily, capturing a number of merchant vessels. The ships were brought into port and moored while their cargoes were unloaded and placed in warehouses under guard.

The main body of the army kept itself busy in the countryside foraging for provisions, capturing slaves, and looking for booty. Some parties were successful while others failed. The Greeks lost one of their best commanders, Cleaenetus, when he was killed with some of his men attempting to take a stronghold in the mountains.

As the Greeks ravaged the countryside immediately around Trapezus, they found they had to range farther and farther away from the protection of their camp and the walls of the city. After several weeks it came to a point where a foraging party of Greeks had to spend two or three nights in the field before they reached a village large enough to raid and then two or three nights on the return. The farther away from the city they foraged, the larger the raiding parties had to be and the slower they moved.

Eventually, a commander had to take nearly half the army with him to forage while the other half remained behind to protect the camp and the city. The Colchians, since most of their villages had been burned and plundered by the Greeks and many of their women carried off, had begun massing in large numbers in the mountains not far from Trapezus and the Greek camp. They would not risk an all out assault against the city, but the mercenaries needed to be particularly careful when they left the safety of their camp.

The leaders of Trapezus were eager to take advantage of the presence of the Greek mercenaries to use them against a particularly troublesome enemy called the Drilae. The Drilae were a warlike mountain people who often raided close to Trapezus. Their country was difficult to reach but the mercenaries were willing to undertake a campaign against them since the prospect of more booty and slaves was promising.

When the Greek mercenaries and their guides reached the highlands, the Drilae set fire to many of their weakest strongholds and fell back to their more secure ones higher in the mountains. The Greeks found little to plunder in the burned-out villages and few people to take as slaves. They found one stronghold, however, in which a large number of people had taken refuge with their animals and goods. The stronghold would not be easy to take since it was built upon an exceedingly deep ravine and the approaches were difficult on every side.

As the army neared the stronghold the peltasts ran about a half-mile ahead of the slower and more heavily armed hoplites. They crossed the ravine and began an undisciplined attack against the stronghold. Behind them followed a large number of Greek spearmen in support. The peltasts who crossed the ravine amounted to more than a thousand men. The Drilae were surprised by the attack and had not had time to bring all their animals within the confines of the stronghold. The spearmen broke off their support of the peltasts and set about trying to capture the animals and anything else they could find of value.

The peltasts were unable to breach the stronghold because it was well-protected by a wide trench and rampart. Upon the rampart the Drilae had erected wooden towers at equal intervals. When the peltasts tried to withdraw, the Drilae left the safety of their fort and chased them. The descent from the base of the stronghold down to the ravine proved difficult and only a small number of Greeks could descend at one time because of the footing.

Xenophon moved up to the ravine with some other officers to assess the situation. The captains were of the opinion that the rampart could be breached and the stronghold probably taken but it would cost many Greek lives. Xenophon concurred, yet they decided to go ahead with the assault since they had come this far and a retreat could cost them high casualties as well. The Greek hoplites were moved forward and then brought up to the ravine in their respective companies for combat. The Greek bowmen, spearmen, and slingers were positioned to provide the necessary cover for the advancing hoplites.

Then Xenophon gave the order and the Greeks struck up the paean. The trumpets sounded and the hoplites moved forward. The missiles began to fly. Spears, arrows, stones, and firebrands were hurled in such great numbers by the Greeks that they cleared the ramparts and towers of the defenders. This allowed the infantry enough time to move to the base of the ramparts and secure their positions.

Agasias the Stymphalian, a captain leading one of the first companies to reach the ramparts, dropped his weapons and clad only in his tunic scaled the walls. He made it to the top and then reached down to pull another Greek up behind him. Meanwhile, other Greek captains, not to be outdone by a Stymphalian, began scaling the ramparts and assisting others to follow. The ramparts were captured and in short order the peltasts and other lightly armed troops had overrun the entire fortification.

Xenophon kept the hoplites outside the gates of the stronghold, for enemy forces were concentrating in ever greater numbers upon the heights above them. The peltasts who had scaled the walls and entered the stronghold only minutes before came rushing out through the main gate. They reported that within the stronghold there was a citadel which was well-fortified and heavily garrisoned. Everyone outside the citadel had been killed or carried off by the Greeks, but the lightly armed peltasts could not breach the citadel.

Xenophon and the officers determined that the citadel was too well-fortified to take without heavy casualties, and the enemy forces massing in the heights above gave them cause for concern. It was agreed to withdraw. As the Greeks began their retreat the Drilae attacked in great numbers. Many of them rushed out from the citadel while others who had been hiding in the houses which lined the narrow streets to the citadel joined them.

Matters became even more difficult for the Greeks because it was getting near dusk. One of the houses in the stronghold was set afire by the Greeks and began to burn vigorously. The fire in that house quickly spread and other houses in the stronghold began to burn. The houses burned quickly as they were made of wood and very dry. People and soldiers who had been hiding in the houses were now forced into the streets where they were caught between the fighting and the raging fires.

The Drilae who had charged after the Greeks now found themselves hampered by their own people in the streets and the burning houses all around them. They broke off their pursuit of the Greeks and directed their attention toward putting out the fires and saving their own people. The Greeks used this distraction to cover their retreat from the stronghold and to escape down the ravine. As the Greeks retreated into the darkness of the mountains they could see behind them that the whole stronghold was burning; everything made of wood—houses, towers, and palisades—was ablaze. Only the citadel, which was made of stone, withstood the fires.

The Greeks marched all through the night with little to show for their efforts. Many of them had been wounded and a few killed. By dawn the mercenaries had come to a steep and narrow trail that led down the mountain. The path led to a plain and then the route to Trapezus was open before them. They reached the city late that morning and while many of the soldiers went straight to their beds others tended to the wounded.

As the days wore on, the situation for the Greek mercenaries at Trapezus was becoming difficult. Cheirisophus had not returned and they had not assembled enough ships in port to transport the entire army home by sea. Provisions were running dangerously low and the cost of foraging in the mountains had become too high. The city would not support them any longer, and since they had ravaged all the land around it there was nothing left to pillage in the countryside. When the Greeks went into the city to buy at the market or drink at the taverns arguments with the merchants over prices were frequent. Relations between the mercenaries and their fellow Greeks of Trapezus were becoming strained.

The officers held a council to consider their further options and it was decided by vote that the army would leave by land and follow the coastal road west to the Greek city of Byzantium. They would put on board their few ships all those soldiers who were sick or wounded, and all those forty years of age or older. The Greeks had taken a number of captive women and children, and those who were not sold in the slave market at Trapezus were also put aboard the ships along with the baggage. In command of the ships they put the two oldest generals, Philesius and Sophaenetus, who were in their fifties. The small fleet set sail while the rest of the army began to march west along the sea.

Within three days the army reached another Greek city on the coast, Cerasus, about seventy-five miles from Trapezus. Some scant remains of this ancient city are still visible in the depressed and bleak Turkish coastal town of Giresun. In Cerasus, the Greeks found a ready market for the booty they had collected along their march from Trapezus and they sold what remained of the captive women and children who were aboard the ships. The money was distributed evenly among the soldiers with a tithe collected for the gods and held by the generals for safekeeping.

When the army finally left Cerasus, those who had been aboard the ships continued to travel in that manner while the rest of the army marched west along the coast. After a few days the army reached the boundaries of a people called the Mossynoecians. They were called "the dwellers in wooden towers" and the Greeks sent forward an envoy with a translator to their main stronghold to ask if they could pass safely through their country.

The Mossynoecians refused to let the Greeks march through their land. The interpreter with the army, a man named Timesitheus from Cerasus, suggested that the Greeks enlist the aid of another tribe of Mossynoecians further west who might be more cooperative than this group. While Xenophon and the main force held their positions around the strongholds, Timesitheus and a small band of Greeks set out for the strongholds of the rival tribe. This group was willing to conclude an alliance with the Greeks if in return the Greeks would aid them in making war on their neighbors. They provided three hundred canoes, with three warriors in each one. They paddled their canoes along the coast and then put ashore to join the Greeks for battle. These warriors carried wicker shields covered with a shaggy ox-hide and shaped like an ivy leaf. Each man carried in his right hand a long lance and in the other a battle-axe. They wore short tunics of linen and leather helmets with a tuft in the middle shaped like a tiara. After they formed their battle lines on the flanks of the Greeks they fell into a rhythmic chant. As the Greeks watched in amazement these warriors began passing through their ranks in a trance-like state and then suddenly charged straight ahead against the stronghold of their enemy.

This stronghold was called Metropolis by the Mossynoecians and lay somewhere between the modern towns of Giresun and Ordu along the Black Sea coast. The Mossynoecians had allied themselves with the Greeks in the hopes of taking this town for themselves and enslaving their neighbors. They led the attack and were followed by a number of Greeks who broke ranks and advanced without orders. These peltasts impetuously joined the attack in the hopes of being the first to loot, rape, and murder.

The defenders within the town launched an unexpected counterattack that drove both the Greeks and Mossynoecians back toward their own lines. Many of the Greeks fell during the retreat and were captured. Their heads were cut off and used to taunt the main body of the army. This infuriated the Greeks and Xenophon called them to assembly.

Xenophon chastised those Greeks who had survived the skirmish, pointing out to them the folly of not staying in formation and fighting under orders. After all, they were Greeks not barbarians. This was the first time during the entire expedition when the Greeks had been forced to retreat in the face of the enemy and it had happened because they had not remained in formation and fought according to plan.

The next day, after a leisurely breakfast and the requisite sacrifices, the Greek army drew up in battle formation and the plan of attack was explained. The barbarian allies were placed on the Greek left flank. The peltasts formed the first rows of the advancing army followed by the bowmen. Behind them came the heavy infantry, the hoplites. The Greek army, proceeding at a walk, moved toward the walls of the stronghold. The barbarians inside sallied forth to meet the attack of the peltasts, but when the hoplites came up the barbarians fell back. Supported by the advancing hoplites, the lighter armed and quicker peltasts pursued the enemy back to the gates of their stronghold. The phalanx, in tight formation, followed behind at a measured pace.

As the main body of the Greek army approached the stronghold the entire barbarian force charged forward against them. The Greeks refused to give way and closed with the Mossynoecians in hand-to-hand combat. The barbarians, no match for the disciplined and skillful Greek infantry, took to flight and abandoned the fortress. The barbarian chief and his commanders took refuge in one of the tall wooden towers and refused to surrender. So the Greeks set fire to the towers and burned them alive.

The Greeks took the city and set about plundering what wealth it possessed and murdering the inhabitants. In the houses they found dolphin meat preserved in salt and laid away in large jars. There were large quantities of walnuts from which the local people made loaves of bread and the Greeks found wine which, when diluted with water, was fragrant and delicious. After the Greeks had finished looting they turned what was left of the city and its inhabitants over to their barbarian allies.

The Mossynoecian allies presented the Greeks with the fattened children of the vanquished as gifts. These children of the wealthy townsmen had been nourished on a diet of boiled nuts since infancy and as a result they were extraordinarily soft to the touch and their complexions very white. The children were so fat that they were as wide as they were high and their backs were tattooed in complex flower patterns. The Mossynoecians began a celebration. After much drinking and feasting they came to the Greeks and asked them to allow them to have intercourse with the few women who still accompanied the Greek army. In return they offered their own women, who were very white in complexion, to the Greeks. The Greeks were surprised and at the same time disgusted by this request. The Mossynoecians pressed the matter and the Greeks continued to hesitate. The mercenaries regarded these people as the most uncivilized they had seen on their entire expedition through Persia. They were eager to do in public those things that the Greeks believed should be done in private. The Greeks found other behaviors among these people strange. When the Mossynoecians were alone they would talk and laugh out loud to themselves. Then for no apparent reason they would break out into spontaneous bouts of wild dancing.

The Greek army left the Mossynoecians and marched several more days along the coast. They reached the Greek coastal city of Cotyora which was a colony of a larger group of Greeks called the Sinopeans. The city of Sinope was nearly two hundred miles farther west along the coast. The army had rested at Cotyora for forty-five days when ambassadors from Sinope came to see them. The ambassadors had been sent by the leaders of Sinope because they were receiving disturbing reports about the mercenary presence in Cotyora and they were concerned about the well-being of their colony.

The ambassadors met with Xenophon and the other generals and they began by praising the Greeks for their victories over the barbarians and their long, arduous journey through the Persian Empire. Beneath their praise and in their manner Xenophon could sense an underlying fear for the safety of their own city. Then the ambassadors turned to a discussion of the matters that had brought them to Cotyora. They criticized the mercenaries for taking supplies from their colonists by force or threat of force. Cotyora, they reminded Xenophon, was their colony. They warned the Greeks that to continue in that manner would cause the inhabitants of all the Greek coastal cities to close their gates and ally themselves with the barbarians for mutual protection against the mercenaries.

Xenophon listened, and when the ambassadors had finished he spoke on behalf of the army. First he recounted how when the army had reached the first Greek city, Trapezus, the inhabitants had welcomed them as fellow Greeks and provided them with a market at reasonable prices. The mercenaries had purchased what they needed and taken nothing by force. Then Xenophon called forth the guides from Trapezus who had been sent with the army and they confirmed the truth of what he said. Then he explained to the ambassadors that at other cities along the route, whether barbarian or Greek, where the inhabitants had refused them provisions, they had had no choice but to take what they needed by force in order to live. What the Greeks took they took because they needed to survive, not to enrich themselves. Among barbarians like the Carduchi, the Taochians, and the Chaldeans, the mercenaries took by force what they needed and more. From people like the Macronians, who provided them with the best market they could, the Greeks paid for everything and took nothing by force. As for the Cotyorites who were complaining, they had at first shut out the mercenaries and would not provide a market. This forced the Greeks to plunder the countryside. Finally, when they had no alternative because provisions were running low and they had among them many sick and wounded, the mercenaries forced their way into the city. They quartered their sick and wounded in the houses of the Cotyorites but they paid for their keep. The rest of the mercenaries remained in their own camp outside the city gates. Xenophon said his mercenaries had spent the last year fighting forces far larger and more dangerous than the Cotyorites and the Sinopeans. If need be they were prepared to fight again, even against Greeks if these stood between them and the road home.

The Sinopean ambassadors became frightened. In an effort to placate Xenophon and the generals they turned on their spokesman, Hecatonymus. They criticized his harsh words and repudiated his threats against the mercenaries. They offered their cooperation and friendship in helping the Greeks return home. The ambassadors offered to welcome the Greeks into their city with friendship and generosity. The mercenaries would be welcomed as heroes who had fought against the Persians, and honored as fellow countrymen. They would be at home in Sinope as Greeks among Greeks.

After this the Cotyorites sent gifts of food and drink to the mercenaries outside their walls. They opened their homes and entertained the ambassadors of the Sinopeans and the Greek officers alike. They engaged in friendly conversations and shared meals together. The Sinopeans offered advice on the rest of the journey home and spoke of the land of the Paphlagonians, the next country to the west. This, they told the mercenaries, was a land of "fair plains and lofty mountains." The Paphlagonians were skilled horsemen and so proud and independent that when the Persian king summoned them to muster they refused to come. Their infantry, too, was formidable on the plains and numbered well over 100,000. Finally there were four wide and deep rivers that had to be crossed—the Thermodon, the Iris, the Halys, and the Parthenius. The best solution, they advised, would be for the Greeks to abandon the land route and sail around

Paphlagonia by sea to Heraclea and from there on to Chrysopolis by land or by sea.

After listening to the advice of the Sinopean ambassadors, the Greeks voted to make the journey by sea. Xenophon agreed, provided there were ships enough to take the entire army at the same time. He would not agree to divide the army, sending half home by ship and forcing the other half to remain behind for the next group of transports. The army had to stay together, for its unity was its strength.

Xenophon passed through the city gates and walked through the mercenary camp. He looked out at this army that had become fit and well-trained through months of fighting and marching. They were well-disciplined and he felt pride as their elected commander. Never before, since the height of the Peloponnesian Wars in Greece, had such a large body of veteran soldiers been gathered together in one place. They had been brought together as brothers by months of fighting, marching, and dying together. They were a proud army of soldiers who lived and shared with each other during the best and worst of times.

Returning to Greece had been the dream, the vision that had kept Xenophon and the mercenaries fighting against the Persian king and Tissaphernes. Even after Cyrus had been killed, it was what kept them marching through the mountains of Armenia during that long, cold winter. It was a dream that many of them had died for and for which many more would still die.

The reality of returning to Greece, however, was something else again. Most of these men had left Greece because of poverty and because they had no hope for a future there. They had joined Cyrus in the hopes of earning enough money to begin a new life. Many of the mercenaries had planned to settle in Persia if Cyrus succeeded in becoming king. It was then that the thought came to Xenophon that they were brothers and it seemed reasonable to him that they could gain glory for Greece and improve their own lives by founding a new city on the coast of the Black Sea. They could settle in the Pontus or even farther west on the southeastern coast of Turkey.

The city he envisioned for his men would become great. He calculated that with the number of mercenaries, the camp followers, the captive women and slaves, and the native people of whatever area they settled in, they had enough people to build a powerful city. The surrounding area would come under their domination and their city would become rich through trade in slaves and grain.

Xenophon sought out the seer Silanus and revealed to him his plans. He asked Silanus to offer sacrifices to the gods to guide him in his thinking and help bring about his vision. Silanus was an Ambraciot who had been the soothsayer to Cyrus. When he learned what Xenophon was thinking he opposed the idea but kept his thoughts to himself. He carried out the sacrifices that Xenophon had requested but he also began to spread rumors among the troops. He let it be known that Xenophon wished to found a city in the Pontus for the benefit of his own prestige and power. He intimated that Xenophon even thought to make himself a king over the Greeks.

When word spread among the mercenaries, a number of them agreed with Xenophon's idea to found a city. They considered it desirable to settle down in this rich land, begin families, and build a new life. The majority of the army, however, wanted to return home to Greece. Factions formed, composed of men for and against the founding of a new city. As a result, tensions rose and tempers flared, forcing Xenophon to deal with the most serious crisis of the expedition. So strong had become the feelings among the mercenaries for or against the founding of a city that the army seemed on the verge of breaking apart. Internal discord threatened to accomplish what the Persians and the mountains of Armenia had been unable to achieve. Xenophon called an assembly.

He rose to speak and the soldiers fell silent to listen. Xenophon explained to them that he had sacrificed to the gods for guidance on his idea of founding a Greek colony, a city on the coast of the Black Sea. He went on to say that it was no more than an idea and that he was not plotting against the army's interests. He had learned that Silanus the soothsayer was spreading rumors among the troops, causing many of them to become angry. Xenophon explained that he never intended to undertake his idea without first getting the consent of the army. He reiterated that the strength of the Greeks lay in their unity and mutual trust. If the army came apart now and they went their separate ways in small groups, they would be defeated by enemies in the weeks and months to come and never reach home.

Xenophon finished by telling the soldiers that he would always abide by their majority decisions in assembly and he now believed that it would be best for the army to return to Greece. It was important that the army remain together, and he asked the assembly to vote that any man who was caught deserting before they reached Greece should be put on trial.

Silanus rose in anger and began shouting that it was only fair that those who wished to leave the army now should be allowed to do so. The soldiers around him pushed him down and would not allow him to speak. They threatened that if they caught him or any of his friends trying to leave they would be tried and punished as deserters. Silanus was anxious to return to Greece as quickly as possible, for he had retained a small fortune in gold coins. Many had been given to him by Cyrus on the trip inland and he had kept them throughout the long march over the mountains. Thorax, a Boeotian, rose and spoke next. He spoke in favor of returning to Greece and told the assembly of his dream of finding fertile land in his own country. It was in Greece that he wished to settle, among the olive groves, rather than here in the lands of the barbarians.

Other soldiers rose to speak. Some spoke for and some against the prospect of founding a new city. Xenophon sensed that the army was on the verge of coming apart and he rose to speak again. This time he spoke to the assembly about the evil of discord that was beginning to reveal itself in the army. It was time for the Greeks to take stock of themselves and bring this evil to light before they stood condemned as wicked and base men, both in the sight of the gods and before men.

Xenophon recounted how when the army had passed through the lands of Cerasus some of the soldiers had bought cattle and other provisions from the people of the area. They had been friendly and had willingly traded with the mercenaries for provisions. Clearetus, a captain, set out one night with some of his men with the idea of plundering one of the villages nearby. Since these people were friendly to the Greeks and trusted them he expected that they would not guard their village against a surprise attack. Clearetus and his men had planned this without a word to any of the soldiers in the army. He had plotted to plunder the village of its treasure and then with a few of his men embark on a ship for home. He had bribed the captain of a merchant vessel, at anchor in the harbor at Cerasus, and expected to be gone before the Greeks learned what he had done.

Late that night Clearetus and his men moved out of the camp without telling the officers. They had not accurately calculated the time necessary to reach the village and they found themselves outside the gates just at dawn. Some of the villagers had already risen to begin their chores for the day and they saw what Clearetus and his men were about to do. The villagers sounded the alarm and mounted a spirited defense of their homes. Clearetus and some of his men were killed but most of these Greeks managed to return to Cerasus. The next day, three elderly men were sent as ambassadors from the village to the Greek army at Cerasus. They planned to come before the general assembly of the Greeks to explain what had happened the day before and to make arrangements for the Greeks to recover their dead.

Some of Clearetus's men saw the ambassadors when they arrived in Cerasus, and to stop them from telling the other Greeks what had happened they murdered the three old men. A few citizens of Cerasus saw the murder and reported it to the Greek generals. While these citizens were conferring with the Greek officers, a mob of soldiers, many of whom were carrying stones, formed around their tents and threatened to kill all those inside. The citizens became frightened and fled the Greek camp with many of the renegade soldiers at their heels. They were driven by this mob into the sea and drowned. Xenophon compared the madness that had descended upon some of the soldiers to the one that strikes dogs.

Xenophon said that things could not continue in this way. The army could not be allowed to form into mobs and stone to death anyone they happened to dislike. Men could not be killed in the streets without trial. The army could not be allowed to dissolve into an unruly mob. If the Greeks had violated a sacred right by killing heralds—ambassadors—how could they expect to send their own ambassadors in safety to others? They could not even ask for the return of their own dead for proper burial.

The Greeks rose as one body and urged that the men who had done these things should be punished and that henceforth no one should be permitted to take the law into his own hands and kill without reason. Any soldier who broke this law should be brought to trial for his own life.

The assembly had been brought nearly to a frenzy by this story and they wanted to see someone pay. So they voted that trials should be held. First it was agreed that the renegade Greeks who had killed the three old men and drowned the citizens of Cerasus should be put on trial. Still the desire of the army for vengeance was not satisfied, and they demanded that trials be held for any soldier or officer accused of wrongdoing since Cyrus was killed at Cunaxa nearly a year before.

A jury of captains was impaneled and upon the advice of Xenophon the soothsayers undertook to purify the entire army before the beginning of the trials. It was resolved that first the generals should undergo an inquiry as to their past conduct in leading the army. Then the junior officers would undergo the inquiry and finally any common soldiers. The soldiers were encouraged to come forth with any grievances against the generals; as a result, two generals, Philesius and Xanthicles, were tried and condemned by the juries for carelessness in guarding some of the common stores. Both generals were fined, and a third, Sophaenetus, was charged and punished for neglect of duty.

Then charges were brought against Xenophon for assault. Certain "common soldiers" accused him of beating them and so brought to the jury the charge of "wanton assault." The men came forward and told the jury how Xenophon had beaten them in the mountains just before the army made its way to the sea and the city of Trapezus. After they testified, Xenophon rose to defend himself before the jury and the assembled soldiers. While Xenophon, as with any Greek, had the right to representation, he chose to defend himself. He began his defense with a cross-examination of his accusers, a tactic he had learned at Athens from his old teacher Socrates. First, he asked his accusers to reveal their rank to the assembly. Were they officers? Were they hoplites or peltasts? The men replied that they were free Greeks, and that they had been detailed to drive the mules. Then Xenophon asked the mule drivers if he had struck them in order to take their rations or did he strike them for their money? Did he strike them because he was drunk, or did he strike them in order to take from them a captive woman? To each question the men were forced to face the jury and answer no.

Then, as the army watched and listened, Xenophon began his defense. He remembered the incident. It was when the army was marching through the snow of the Armenian mountains and he was in charge of the rear guard. After a particularly brutal fight against the mountain tribes, he had ordered these mule drivers to unload their goods and carry his wounded soldiers instead. When they refused, he beat several of them into submission. Later that day, when he came upon these mule drivers farther in the line of march, he found that they had unloaded the wounded soldiers and left them covered by snow along the side of the route to die. They had left fellow Greeks, brave soldiers, to die because they valued their own goods more than the lives of these men. When Xenophon saw what they had done he set about beating the mule drivers again with his whip and often with his fists.

When he went back to find the wounded left by the side of the road many had already died and this caused him even greater anger. Some of the drivers shouted out to the jury in their own defense that the wounded men being carried on their mules either had died already or would have in short order. Xenophon replied that perhaps they would all have died that day, for it was the darkest period of the march, when the cold, snow, and hunger threatened to finish them all. But no matter, he recounted to the jury, he would not stand to see sick and wounded men, men who had fought bravely, left behind to die buried alive in the snow by the mule drivers.

The army had heard enough. They rose en masse over the objections of the jury for order and demanded the punishment of the mule drivers. When the assembly finally quieted down once more, Xenophon began his summation. He had indeed struck men on the march. When he struck men it was for their insubordination, not out of wantonness on his part as a commander. If every man in the army had behaved like these mule drivers, all would have perished. It was only discipline and care for each other that got them through that difficult time in the mountains.

Xenophon volunteered that he had struck men who had fallen from the line of march and would not move on. There were men he came upon who lay by the side of the road and refused to follow orders. They needed a beating to make them move. He asked the jury what alternative he had. Should he have left them along the route to be captured, tortured, and killed by the enemy following the column? Men who stopped and lay by the road after a time could not move again. Men froze quickly in the brutal cold. He pointed out to the jury that men who sat by the wayside found their legs would no longer function and their toes rotted off.

Moving was the only alternative to dying. Xenophon admitted he had struck men who malingered. He had struck them with his fists and with his whip. Better that they be struck by him and forced to move than to be struck by the battle-axes of the mountain tribesman following behind. Those who came forth today to complain of harsh treatment at his hands would have been dead if not for him and the rear guard. Xenophon summarized to the jury that what he had done on the march was necessary for the good of the army and if they felt he abused his power of command then he was prepared to accept his punishment.

By now Xenophon was angry and he turned to the assembly and shouted that he never struck a man in his command without reason. There were Greeks in the column that day, with swords in their hands, who had witnessed him strike the malingerers, but they never raised a hand in the stragglers' defense. Xenophon noted that the men who were the worst malingerers among them during the march through the mountains were now the ones causing dissension in the army. Those who had been most cowardly on the march had become, in easier and safer times, the most criminal among them. He pointed to Boiscus, a boxer and mercenary from Thessaly. This man, Xenophon recounted, had tried to get out of every hardship on the march, even finding other men to carry his weapons. The officers had even come upon him after a skirmish stripping the dead bodies of Greeks of their valuables.

Then Xenophon called for the soldiers he had saved on the march to come forward. He called for the men he had protected from the cold and certain death, the men he had helped when they were sick or wounded, the men to whom he had provided extra food and praise for deeds well-done. He demanded they come forward in his defense. Then, many of the men among the hoplites and peltasts, cavalry and common porters alike, rose and spoke in his defense. They recounted incidents on the march when Xenophon had helped them, and in the end the assembly rose as one body and praised the leadership of Xenophon. When the assembly ended Xenophon was once again confirmed as their leader and all charges against him dismissed.

The Greeks remained at the coastal city of Cotyora for some time. Soldiers who had money lived by purchasing from the merchants of the city while others took to pillaging the nearby villages of the Paphlagonians. The Paphlagonians in return took to kidnapping Greeks at night. They would sneak into the Greek camp and either injure or kidnap any soldiers they found sleeping near the perimeter.

Corylas, the ruler of Paphlagonia, finally sent ambassadors to the Greek camp to propose a truce. He sent his ambassadors with gifts of horses and clothing for the Greek officers, and gave his word that the

mercenaries would suffer no harm at his hands. The Greek officers
replied that they would take counsel on the matter, and invited the
Paphlagonian ambassadors to dine with them as their guests. By sacrificing some of their cattle, the Greeks provided dinner for their
guests. The ambassadors and the Greek officers reclined on couches
and drank large amounts of wine from cups made of horn. These were
the very same cups and wine that the Greeks had looted from the
Paphlagonian villages.

Then, as the meal was ending, the entertainment commenced. Two
Thracian officers rose from their dinner couches and began a ritual
dance of combat and death from their native land. The men danced in
their full body armor to the accompaniment of a flute. So skillful was
their dance, and so deftly did they use their swords that the Paphlagonian ambassadors believed that one dancer had actually struck
down the other. When the two had finished, some officers from
Mantineas and others from Arcadia arose, arrayed as well in their
finest armor. They performed the dances of their land and the
Paphlagonian ambassadors marveled that all these Greeks danced in
their armor and carried swords.

The final entertainment of the night was a young girl, a slave of
one of the Arcadians. She entered the tent and performed the most
sensual dance for the guests. With all the grace and beauty of a youth-
ful, supple body she captivated the men who watched. When she finished there was great applause. The Paphlagonian ambassadors asked
if Greek women fought by the sides of their men. The Greeks replied
that it was their women, not they, who had put the Persian king to
flight at Cunaxa. With that joke the evening ended and the group
parted company. The next day the ambassadors reviewed the Greek
army and received pledges from the generals that no harm would
come to any of their people at Greek hands.

The ambassadors departed by land for their homes and the next
day the Greek army put out to sea. For a day and a night the flotilla
carrying the Greeks sailed west off the coast of Paphlagonia toward
the port city of Sinope. When the Greeks landed, the Sinopeans sent
them gifts as expressions of their hospitality. There were five thousand
bushels of grain and fifteen hundred jars of wine.

At Sinope, Cheirisophus rejoined the Greeks, but instead of bringing a fleet, as he had hoped, he arrived on a single warship. He
reported that his friend, the Spartan admiral Anaxibius, had sent his

compliments and further promised that once the mercenaries had left the Black Sea they would be put on regular wages. The Greeks remained outside of Sinope at a place called Harmene for five days as they prepared for the journey to Byzantium at the mouth of the Black Sea.

While the army contemplated its return to Greece, many soldiers complained that they had nothing to show for their service in Persia and all the fighting they had endured. Most of what they had plundered along the way had been used up buying supplies. Some of the soldiers suggested it might be wise to change the structure of command from several generals to one commander in chief. Thus, they argued, there would be less need for the endless conferences of officers and the submission of every issue to the majority vote of the assembly. It was agreed in the assembly to elect for the time being one supreme commander until the army returned to Greece.

The captains and many of the common soldiers looked to Xenophon to fill this role because they had gained confidence in his ability to lead. To Xenophon, the idea was appealing. He was flattered and honored to be nominated to lead the army and genuinely felt he could be of service. But while he desired to become the sole commander, he knew the army could be fickle. If things took a turn for the worse, his reputation would suffer and he could lose his life at their hands. Unable to reach a decision, Xenophon did what any good Greek would do—he turned to the gods for advice. He offered sacrifice to Zeus on the question, for the oracle at Delphi had instructed him to follow the signs of this god above all others. Xenophon made sacrifice and the signs indicated that he should neither vie for the command of the Greeks nor should he accept it should it be offered to him.

The army met in assembly, and the speakers that day urged a unanimous vote in favor of Xenophon. It seemed certain that Xenophon would be elected as he rose to address the assembly. He explained that he was honored at their confidence in him and that he indeed wished to serve the army as he had over the past months. Still, he thought it best that the soldiers elect a Spartan, a Lacedaemonian, for their leader. He explained his fear that if the army emerged from Asia led by an Athenian it would not be well-received by the Spartan authorities. Neither was it safe for him personally if the Spartans thought he refused to recognize their supremacy. After he had spoken, the army restated its support for him. A number of speakers disparaged the Spartans. Agasias the Stymphalian rose and mockingly asked the crowd it they were now inclined to elect a Lacedaemonian master of ceremonies at every feast lest they offend the fragile Spartan ego.

Then Xenophon, fearing the situation might anger the Spartans in the ranks, explained to the soldiers that he had sacrificed to Zeus for guidance on the matter and that the signs were against his becoming their commander. The soldiers then accepted his decision and chose Cheirisophus as their supreme commander. Cheirisophus commanded the troops that Sparta had dispatched to join the army at the beginning of the expedition, the only "official" Greek aid to Cyrus, so choosing him as overall commander at this point was prudent. Cheirisophus stepped forward and proudly accepted the title. He spoke to the army and told them that even if they had chosen Xenophon he, as a loyal soldier, would have supported him. Then he warned the army that Xenophon was in danger. The deserter Dexippus had arrived at Byzantium and had falsely accused Xenophon of treason before the Spartan authorities.

Cheirisophus took command and ordered the army to prepare to set sail for Heraclea the next morning. Heraclea was a Greek city near the place where Hercules was said to have slipped past the three-headed dog Cerberus and descended into Hades. When the Greek fleet sailed into port, the people of the city sent them five thousand bushels of grain, two thousand jars of wine, twenty cattle, and a hundred sheep as tokens of their friendship and hospitality.

At Heraclea, the army gathered together and discussed whether the remainder of the journey should be by sea or on land. The Greeks were close to Byzantium and even though they had elected a new commander they still would not give up their right to meet in assembly to discuss and vote about their course of action.

Lycon the Achaean was the first to rise and address the army. He pointed out that they had only three days' rations left, even with the gifts from the citizens of Heraclea, and little money to buy additional provisions. He proposed that they extort from three to ten thousand cyzicenes (a coin minted in the city of Cyzicus) from the people of Heraclea to spare them the looting and burning of their city. The army nominated Cheirisophus and Xenophon as ambassadors to present their demands to the citizens of the city.

Both commanders disagreed with the army's proposal. They argued that the city was Greek and that they should not demand, under threat of reprisal, what these people were not willing to give freely. So the army sent Lycon, who had first proposed the matter, with Callimachus the Parrhasian and Agasias the Stymphalian to present their demands.

These men went as ambassadors to Heraclea and issued their demand to the leaders of the city. Lycon even added stronger and more ominous threats in case the townsmen were considering a negative response. The city leaders were gracious and agreed to take the matter under consideration, promising to give the Greeks a reply in short order. As soon as Lycon and the other ambassadors had left the city, however, the gates of Heraclea were drawn shut and bolted and guards were posted on the walls.

Lycon and Callimachus returned to the Greek camp where they accused Cheirisophus and Xenophon of having sabotaged the undertaking. The two sides argued and the mood turned serious. The army started to disperse into opposing groups that threatened to elect their own officers. There was talk among some of the soldiers that it was shameful for Peloponnesians to be under the command of an Athenian. Xenophon, they argued, was a man who had come to the army with no troops of his own and no experience in military command. This argument began to gain support and eventually the army broke into hostile factions.

The Arcadians and Achaeans, who made up more than half of the army, joined forces and elected ten of their own generals to command them. These generals were to vote among themselves on all issues and were obliged to follow the will of the majority. So the supreme command of Cheirisophus the Spartan came to an end just seven days after the Greeks had unanimously elected him.

Xenophon decided he would complete the journey back to Greece with the Spartan, Cheirisophus. It was better, he believed, than each one going his separate way with his own band. Cheirisophus's lieutenant, Neon, however, urged Xenophon to make separate plans, for he had heard that Cleander, the Spartan governor at Byzantium, was sending ships to fetch the Lacedaemonian element of the army. At worst, to Neon, Xenophon's men would take up valuable space on the ships; at best, they would be left on their own anyway. Cheirisophus had become withdrawn and bitter after his rejection by the army, and soon fell ill. In the meantime he let Neon act as commander of the Lacedaemonian contingent.

Xenophon thought about simply deserting the army and sailing home to Greece alone. He sacrificed to Heracles for advice and the reply was that he should remain with the men who had been loyal to him to see them safely home. Thus the army split into three parts. The first faction was made up of the Arcadians and Achaeans, more than 4,500 hoplites from the central and northern part of the Peloponnese. The second was 1,400 hoplites and 700 peltasts under Cheirisophus and Neon from the southern part of the Peloponnese, the region of Sparta. The final group of 1,700 hoplites, 300 peltasts, and 40 horsemen from various parts of Greece remained with Xenophon.

The first group, the Arcadians and Achaeans, set sail from Heraclea and intended to land outside Chrysopolis, which lay across the Bosporus from Byzantium, and make an attack upon the Bithynians. They intended to burn the villages and towns to secure as much plunder as they could before returning home. They landed at Calpe Harbor about midway along the coast between Heraclea and Chrysopolis.

Cheirisophus and his group of Spartans marched by land from Heraclea across country toward Chrysopolis. Xenophon and his group took ships as far as the boundary of Thrace and then moved over land through the backcountry toward Chrysopolis. The Arcadians landed and immediately launched their attacks on the villages and towns of the area just before dawn. The attacks were unexpected and the heavily armed hoplites easily took the villages. The Greeks gained much plunder and many slaves. As the Greeks withdrew along their route, burdened with plunder and hampered by slaves, the Thracians began to harass their lines. These guerrilla tactics proved effective as a number of Greek commanders were killed in the skirmishes. In one ambush, an entire company of Greeks was wiped out as it attempted to cross a particular gorge. A second company was ambushed and only eight of its number survived. The other companies succeeded in coming together and forming a protective ring around their camp. All night, the Thracians massed outside the Greek perimeter, shouting and calling to one another in an attempt to shake the nerves of the Greeks within the camp. By daybreak, the Thracians had amassed a sizable force, primarily light troops and cavalry.

The Greek force had no light troops of its own, and its armored hoplites were ineffective against the Thracian horsemen, who were able to charge, dispatch their missiles, and then ride quickly out of range. Many of the Greeks were wounded in these attacks and the force soon found itself surrounded, unable to move, and critically short of water. The Greeks were forced to ask the Thracian commanders for a truce. This was the first time during the long campaign that a sizable contingent of the mercenaries had been defeated.

Cheirisophus proceeded along the coast with his forces without incident and arrived at Calpe Harbor. Xenophon, moving through the backcountry, sent his horsemen ahead as scouts. They returned with some old men they had found along the road, who informed Xenophon what was happening to the Arcadians.

Xenophon gathered his troops and described the situation of their former comrades. He urged his men to go with him to the Arcadians's rescue, for if these Greeks were defeated they would all be in danger. Only when unified were they strong. Breaking apart had been a mistake and they must put aside any ill feelings and hurry to rescue their comrades.

Timasion, at the head of the cavalry, was sent ahead to act as the eyes of the army. Xenophon took up his arms and set out, followed by his most loyal men. On each side of his main force he dispatched scouts and flankers to protect the main column from attack. He ordered these forces to burn every village, house, and field they encountered on the march.

The result was what Xenophon had intended. When the Thracians looked behind them, the entire country seemed on fire, the swathe cut by Xenophon's army enormous. Thus his forces appeared much larger than they actually were. The scouts rode up a hill and some half a mile away saw the camps of the Thracians. That night, Xenophon camped his army and at daybreak the Greeks offered prayers to the gods. They ate breakfast and formed their lines for the impending battle. When they arrived they found that the Arcadians had departed. And the enemy was nowhere to be seen. A few old people hiding in the woods were captured and reported to the scouts that the Thracians had left their camps during the night and that the Greeks, no longer besieged, left shortly thereafter.

Xenophon, hearing this, pushed the troops in a forced march to Calpe Harbor to join the other Greeks. As they proceeded along the road they could see the tracks of the Arcadians and Achaeans leading to Calpe. When the soldiers of Xenophon caught up with the rear guard of the retreating Greeks, there was joy as the two groups reunited. The Arcadians explained that the Thracians feared a night attack by Xenophon's men and were afraid of being caught between two hostile forces of Greeks. So in the night they retreated. When the attack did not come at dawn, the Arcadians decided to take advantage of the situation and make good their escape to the sea.

IX
GREEKS AMONG GREEKS

In the ancient world, Thrace was the name for a large and very wild area that extended from the northeast corner of Greece to the shores of the western portion of the Black Sea. A portion of Thrace began at the mouth of the Bosporus and extended along the Turkish coast of the Black Sea east as far as the city of Heraclea. The Greeks feared the Thracians who lived along the sea, near the Persian province of Bithynia. They would abuse in the most sadistic and barbaric manner any Greeks they found shipwrecked along their coast.

Calpe Harbor is a small piece of land jutting into the Black Sea midway between Heraclea and Byzantium. A part of this land mass is an isthmus that extends seaward and consists of a precipitous mass of rock a hundred or so feet high. The beach to the seaward of the isthmus is large and safe enough for several thousand men to have camped in relative comfort. At the foot of the great rock is a harbor whose beach faces west. It is an excellent place for an army to camp because it is secure from the elements and there is an abundant supply of fresh water close to the shore. The army bivouacked on this beach at Calpe Harbor and as the soldiers reconnoitered the area they found many prosperous villages nearby, and thick forests from which they could obtain timber for building new ships or repairing old ones. The Greek scouts also discovered that the land all around them was rich in barley, wheat, beans, millet, sesame, figs, and grapes. They found that the grapes, when pressed and mixed with water, yielded a good sweet wine. This land lacked only olives to remind the mercenaries of their homeland. Today, the site of Calpe Harbor is occupied by the sleepy resort town of Kerpe.

The soldiers took up quarters on the beach and in a short time had established a relatively permanent camp. As the tedium of daily life in this peaceful place set in, the Greeks, not for the first time, began arguing among themselves. Some of the soldiers were anxious to set out for home and they complained that Xenophon had brought them to this place so that he could realize his dream of founding a city. They were angry over what they perceived as his deception and said they would have no part of settling there. Others among the mercenaries favored the idea. As at Cotyora, the men were divided along the lines of those who had homes or families to return to and those who had become rootless, fully inclined to begin new lives abroad. A third faction was made up of Spartans, who as always considered that their first duty was to their city-state.

The entire army had reunited at Port Calpe after the fiasco in the Thracian countryside that got many of the Greeks killed. Whether in spite of or because of being reunited, they were busy quarreling and bickering among themselves. The mercenary army had held together the past year because of common adversaries, both human and natural, and their sense of identity as Greeks alone together in a vast, foreign land. Now that they were nearer to home and in more secure conditions, the traditional political rivalries of the Greek mainland were making themselves felt among them.

Xenophon proposed that they offer sacrifice to the gods with a view to an expedition into the countryside. The army was dangerously low on provisions and the Greek dead who had been left behind in the recent fighting needed to be recovered and properly buried. The sacrifices proved favorable and an expedition was formed. The Arcadians joined primarily to recover their dead and give them proper burial, while other Greeks joined simply in the hopes of finding some booty.

As the expedition moved into the surrounding countryside the Greeks came upon their dead. Many of the mercenaries who had fallen during the recent fighting died where they had fought. It was a depressing sight for the Greeks to come upon their dead friends and comrades lying by the side of the road, some in bushes and others among rocks. They searched in all directions and found more bodies. There was evidence that some of their comrades had been captured during the fighting, brutally tortured and then killed. Since the dead had already lain for five days in the sun it was not possible to carry their bloated and decomposing bodies back to the Greek camp for burial. So mass graves were dug, the proper prayers were said, and the earth consecrated. As the Greeks moved through the countryside on their way back to camp they marched in line and mostly in silence.

There was little talk among them, and none of the bantering that they usually engaged in to relieve the boredom of a march. It had been grim work for the soldiers that day. When they finally arrived in camp that night most took their dinner early and went directly to sleep.

The next day the army was called to meet in assembly. Agasias the Stymphalian, Hieronymus the Elean, and some others from among the elders of the Arcadians had a resolution they wished the army to debate and vote on. They proposed that there should be no more talk of dividing the army until they reached Greece. Any man who spoke of dividing the army from this point on should be killed on the spot. The army should return to the unified style of leadership that it had enjoyed under the old system of command when they first entered Persia in the service of Cyrus. Cheirisophus was not there as he had died from the effects of a medicine he had been given to break a fever and Neon had taken his command. There were no objections from any of the other Greeks.

After everyone who wished to had spoken on the subject, Xenophon rose to address the assembly. They had agreed on the structure of command and now they needed to decide on the route home. Xenophon proposed a journey by land since there were not enough ships in port or even under construction for all the soldiers to embark at once. They had agreed not to divide the army again, so to march was the only alternative. He warned the Greeks that they must prepare to leave Calpe Harbor soon since they were nearly out of provisions. Lastly, he warned that the army must prepare to meet fierce resistance from the Thracians along the route. These were a people who hated Greeks and they could be expected to offer intense resistance at every opportunity.

The Greeks called for sacrifices before the army set out, and a soothsayer, Arexion the Arcadian, came forward to interpret the results. The soothsayer Silanus had deserted the Greeks several days before on board a ship with a chest of gold. He had secretly bribed a merchant ship's captain at Heraclea to take him and his money home to Greece. However in those days, a long voyage by sea for a man with a sizable purse could be a fatal venture. Lone travelers had a way of falling overboard when their ship was out of sight of land and their purses had a way of disappearing among the crew before the ship reached port.

The sacrifice of the victims on the beach that day proved unfavorable. Arexion said that all the signs for the march home were wrong. Many of the Greeks who were already disgruntled began to criticize Xenophon openly. They contended that he had arranged for the sooth-sayer to pronounce the sacrifices unfavorable so as to force the army to remain at Calpe Harbor to found his city. Provisions had nearly run out and men had started fighting over what little remained. There was considerable anger among many of the Greeks and so Xenophon called them into assembly. He invited any of the soldiers to inspect the sacrificial victims and see for themselves that the signs were not favor-able. Then he suggested another sacrifice to determine signs for a shorter expedition into the countryside to search for provisions. A man rose in assembly and said word was circulating among the troops that warships from Byzantium would arrive soon, along with mer-chant ships filled with provisions to feed them. Then the ships would take them home.

Hopes rose with that rumor, as they usually do among desperate men, and the assembly voted to stay at Calpe Harbor a little longer. But it was still necessary to send men to find provisions, so Xenophon ordered another sacrifice. Three times the soothsayer sacrificed to the gods and each time the sacrifice was unfavorable. Men complained openly that their bellies were empty, but still Xenophon, a pious man, would not allow an expedition to leave camp unless the sacrificial signs were favorable.

The next morning Xenophon undertook to sacrifice again and this time nearly the entire army, hungry and angry, turned out to watch the proceedings. The reading of the entrails of the victims was once again unfavorable. Then some of the more disgruntled and aggressive of the Greeks brought forth a great bull that had been yoked to a wagon. They proceeded to sacrifice the beast and again Arexion interpreted the signs as unfavorable.

Finally Neon, who now commanded the men from the southern Peloponnese, saw the terrible state of the army and announced that he would ignore the omens and lead an expedition into the countryside. He set out for some villages with a raiding party composed of about two thousand of his own troops. Eventually his force divided itself into smaller parties because the villages were spread out over a great distance. Then, as an object lesson in the perils of not heeding the signs of sacrificial entrails, Persian horsemen suddenly appeared and attacked one of the Greek raiding parties that was in the process of looting and burning. The Greeks had no idea that the Persians were in the area and they had anticipated only light, if any, resistance from the villagers. The attack came as a complete surprise and casualties among the Greeks were heavy.

The Persian cavalry that attacked the Greeks that day was under the command of one of their old enemies, Pharnabazus, satrap of Phrygia. Phrygia was one of the larger satraps in Asia Minor and had once been under the control of Cyrus. Pharnabazus had returned to the province of Phrygia after the battle of Cunaxa and joined forces with the Bithynians to await the Greeks. Over five hundred of the soldiers in the raiding party were killed in the attack, while those who survived were scattered throughout the countryside. The survivors managed to return to Calpe Harbor and report what had happened just as the Persian cavalry arrived at the perimeter of the Greek camp. The sentries raised an outcry, and the soldiers took up arms. The Greek battle line forced the Persians away from the camp, but the Greeks spent that night under arms waiting for another attack. Few Greeks slept that night. This was the second defeat for the mercenaries, and Xenophon began to fear they might be losing the fighting edge that had previously served them so well against their enemies.

At daybreak, the Greeks decided to dig a wide trench in front of their camp as an obstacle to the Persian cavalry. The officers decided that here at Calpe Harbor they would make their stand against Pharnabazus and his infantry. With cliffs on either side of them and their backs to the sea, the Greeks had nowhere to go. They wondered where Tissaphernes might be and if he would join forces with Pharnabazus. In either case, the Greeks were resolved to face whichever enemy came before them and in whatever numbers. As the Greeks waited for battle, a ship appeared in the harbor filled with provisions sent by the Greek colonists of Heraclea.

The soldiers were elated and Xenophon performed a sacrifice with a view toward another expedition into the countryside. This time the signs were favorable. Just as the sacrifice was finishing, the soothsayer Arexion pointed out an eagle circling the camp. It was another favorable sign and Arexion urged Xenophon to lead the expedition against the Persians. The Greeks took up their arms and formed into ranks. Neon volunteered to remain behind to guard the camp and a contingent of men was formed from the soldiers who were older than forty-five.

Before the Greeks had marched two miles from their camp, they began to see the bodies of their dead along the road. They buried all of the Greek corpses they found but there were so many that individual burial was not possible. At the closest village they found the greatest concentration of Greek bodies and they buried them in a common grave. It was late afternoon by the time the burials were completed and elements of the army were still trying to find provisions from among the burned-out, deserted villages. Then some of the Greek scouts caught sight of the enemy cavalry passing over some hills that lay opposite the villages. There were horsemen in large numbers followed by foot soldiers in battle formation.

The commanders of the Persian forces that day were Spithridates and Rhathines, experienced generals who served under Pharnabazus. The Persian force halted some two miles from the Greeks, ready for combat. Arexion, the soothsayer, immediately offered sacrifice and the first omens proved favorable. Xenophon ordered three battalions of about two hundred men each to stay behind as the reserve line. Their purpose was to support the main line, or phalanx, in combat and, if necessary, cover their retreat.

As the main line of Greeks moved forward against the Persians, they came to a particularly difficult ravine. The vanguard stopped, unsure of what to do since the ravine was in sight of the enemy. They sent for the generals to come forward and advise them. Xenophon with several other officers rode to the front and they discussed whether to risk crossing the ravine in the face of the enemy or to withdraw. Xenophon pointed out that a retreat in that exposed terrain, because of the Persian cavalry, could prove to be as dangerous as crossing the ravine.

All agreed that the army should advance and Xenophon volunteered to lead. Calling to many of the soldiers by name, he urged them to cross the ravine wherever they happened to be along the battle line. There was a narrow bridge over the ravine but for the entire army to defile along it would take too long. The soldiers crossed to the other side without incident and Xenophon quickly organized the peltasts into position on either flank for protection. Once they were securely in position he ordered the main force of hoplites to advance against the Persians.

As the Greeks marched forward they were under standing orders to keep their spears on their right shoulders. Once a signal was given they would lower their spears for the attack. The troops were ordered to move forward slowly and keep in formation without breaking into a run. The orderly, measured advance of the Greek mercenaries was their modus operandi and it gave them the advantage over their more excitable adversaries. This time, however, the Persians did not break and run. They were standing their ground because they believed their defensive position could hold back the Greek attack.

As the Greeks advanced, some of the peltasts on the flanks raised the battle cry. They broke ranks and charged against the enemy without waiting for orders. The Persians rushed forward to meet them in strong numbers and the Greeks who attacked were turned back with many casualties. The Greek phalanx of hoplites, however, kept moving forward in disciplined fashion. Upon the proper signal they struck up the paean and, at the very last minute before the two sides engaged, they roared the battle cry. They lowered their spears and closed for combat. Seeing the Greek hoplites' ominously advancing wall of spears and shields suddenly erupt into a violent charge, the Persians panicked. The panic spread through their ranks and men began to desert their positions in droves. Within a few minutes there was a disorganized Persian retreat.

The small contingent of Greek cavalry, under the command of Timasion, pursued the retreating Persians, killing many as they fled. The left wing of the Persian infantry had come apart completely in the panic and many men were killed, but the right wing, untouched by the Greek cavalry, suddenly stopped its retreat and regrouped around a hill. These Persians intended to stand their ground against the Greeks, but the hoplite phalanx veered directly toward them and the Persians chose the better part of valor. This time it was the peltasts who pursued until the entire right wing had been dispersed with heavy casualties.

Having broken the Persian infantry, the Greek commanders could now see the Persian cavalry under Pharnabazus standing in reserve on nearby hillsides. Bithynian cavalry had joined the Persians in large numbers and the Greeks anticipated a mounted attack that could come at any time. Though the Greeks were tired from the fight, they nevertheless decided to seize the initiative. They re-formed their lines, and when the order came they moved forward against the horsemen.

The Persian cavalry had the advantage because of the terrain but like their infantry they, too, refused to stand against the advance of the disciplined Greeks. They retreated at full speed into a ravine behind the hills. The Greek foot soldiers were neither able nor inclined to pursue cavalry, and further, could not be sure whether the terrain beyond the hills would favor their continued advance or lead them into a trap. By now the Greeks were exhausted, so they broke off their attack. It was late in the day, they were hungry, and they wanted to return to the security of their camp before nightfall.

The Greeks began the march back to their camp, a distance of six or seven miles, at sunset. As soon as they left the field, the Persians regrouped. They moved their slaves and other property to more secure positions, as far away from the Greeks as they could. The Greeks returned to their camp that night and prayed for the quick arrival of Cleander's triremes to take them home. The next morning, driven by hunger, some of the Greeks went out into the countryside in small groups to search for what was left of any food in the countryside.

The Greek cities along the coast, from Byzantium to Sinope, had continued to send limited provisions to the mercenaries, and ships passing the area would stop at the Greek camp to trade. Word had begun to spread along the coast of the Black Sea that a new city of Greeks was being founded at Calpe. Even nearby tribes who had formerly been hostile became friendlier the longer the Greeks stayed in the area. Aside from possibilities for trade, the powerful mercenary army could be just as valuable an ally as it was a dangerous opponent. Envoys came from tribal chiefs who told Xenophon they had heard he was the man who was building a new city, and they desired to be his friends. Xenophon always made it a point to present these envoys to the soldiers and had them state their purpose in front of the general assembly. In that way no disgruntled soldier could accuse him of plotting secretly behind the backs of the army.

A few days after the battle with Pharnabazus, two Spartan war triremes sailed into Calpe Harbor. Aboard one of them was Cleander, the Spartan governor of Byzantium. When the Greeks saw the warships sail into the harbor they became concerned because there were no transport ships with them. When the governor came ashore, the Greeks were surprised to see Dexippus in his company. Dexippus was the man who had deserted them at Trapezus some weeks before after he had been given charge of the fifty-oared warship. Instead of bringing in more ships for the aid of the army, he had used the opportunity to save himself.

Dexippus came ashore at Calpe that morning under the protection of the governor. Soon he was in a dispute with some of the soldiers over plundered livestock, and he reported to Cleander that there had been a robbery. The Spartan told him to arrest the guilty party, so Dexippus went back and seized a man who served under Agasias. When Agasias happened to come upon the scene he freed his man, and other mercenaries who had witnessed the incident began to stone Dexippus. As Dexippus fled through the camp more and more Greeks joined the chase. They called him "traitor" and by the time he reached the safety of his ship the number of soldiers chasing him had grown to a large mob of angry men. When the sailors aboard the ships saw what was happening, many became frightened. They urged their captains to pull up the anchors and set sail before the enraged mob killed them all.

The Spartan governor and a few of his men arrived at the shoreline and a tense standoff ensued with the Greek mercenaries. The governor became fearful of the soldiers and retreated to the safety of his ship at anchor. Cleander was not pleased with the way he had been treated by these soldiers and he sent for Xenophon to report to him aboard his ship.

Xenophon had been away from camp with a foraging party during the incident, and when he returned to camp the mob was beginning to disperse. He boarded the war trireme and assured Cleander that he had nothing to fear from the Greek soldiers. Dexippus, however, who was standing nearby, was angered and frightened by the incident. He urged Cleander to sail away from the Greek camp quickly before these men turned even more violent. Cleander, his dignity as Spartan governor of Byzantium impinged and his authority challenged, threatened to issue a proclamation branding these Greeks as renegades and ordering that no Greek coastal city could receive them or offer them provisions.

Cleander, from Byzantium, controlled the narrow passage between the Black Sea and the Aegean. He was a powerful man in the region and not one to have as an adversary. Xenophon did his best to defuse the situation but Cleander became increasingly resolute. He demanded that the Greeks turn over the men responsible for menacing him and for stoning Dexippus. These men would be held for trial and subsequent punishment.

Dexippus took advantage of the situation and continued to agitate against his former comrades. He identified Agasias to Cleander as the instigator. He urged Cleander to order his immediate arrest as an example to the other mercenaries that the authority of a Spartan governor could not be challenged without serious consequences. Agasias was a close friend of Xenophon and during the long march from Cunaxa had proven himself to be a brave and loyal officer. There had been ill-feeling between Dexippus and Agasias from the early days of the march, and now Dexippus, taking advantage of the Spartan governor's wounded pride, persuaded Cleander that Agasias be arrested.

The Greeks called an assembly to debate and vote on Cleander's demand. As the assembly debated, many of the speakers made fun of Cleander and Dexippus. When Xenophon spoke, he warned the assembly that Cleander was a powerful man who could injure their cause and prevent them from returning home to Greece. The Greek coastal cities, Xenophon reminded the assembly, were in alliance with the Spartans, who, since their defeat of Athens in the Peloponnesian War, had become the virtual rulers of Greece. Xenophon feared Cleander would shut them out of Byzantium and send word to other Greek governors not to receive them or provide aid. Any hopes that the Spartan admiral Anaxibius would send them the ships they needed to return home would disappear. Cleander could brand the mercenaries as disobedient to the laws of Greece and they would become outcasts or exiles, forced to roam in the lands of the barbarians.

Xenophon had to bring a difficult choice before the assembly. What he presented to them that day was the possibility that a few of their comrades might have to be sacrificed to Spartan pride so that the entire army could remain in good standing. Rumors circulated among the Greeks that Dexippus had told Cleander that the soldiers who threatened him, including Agasias, were under direct orders from Xenophon. It was feared that Cleander might demand the surrender of Xenophon as well.

Agasias rose and spoke. He told the assembly that he had not acted under orders from Xenophon. Xenophon was out of the camp at the time of the incident. When Agasias saw Dexippus, the traitor who had betrayed the army at Trapezus, trying to steal from them a second time, he was outraged and attacked him. Other soldiers saw what was happening and joined in.

Agasias offered to surrender for the sake of the army, but asked that his fellow Greeks not turn him over to Cleander in chains. He would surrender to Cleander but only as a free man. He told the army not to make war upon the Spartans on his behalf, and asked only that the army he had served so loyally and bravely these past months send him to Cleander accompanied by soldiers and officers who might speak in his defense. The army allowed him to choose those he wished to accompany him.

Agasias set off to Cleander's camp accompanied by a number of soldiers and generals. They approached Cleander in his tent and Agasias spoke first. He told the Lacedaemonian governor that he was the officer who had ordered the stoning of Dexippus. He explained how Dexippus had betrayed the Greeks at Trapezus and taken the fifty-oared warship to escape rather than help his fellow Greeks. Agasias told Cleander that it was the coward and traitor who should be killed instead of a good and brave soldier.

Cleander listened attentively to all that Agasias said. Then he listened carefully to the speeches in support of Agasias made by the other Greek generals and soldiers. When all had been said, Cleander rose to speak. No matter how base and treacherous Dexippus had been, as a Greek, he had a right to a trial. For a trial was the right of every free Greek and Agasias had violated that basic right in trying to stone him to death.

Cleander pointed out that Agasias himself had come forth today to demand that right. As a free Greek he sought a trial on the charges, yet he had sought to deny that same right to Dexippus. Cleander ordered Agasias to return to the Greek camp and present himself for trial when summoned. As for the rest of the Greeks, Cleander would bring no further charges against any of them and the matter would end with the trial of Agasias. Cleander dismissed the Greeks and proceeded to his breakfast with his aides.

When Xenophon heard the result he proposed sending another delegation to Cleander on behalf of Agasias. In an effort to impress the governor, this delegation was composed of the mercenary army's highest-ranking Spartan officers. Xenophon, though he was an Athenian, volunteered to lead them to Cleander.

Xenophon came before Cleander just as the governor had finished his breakfast. Cleander agreed to hear them and Xenophon was the first to speak. He began by placating the pride of the governor. Xenophon pointed out that the entire Greek army was now anxious to submit to the wishes of the Spartan governor. The Greeks had agreed to surrender all those he wished to punish and now they asked—in fact, begged—him to spare the life of a noble soldier and comrade. In return they promised to recognize Cleander as their leader and would demonstrate obedience to his authority. They asked only that he put Dexippus on trial as well and compare for himself how the conduct and lives of the two men differed.

After hearing the words of this delegation and seeing among them so many Spartans, Cleander agreed that by the twin gods Castor and Pollux, the special protectors of the Lacedaemonians, he would pardon Agasias. He recounted how the words of the delegation, especially those of Xenophon had moved him to compassion and now he distrusted the rumors he had been hearing that this army of mercenaries was composed of renegades disloyal to the laws of Greece and the authority of the Lacedaemonians.

The delegation thanked him and departed, taking Agasias with them. Cleander ordered sacrifices with a view to the journey back to Greece. Over the next few days, Cleander and Xenophon became close friends. Cleander was invited by Xenophon to review the Greek troops, and when he saw the disciplined way they paraded before him, and their salute of loyalty to his leadership, he was so impressed that he offered to lead them home to Greece himself. Yet in spite of his good will and friendship, the sacrifices were not favorable to his taking command.

For three days, victims were sacrificed and the soothsayer read the entrails. Yet each time the findings augured unfavorably for the journey home. Finally Cleander told the Greeks they should return home with Xenophon as their commander. The Spartan governor promised he would send word ahead so that they should be received as heroes by the Greek cities along their route.

The mercenaries voted to present Cleander with the gift of their livestock from the army's common property. The Lacedaemonian governor acknowledged their generosity, and in turn gave the animals back to the army. After Cleander sailed away, the army took its leave of Calpe Harbor, marching west through Bithynia. Their destination was Chrysopolis, a great city located on the Asian coast of Turkey just across the Bosporus from Byzantium. There was little to plunder along the way, and so as not to emerge from barbarian territory empty-handed, the army made a diversion of one day and night to enrich itself with loot and slaves. On the sixth day, the men reached

Chrysopolis, where they stayed for a week, resting and selling their plunder.

The Greek mercenaries now found themselves close to where they had begun their journey with Cyrus over a year earlier. They were on the borders of the Persian provinces of Lydia and Phrygia. They had come nearly full circle in their long march, during which they had humiliated the "king of kings" and made enemies throughout the Persian Empire. They had shown the world what a small yet well-disciplined force of soldiers could do against armies many times their size, and how easily penetrations could be made into the heart of the Persian Empire.

With the "Ten Thousand" so close to the borders of his province, the Persian satrap Pharnabazus became fearful. The Greeks might turn once more and march into his province to plunder and burn his cities and villages. In an effort to prevent this he sent word to Anaxibius, the Greek admiral who was at Byzantium. Pharnabazus asked him to transport the mercenaries out of Asia Minor, across the Bosporus to western Thrace. If the Persians could not destroy the Greek army, they could at least pay to have it removed from their territory. Anaxibius summoned Xenophon and the senior Greek officers to a meeting. He promised that if the mercenaries consented to cross over to Europe they would receive regular wages in his service. The officers agreed to consider the matter, but Xenophon took the opportunity to announce that he would part company with the army and sail back to Athens. Anaxibius urged him to stay with the army until it reached western Thrace and then take his leave if he so chose. The other officers prevailed upon Xenophon to stay, and feeling a strong sense of obligation and loyalty to the army, he agreed.

Soon thereafter, Seuthes, a Thracian from the European side of the Bosporus, sent an envoy to Xenophon. The envoy, Medosades, urged Xenophon to use his influence to bring the army across the Bosporus. For his services, Medosades promised that Seuthes would pay Xenophon well. Xenophon was puzzled at the offer since the army was inclined to cross anyway, so he suggested that Seuthes save his money. Once the army crossed the Bosporus, Xenophon suggested, Seuthes could negotiate terms with the new leaders himself. Following this conference, the army crossed over to the city of Byzantium on the ships of Anaxibius.

When the army reached Byzantium, Anaxibius would not pay

them wages as he had promised. He ordered the mercenaries to camp on a plain outside the city walls and prepare themselves to be counted and then sent home.

The mercenaries were angered at this turn of events since most of them had no money with which to secure provisions for the march to Greece. They had counted on wages from Anaxibius and the possibility of plunder in the countryside around Byzantium to give them something to show for their past year's service as mercenaries. They made their way into the city where they remained, making a general nuisance of themselves, drinking and carousing.

Xenophon, meantime, had made his preparations to sail home to Athens and he went to the governor, Cleander, to say farewell. Cleander urged Xenophon not to leave yet because of the tension that was developing between the army and Anaxibius. Cleander warned that even now certain powerful factions in the city were blaming Xenophon for the refusal of the mercenaries to leave Byzantium. Once more, Xenophon was caught up in the intrigues of Greek politics.

Xenophon defended the mercenaries and explained that the soldiers lacked provisions for the journey home. Nor had they been paid the wages promised by Anaxibius. Many were without money at all and unable to buy food. Cleander advised Xenophon to lead the Greek mercenaries as far away from the city as he could and only then take his leave and set sail for home. Xenophon proposed that they arrange a meeting with Anaxibius and discuss the matter before it became more serious and violence broke out.

A meeting was arranged but Anaxibius proved obstinate. He insisted that Xenophon was to leave the city with the army as quickly as possible and he refused to discuss the matter of wages. Then he threatened that any soldier or officer who was absent when the count was made on the plain in a few days would suffer the consequences.

Xenophon agreed to everything that was demanded of him. That night he was tired and despondent when he returned to the army. As a minor compromise, Anaxibius had agreed that the army would be honored by being allowed to march through the city before heading to the surrounding countryside. The parade was held while Eteonicus, an aide to Anaxibius, waited with a guard by the main city gates, prepared to "thrust in the crossbar" once the mercenaries were outside the city walls.

Anaxibius then addressed the Greeks from atop the city walls and ordered them to obtain their provisions by looting villages deep inside Thrace. They should then march to an area of southern Thrace called the Chersonese (the modern Gallipoli Peninsula). There they would come under the jurisdiction and pay of Cyniscus, another Lacedae-monian general who was engaged in a war with the Thracians. He had use for the Greek mercenaries in his war and would pay them a daily wage for their services. The Greek officers were uneasy and their doubt spread through the army. Suddenly, some of the soldiers took up their arms and rushed the city in an attempt to get back inside the walls. Eteonicus and his guard bolted the gates shut in their faces, and the mercenaries set to shoving or hammering their way back in. Some were demanding and others were pleading. More Greek mercenaries arrived at the gates and threatened to break through if they were not opened. Others ran down along the shore and made their way along the coast looking for another way into the city.

A small group of mercenaries that had intended to desert the main force remained hidden within the city walls when the gates were bolt-ed shut by Eteonicus. This group rushed the surprised guards, cut through the cross bolt with axes and opened the gates, to the delight of their comrades outside. When Xenophon saw what was happening he feared the soldiers would loot the city and their chance to return home to Greece would be lost. He ran toward the gates to try and take command but was swept in with the shouting mass of soldiers.

When the Byzantines saw the Greek mercenaries coming through the gates many fled to their homes in panic and locked themselves inside. Others deserted the city altogether and sought refuge aboard ships at anchor or fled into the countryside. A general panic spread throughout Byzantium. The citizens feared the angry mercenaries would slaughter them and put their city to the torch.

Eteonicus and his men retreated to the city's heavily fortified citadel. Anaxibius ran down to the shore and was able to reach the citadel by circling around on a fishing boat. He sent for reinforce-ments from Calchedon, farther down the coast, because his garrison was outnumbered by the out-of-control mercenary army.

When Xenophon made his way to the citadel he was surrounded by many of his most loyal men. They urged him to prove that he was a man and seize the city and all its ships at anchor. Now, they told Xenophon, was his moment to become great. With the city of Byzantium theirs, the mercenaries believed they could hold out indefinitely against any Greek forces sent from the mainland to dislodge them.

Xenophon moved to the Thracian Square, a large plaza within the city that was free of any houses or buildings and ideal for assembling the army. Xenophon ordered the Greeks to "ground your arms in line of battle." They obeyed and within a short time the hoplites had fallen into a line eight deep and the peltasts had moved into position on the wings, as was their habit. The army was brought to attention, arms grounded, and they became quiet to hear Xenophon speak.

Xenophon explained that he understood their anger and their feelings that they had been mistreated and deceived by Anaxibius. In the name of the gods, Xenophon begged his comrades not to give into this momentary fit of madness. He urged the mercenaries to give some thought to the long-term consequences of taking the city of Byzantium. Xenophon warned the men that if they sacked the city, killing fellow Greeks, looting, raping, and burning, they should be declared renegades by all the Greek city-states. They would be at war with all of Greece, not just the Spartans.

They would become enemies to their kinsmen. He emphasized that they would eventually lose against the greater resources and power of mainland Sparta. He reminded the Athenian mercenaries among them how Athens, a strongly fortified city with vast treasure and a fleet of three hundred triremes, had been defeated by the more powerful Lacedaemonians. What fate other than defeat could they, too, expect at the hands of the Spartans? They would be killed or made slaves. Where would they go, even if they could escape? Where would they find refuge? Surely not in the land they had just left and from a king who hated them. All over Asia, Tissaphernes, Pharnabazus, Mithridates, Orontas, Abrocomas, and the other barbarian satraps were poised against them. Was there one among the Greeks in this army so stupid as to think they could ultimately win against such odds?

All the Greek city-states would band against them and bolt their doors. He reminded his soldiers how they had refrained from taking barbarian cities, even though they were victorious. They had shown restraint before against barbarians, and now should they pillage the first truly Greek city they had come to?

Xenophon finished his speech by saying he would rather be drowned at sea than to have to witness the pillage of this city by his own men. He bade them to seek justice and their rights through obedience to the laws of Greece. The mercenaries, even if they could not obtain their just rights here in Byzantium, even if they were wronged and cheated by Anaxibius, must not risk losing their chance to return home to Greece. Xenophon proposed sending a delegation to Anaxibius asking once more for provisions; but if these were not to be had, the army would still depart peaceably, not as a victim of deceit but as proof of its discipline and obedience.

The soldiers agreed with Xenophon. Hieronymus the Elean, Eurylochus the Arcadian, and Philesius the Achaean were sent as bearers of the message to Anaxibius. While the messengers went in search of Anaxibius, a self-designated general named Coeratadas from Thebes arrived in the city. He approached Xenophon and the other officers and offered to lead the Greeks to a portion of western Thrace behind Byzantium. Here he promised the Greeks they would find plenty of villages, and he offered to supply them with provisions from his own coffers until they could secure their own. The next day he sent twenty of his men loaded with barley meal, twenty more loaded with wine, three men loaded with olives, one with garlic and one with onions. He held a sacrifice to the gods in front of the army, yet he would not distribute the provisions to them. On the next day he held sacrifices again and still he would not distribute the provisions.

The Greeks tired of Coeratadas quickly and on the second day decided his provisions were too meager to supply the army for even a day. They sent him away. In the meantime a reply had come back from Anaxibius. He accepted the proposal of the mercenaries on the condition that they leave the city and await his further orders outside the walls. Anaxibius warned that he would report what had happened at Byzantium to the ephors at Sparta and await their decision. He offered to write favorably on behalf of the mercenaries. The army left the city, and Anaxibius returned and ordered the gates shut and bolted once more. The Greeks were warned that any of their number caught within the city walls would be taken and sold as slaves. Xenophon, as a friend of Cleander, was allowed to come within the city walls and arrange for his own departure to Athens by ship.

The commanders of the army were now Neon the Lacedaemonian, Phryniscus, Philesius, and Xanthicles, all Achaeans, and the Dardanian Timasion, who had commanded Xenophon's cavalry. They led the army to some villages not far from the city and established a camp. The generals debated among themselves. Phryniscus wanted to join Seuthes in Thrace and enter into his service. Neon wanted to go to the Chersonese because, as the only Spartan among the generals, he might then become commander of the entire army. Neon and his men, most of whom had not begun the expedition with Cyrus as mercenaries but as regular troops dispatched from Sparta, were also inclined to do whatever the Lacedaemonian authorities requested. Timasion, as did many of the soldiers, desired to return to Asia. Residing in friendly territory under Spartan control was in many ways more difficult than living at the fringe of Persian territory. In Persia, the army could at least plunder and enrich itself at will. For many of the soldiers, acquiring wealth was a prerequisite for returning, or even wishing to return, home.

As the days and then weeks wore on, the tedium and poverty of life outside Byzantium began to wear on the soldiers. Some of them sold their weapons and made enough money to book passage on merchant ships heading to Greece. Others became absorbed into the life of neighboring Greek cities and towns. They married local women and settled down. Some fell sick and others turned to drink. It pleased Anaxibius to see the army coming apart, not only because it relieved his own anxiety but because it more than fulfilled his part of the deal with Pharnabazus.

At this time, Anaxibius's term as admiral had expired, and Xenophon took passage with him on a ship bound for Greece. Along the way, Anaxibius encountered the new governor of Byzantium, who had been sent to replace Cleander. The new Spartan governor, Aristarchus, informed Anaxibius that his replacement as admiral, Polus, was already at or near the Hellespont. Anaxibius suggested to Aristarchus that as his first official act he capture and sell as slaves all the mercenaries who had stayed behind at Byzantium. Cleander had actually taken pity on many of the sick and wounded mercenaries who remained behind, and had compelled citizens to care for feeble soldiers in their homes. Aristarchus, when he took office, ordered the arrest of any mercenaries found within the city walls. Nearly four hundred of them were captured and sold into slavery.

Anaxibius crossed over to the Asian side of the Hellespont at Parium and sent word to Pharnabazus that the terms of their agreement had been carried out. The Greek mercenary army had been removed from Asia Minor; now Anaxibius wanted full payment.

Pharnabazus, however, had learned that Anaxibius was being replaced. He abandoned his promises and instead sent envoys to establish ties with Aristarchus, the new Spartan governor.

When Anaxibius learned that Pharnabazus was reneging on their deal he summoned Xenophon and urged him to return to the mercenary army and lead it back to Asia. He put a thirty-oared warship at Xenophon's disposal and sent word to the coast that he be provided horses and an escort to hasten his return to his men. He also warned Xenophon of the danger for the mercenaries implicit in an arrangement between Pharnabazus and the new Spartan governor. Such an alliance was sure to be formed at the expense of Xenophon and those who remained in the army. Xenophon crossed the Propontis (Sea of Marmara) and arrived at the city of Perinthus. From there he rode to the Greek camp outside Byzantium. When he rejoined the army he was distressed to see the state of his soldiers. But they welcomed him back as their commander and were only too glad to follow him back to Asia Minor.

X
LIVING BY THE SWORD

Ironically, after their epic march through the Persian Empire, the mercenaries voted to return to Asia after just a few months' stay in Greek territory. Xenophon led the army southwest from Byzantium along the Sea of Marmara until they arrived at Perinthus. There they established a camp just outside the city walls, though the Lacedaemonian commander Neon, with about eight hundred soldiers, set up his own camp farther away. Xenophon had begun negotiations for ships to transport the army across to Asia when Aristarchus, the new Spartan governor of Byzantium, arrived at Perinthus with two triremes. He had already been contacted by the Persian satrap, Pharnabazus, with whom he had agreed to keep the mercenaries in Europe.

Aristarchus summoned Xenophon and warned him not to return to Asia. The governor threatened to intercept and sink any ships that tried to transport the mercenary army across the Hellespont. Xenophon replied that it was Anaxibius, the Spartan admiral, who had instructed him to lead the army back to Asia. Aristarchus reminded Xenophon that Anaxibius had been relieved of his command and that, he, Aristarchus, was now in charge. After issuing his blunt warning, the governor departed the mercenary camp and took up quarters within the walls of Perinthus.

The next day, Xenophon and a number of his officers were summoned to enter the city to appear before Aristarchus. Xenophon suspected treachery, having heard from an informant that the governor planned to seize the mercenary leaders and hand them over to Pharnabazus. He refused to attend under the pretext that he was in the middle of a sacrifice. Soon the other officers returned with word that Aristarchus had rescheduled the audience for later that afternoon. Now Xenophon would have no excuse for evading the summons, even

195

as he became more convinced than ever it was a trap. The officers discussed their situation. Xenophon did not want to risk crossing the strip of sea that separated Europe from Asia since Aristarchus had a large number of warships. Nor did he want to lead the army to the Chersonese, as the Spartans wanted, where it might find itself in remote territory at the mercy of a hostile governor. On the other hand, the Thracian warlord Seuthes had persistently tried to entice the mercenaries into his service, and the signs for this prospect from the sacrifice that day had been favorable.

Xenophon, along with trusted lieutenants of each of the army's generals except Neon, left camp and rode to meet with Seuthes. They reached the Thracian camp well before dawn and were stopped at the picket line. Xenophon requested to be taken to see Seuthes, whereupon about two hundred peltasts appeared out of the darkness to escort him. They led him to a stone tower where Seuthes was quartered. Around the tower were armed men and a large number of horses. When the Greeks drew near, Seuthes called to Xenophon to come forward with any two officers of his choosing.

Inside the tower, Seuthes and Xenophon greeted each other, and in the Thracian fashion drank to each other's health from horns of wine. They sat in the great hall of the tower and Xenophon recounted how Medosades, who was present, had come to the Greeks a few weeks earlier at Byzantium and asked them to join Seuthes. Xenophon asked Seuthes why he needed the army and Seuthes explained that many years ago his father had been king of Thrace. His father had been driven out with his family and died several years later in exile. The throne had since been vacant and Seuthes wanted to reclaim what had once belonged to his father. His army was small and inexperienced so he needed the help of the Greeks.

Xenophon listened to what Seuthes had to say and then asked what he could give to the Greeks, soldiers as well as officers, if they entered his service. Seuthes promised to give each soldier a cyzicene coin, with double for captains, and four times as much to generals. In addition he offered land to all those Greek soldiers who wished to remain in Thrace after he became king.

Then Xenophon asked what would happen if the attempt to take the throne failed. Seuthes avoided a direct answer to the question and instead offered his daughter to Xenophon in marriage. As the dowry Seuthes proposed a city, Bisanthe, which lay on the coast west of

Perinthus. This city was reputed to be among the most beautiful places along the seacoast and today is the site of the modern Turkish city of Tekirdag. Xenophon was concerned about the Lacedaemonians in Byzantium and how they would view the mercenaries in the service of Seuthes. Seuthes promised to accept any of the Greek soldiers who joined him as his brothers. He promised to protect them from Lacedaemonian reprisals and welcome them as honored residents in his own land.

Xenophon and his officers left Seuthes and returned to the army to make their report. An assembly of the soldiers was called the next day, though Neon and his men refused to attend. They remained sequestered in their own camp, about a mile away from the main body of soldiers. Xenophon rose and addressed the assembly. He explained to the soldiers the available alternatives but argued against their crossing by sea to Asia because the threat of attack by Aristarchus and his triremes was too great. He outlined a possible march to the Chersonese to serve with pay under the Spartans and explained how Aristarchus had promised not to sell any more of them into slavery. Finally, Xenophon described Seuthes's proposal to hire the mercenaries to help him recover the throne of his father. Seuthes's part of Thrace comprised all the territory that lies between the Chersonese and the Black Sea coast.

Xenophon suggested that before the soldiers decided anything they should march into the countryside to find provisions. The assembly agreed and the soldiers went back to their companies to begin preparations for the next day. When word reached Neon of what the mercenaries were about to do he rode into the camp and tried to persuade Xenophon not to set out against the villages. Aristarchus sent heralds to Xenophon with orders that the mercenaries were not to leave their camp. Xenophon and the army ignored the orders and set out. Time and again heralds were sent to Xenophon as the army moved through the countryside around Byzantium, commanding them in the name of Aristarchus to turn back. Each time the mercenaries refused and continued to move inland, looting and burning every village and town in their path.

After a day Seuthes rode out to find the Greeks. He asked if they had reached a decision on his offer and Xenophon replied that they were too busy plundering the countryside to consider it. When the Greeks had sufficient provisions and slaves they would meet in assembly and consider his offer. Then Xenophon told Seuthes that the mercenaries had received a proposition to enter into the service of Aristarchus as well and that they would consider both offers. When Seuthes heard this he attempted to win the favor of the Greeks by offering to lead them to a number of richer villages nearby where they could plunder and take more slaves, especially women. The army followed his scouts and by early afternoon had arrived at the largely defenseless villages. When the Greeks had finished plundering, murdering, and raping they called an assembly and proceeded to listen to what Seuthes had to offer.

The Thracian made many promises to the assembly that night, and many of the Greeks commented how much he sounded like Cyrus, over a year earlier at Sardis. Before them stood another man who wanted to be a king. As he had described to the Greek officers, Seuthes promised to pay the troops in cyzicenes. He said the Greeks could take their provisions from the countryside, but any captured booty had to be turned over to Seuthes so he could sell it to provide the mercenaries' wages. Then he promised the Greeks they would never find themselves more than seven days march from the sea and they would often be campaigning much closer to the coast. After their long march through Persia many of the soldiers found this aspect of his proposal appealing.

When he finished, Seuthes encouraged the Greeks to speak their minds directly to him in assembly. Many of the soldiers rose either to ask questions or to speak in favor of his offer. It was now nearly winter and some of the soldiers argued that the season to sail home safely had passed. They were blocked from Asia by Spartan warships; they had no wish to enter Spartan service in the Chersonese, and many disliked the idea of the army roaming the wilds of Thrace on its own auspices. It would be better, they reasoned, to wait out the winter with a strong Thracian ally, guaranteed provisions, and even an extra bonus—pay.

Xenophon asked if anyone had a contrary opinion to express, and when no one came forward he put the matter to a vote. The majority of the Greeks voted to take service with Seuthes. Seuthes was pleased and invited the Greek captains and generals to dine with him and his officers the next night in a nearby village. When the officers arrived the next evening, a fellow Greek, Heracleides greeted them outside Seuthes's tent. Heracleides was from a Greek city in Thrace, and he had entered Seuthes's service as an advisor some months before. He assembled the officers, including Xenophon, and explained to them that it was customary when Seuthes invited someone to dinner that the guest bring a present. Heracleides pointed out that once Seuthes became king he would be inclined to reward any generosity shown to him. Even the most modest gesture made now, Heracleides advised, would make many of the Greeks richer men later.

Heracleides told the Greeks that they would become wealthy men if they helped Seuthes become king. For the moment, however, Xenophon and the others must lavish gifts upon Seuthes first. Xenophon was embarrassed by this request and dismayed. He wanted to impress Seuthes favorably that night but all he had with him were a young male slave serving as an attendant and a very small sum of gold in his purse.

The Greek officers entered the tent and each one presented to Seuthes whatever modest gifts he had. Then, with the guests seated in a circle, the first course of the dinner was served. The slaves brought three legged tables with massive platters upon them filled to overflowing with roasted meat. The meat had been cut into chunks and then fastened to pieces of leavened bread with skewers and roasted over the fires. Seuthes followed a Thracian royal custom and stood before the guests. He took pieces of the meat and bread from his own platter, which was the largest and most lavish of all, and then proceeded to throw them to those among the assembled guests who pleased him most. When he had finished, all that he left for himself was the most modest portion. Other guests rose and followed suit. Soon great quantities of meat and bread were being thrown around the room, to the amusement of the Greeks. Then slaves brought in great horns filled with wine from which the guests drank copiously.

When the drinking was well underway, for it was the custom of the Thracians to eat first and then begin serious drinking afterward, a noble and friend of Seuthes entered the tent leading a beautiful white horse. He drank to the health of the future king from the great horn of wine and then offered the horse to Seuthes so that he might ride to victory over his enemies. There was wild applause and cheering among the guests as Seuthes rose to accept the gift. More meat and bread was thrown about the room and more wine consumed from the great horn. Another noble brought into the tent a fair young boy and offered him as a gift to Seuthes. This noble drank as well to the health of the new

king from the large horn of wine. A number of Thracian nobles came
forth after that with more gifts. Some offered elegant clothes for
Seuthes's wife, while others offered gifts of silver bowls and magnificent carpets from Persia.

Then Gnesippus, an Athenian advisor to Seuthes, rose and
explained to the Greek guests that it was the custom in Thrace that
those who could afford to give gifts to the king should, while those
who had nothing to offer could expect gifts from him. Xenophon was
seated nearest to Seuthes in a place of honor and he was embarrassed
by the words of Gnesippus and by the parade of Thracian nobles
offering such beautiful gifts. Xenophon had nothing to offer and was
at a loss to know what he should do at this moment. Heracleides, sensing Xenophon's unease, directed the cupbearer to offer him the great
horn of wine. Xenophon rose and took the horn. Being already slightly intoxicated from the large amount of drinking at dinner, he stood
before the group trying to find the words with which he could make a
toast to his host and hide his embarrassment.

The group fell silent and waited for Xenophon to speak. He began
by explaining that he had only two things of value that night to present to Seuthes—his friendship and his loyalty. Xenophon, speaking
for all the mercenaries present, pledged to be a true friend to Seuthes
and to help him regain the throne that had been taken from his father.
He proclaimed that Seuthes was the rightful ruler of Thrace and the
Greeks were prepared to fight and die by his side in defense of his just
cause. Xenophon promised that the mercenaries would endure hardship and danger for Seuthes and win for him not only the territory that
had belonged to his father but much more. There would be more land
for the new king of Thrace, more slaves, horses, and vast quantities of
gold.

The words about friendship and the promises of wealth pleased
Seuthes. He rose and stood next to Xenophon. Taking the great horn
he drank the wine to show his acceptance of the Greek offer of friendship. Then what remained in the horn, again in the Thracian custom,
he sprinkled over the heads of the guests closest to him. Suddenly,
music filled the room from horns, trumpets, and harps. In response to
the music Seuthes jumped onto one of the tables and gave out a fierce
war cry. Then he began a nimble war dance to the delight of all the
guests. When the dancing had finished the Greeks prepared to leave
the feast. It was time, they told the Thracians, to return to their camp

and post the sentinels. They still had to pass along the watchword and secure their camp for the night. Each Greek officer embraced Seuthes as he left the tent and pledged his loyalty and friendship.

The officers suggested that none of Seuthes's men come near their camp that night since the Greeks could not tell as yet who among the Thracians were friends and who were enemies. Seuthes told the Greeks that since none of their enemies in Thrace knew of their alliance it would be well to move quickly while they had the advantage of surprise. Seuthes told Xenophon he would come to the Greek camp very soon to lead them on the first leg of the campaign. Seuthes accompanied the Greeks to the perimeter of his camp and they marveled at how a man who had consumed so much wine that night could move with such stability and poise.

Shortly after midnight, Seuthes arrived at the Greek camp, accompanied by his cavalry and followed by his peltasts. The Greek units were assembled and each one was assigned a Thracian guide. The guides were older men who had lived in the region for many years and knew it well. Xenophon suggested that as the army moved out that night into hostile territory Seuthes might consider adopting the Greek practice of marching. During the day the Greeks put in the vanguard that element of the army that was most adaptable to the terrain and weather conditions. If the Greeks marched at night, experience had taught them it was best to put the heaviest and slowest element of the army in the vanguard. At night men could easily become separated from the column and then lost. This occurred often when the faster and lighter infantry units were leading the column and moved ahead of the others too quickly.

Seuthes acknowledged the experience of the Greeks in military matters and agreed to place their hoplites first in the column and his cavalry in the rear. It was agreed that "Athena" would be the password if they separated, and then the army moved out into the star-filled night of the Thracian winter. The column marched all that night and halted just before dawn. As the sun rose, Seuthes and his cavalry moved to the front and he complimented the Greek commanders on how well their units had stayed together in the darkness. Seuthes suggested the Greeks stop for a rest while his cavalry went out to scout the land ahead.

As the road ahead of them wound its way into the mountains it became covered in snow. The scouts looked for footprints or tracks to see if anyone had recently passed that way. Seeing nothing in the fresh snow, they reported to Seuthes that they were sure the army had entered the region undetected. As a precaution, Seuthes sent the cavalry ahead with instructions to capture anyone they might come upon to prevent them from warning the villagers. The army still had a distance to cover over the mountains that day before they would come to the first valley that contained villages.

By midday the scouts had reached the heights of the last of the mountains and were able to look down at the peaceful villages in the valley below. Seuthes ordered the cavalry to secure both ends of the valley to cut off any avenue of escape. Then the peltasts would move against the largely unarmed and helpless villagers while the heavily armed hoplites would follow behind as support in the unlikely event the raiding units encountered serious resistance.

The attack on the unsuspecting villages went as planned, and by late that afternoon Seuthes and the Greeks had captured over a thousand people and a great quantity of cattle. The soldiers spent the night in the villages but the next day when the army was ready to leave Seuthes ordered that everything in the valley be burned. He wanted the destruction to serve as an example to the people of the price to be paid if they refused to accept him as their new king. Heracleides was sent to the city of Perinthus with a small detachment of soldiers to sell the booty and slaves the army had taken in the villages. With the proceeds from the sale Seuthes hoped to raise the money necessary to pay the Greeks their first installment of wages.

Seuthes and the Greeks moved further west and north into the interior of Thrace and established their next camp on a large plain. It had become so cold by now that water began to freeze in its containers and many of the soldiers suffered frostbite on their ears, noses, fingers, and toes. The Greeks looked to the native Thracian guides for advice on how to dress for the cold. They noticed that the guides wore foxskin caps on their heads that covered their ears, and they wrapped their feet in several layers of animal skins. In this plain, Seuthes and the Greeks found more villages but most of them were deserted. Heralds were sent into the mountains where many of the villagers were hiding and they announced orders from Seuthes commanding them to come down and surrender. The people were warned that if they did not obey Seuthes would burn every village in the plain. Burning a village in the winter meant destroying the food supplies for the cold months ahead and leaving the villagers without shelter.

As a result of his threats, large groups of women, children, and old people came down onto the plain to surrender. The younger men of fighting age stayed on the mountain and Seuthes assembled a detachment of Greek hoplites to go up and find them. During the night the Greeks set out and caught the unfortunate villagers at dawn the next day just as they were waking. Most of the villagers had no chance. When the attack began, a few of them made their escape to higher ground but most were captured. Those who were captured were taken down to the plain where Seuthes ordered them put to death in front of their families as an example.

An exceptionally handsome captive boy was about to be executed when a Greek hoplite, Episthenes from Olynthus, broke ranks and ran forward. He put his arms around the boy to protect him from the executioner and begged Seuthes to spare his life. The Greek confessed that he had come to prefer young boys to women. He was so taken by the beauty and innocence of this boy that he offered his own neck to the executioner if Seuthes would spare the boy. This amused Seuthes and in a display of generosity he agreed to spare both the boy and the hoplite, to the delight of the mercenaries.

After the executions had been carried out Seuthes moved his main force further down the mountain and onto another large plain. Xenophon remained with a detachment of hoplites in some of the villages that were located higher up on the mountainside. After a few days, Thracians who were living higher on the mountain and in more remote villages sent envoys to Seuthes to ask for a safe conduct if they surrendered. Xenophon also came down from the mountain, preferring the security and comfort of the general camp on the plain to the villages in the heights.

As it turned out, these envoys had not come to ask Seuthes for peace. They had come to spy on his camp in preparation for a surprise attack. The first part of the attack was directed against the Greek contingent that Xenophon had left quartered in the mountain villages. The attack against the Greeks came late that night and ended only when Seuthes and a large column of his soldiers arrived the next morning.

As the days went by, more and more people from the surrounding region heard how successful Seuthes had been against the mountain people and came to the plain to join his army. The army grew over the weeks and eventually increased to three times its original number.

More and more people came to surrender to Seuthes and hail him as their new king. With this large army Seuthes now moved over to the area of Thrace that lay beyond Byzantium on the coast of the Black Sea. Heracleides rejoined them there, bringing with him profits from the sale of the booty and slaves in Perinthus. Wages were distributed to all the Greeks but there was only enough money to pay them for the equivalent of twenty days of the month.

Xenophon became angry and accused Heracleides of holding back much of the money for himself. As a result, Heracleides became openly hostile toward Xenophon and never missed an opportunity to say something derogatory about him to Seuthes. The mercenaries in turn became angry with Xenophon because they had not received their full measure of pay, and they blamed him for urging them to join Seuthes in the first place. Seuthes turned cold toward Xenophon, probably for his accusation against Heracleides, or perhaps because he was not able to pay the mercenaries in full and his pride had been injured. A strain developed in their relationship and from that day forward Seuthes never again mentioned giving Xenophon his daughter for a royal wife or a city within his kingdom.

Heracleides continued to agitate against Xenophon. He warned Seuthes that it would not be in the new king's best interests to allow Xenophon to stay in Thrace once the war ended, especially if Xenophon kept with him a large number of his veteran Greek mercenaries. Heracleides moved among the mercenary generals as well, urging them to take command of the army away from Xenophon. They in turn took every opportunity to complain to him that they had not been paid. Heracleides made promises on behalf of Seuthes and told the Greeks that their pay would come in full within a few days. He cautioned them to remain loyal to the new king.

The Greek officer Timasion was the first to challenge Heracleides. He announced that he would remain loyal to Xenophon even if Seuthes offered to double his pay. Phryniscus and Cleanor followed suit and agreed to continue their support of Xenophon as commander of the army. It became evident that the Greek officers would remain loyal to Xenophon, so Seuthes turned on Heracleides and became friendlier toward the Greeks. The Greeks continued in the service of Seuthes and Xenophon remained their commander, but the breach between the two leaders widened more with each passing day.

The army marched farther inland, suppressing resistance to

Seuthes's authority as they went. They burned and looted villages and towns in the name of the new king and amassed for themselves a considerable number of slaves. They kept the Pontus to their right and finally arrived at an area along the Black Sea called the "jaw of Salmydessus." In this land, some fifty miles northwest of the entrance to the Bosporus, ships would often run aground along the treacherous coastline. There were shoals that extended from the coastline far out into the sea. The Thracians who lived along the coast would plunder these ships when they ran aground, killing all aboard. The various tribes of the area often fought among themselves over the contents of the ships so they eventually set up great stone markers along the coast to divide the territory into sections for plunder. These boundaries were used to keep peace among them. When Xenophon and the army passed along the coast they found great quantities of boxes, many of which contained books, as well as other articles from wrecked ships scattered along the beaches.

The army of Seuthes continued to grow. Each day more and more people from the interior and those who had been conquered joined him. Most joined Seuthes as an alternative to being killed or sold into slavery, not because they believed in him. By late winter, Seuthes's army had become larger than the Greek mercenary force. The Greeks became concerned at the size of the army and that the next round of their pay was not readily forthcoming. Xenophon agreed to speak to Seuthes on behalf of the mercenaries. When Xenophon arrived at the camp, Seuthes sent an aide to tell him he was occupied. Relations between the two men continued to deteriorate. It had been more than two months since the Greeks had joined Seuthes and the euphoria of the early stages of the campaign was gone. Forgotten were the feelings of comradeship and the mutual pledges of eternal friendship and brotherhood that had characterized that first night of drinking in Seuthes's tent.

One day a delegation of Lacedaemonians arrived in the Greek camp and demanded to see Xenophon. They brought word that Thibron, a Spartan commander, was undertaking a new war against the Persians and that he had need for experienced Greeks. The offer was a daric per month for each soldier, two for each captain, and four for each general. With Cyrus dead, Tissaphernes had been reinstated as satrap of his former possessions in the west. Tissaphernes had moved quickly to retaliate against the Ionian cities that had supported

Cyrus, and the Greek colonists had appealed to Sparta for aid. In 399
B.C. the Spartan ephors voted a new war against Persia and Thibron
was sent to Asia Minor with an army to protect the Greek cities.

Heracleides brought the news of the Spartan offer to Seuthes, who
was only too glad to be rid of the Greeks now that his own army had
grown and the serious fighting was finished. That night Seuthes invited the Lacedaemonian envoys to a lavish dinner. Xenophon and the
other Greek generals were not invited to the feast. Over dinner, the
Spartans asked Seuthes about Xenophon's character. He replied that
Xenophon was a good man on the whole but he was an officer who
was a "friend of the soldiers." Heracleides agreed and warned the
envoys that Xenophon was a man who "played the demagogue" and
hence was dangerous to people in authority.

The next day, Seuthes and Heracleides accompanied the Lacedaemonian envoys to the Greek camp, where the mercenaries had
gathered to listen to the Spartan proposition. The envoys began by
telling the assembled soldiers that the Lacedaemonians had decided to
wage war on their old enemy, Tissaphernes, the man who had treach-
erously murdered their generals after the battle of Cunaxa. They urged
the mercenaries to join with their fellow Greeks and avenge themselves
on the Persians who had wronged them. The theme of their speech
was punish your old enemy, earn your wages, and chance upon your
fortune a second time. It was the same recruiting speech they had
heard two years ago with Cyrus, yet the mercenaries were pleased at
the prospect of service in Persia. Then one of the Greeks, an Arcadian,
rose to speak. He brought a serious accusation against Xenophon,
while Seuthes listened intently with an interpreter at his side. It was
always suspected among the mercenaries that Seuthes understood
Greek or at least could comprehend for himself most of what was said.
Still, he always spoke through an interpreter.

The Arcadian soldier accused Xenophon of having led the army
on a worthless expedition for which they had received little pay and
undertaken much hardship. They had suffered through a cold and brutal winter and had little or nothing to show for it, while Xenophon
had profited with gifts from Seuthes. He blamed Xenophon for the
failure of the Greeks to be paid but stopped short of accusing him of
taking the money for himself. The Arcadian proposed to the assembled Greeks that Xenophon should be stoned to death as punishment
for his incompetence. The sight of Xenophon being executed, said the

spiteful mercenary, would more than compensate for the loss of back wages. Two more soldiers from Arcadia rose to support the proposition that stoning Xenophon would discharge Seuthes's debt to the army. The idea seemed to please Seuthes, and perhaps Heracleides had bribed these Arcadians to bring the charges against Xenophon.

Faced with the prospect of execution by stoning from the very men he had led for over a year, Xenophon rose to address the assembly. He began by sighing that in life a man must prepare himself to expect anything and everything. He had now learned that a man could count on nothing but himself. Here he stood, facing the prospect of death by stoning for something over which he had no control. If there was any fault on his part it was that he tried too hard to do what was best for the army. He recounted to the assembly how as he prepared to sail home to Greece he heard that many of them were sick and others sold into slavery. He had returned to lead them out of Byzantium.

He reminded the assembly that Seuthes had urged him several times to bring the Greek army into his service and that Xenophon had declined. Xenophon recounted how in open forum, as was their custom, the Greeks had debated service with Seuthes and voted to go with him of their own free will. As free men they had made a collective decision and now they were considering stoning him to death because they did not want to accept responsibility for their own blunder. As their commander he had led them where they wanted to go. Xenophon found himself blamed for being too good a friend to Seuthes and not to the Greeks when in fact the reverse was true.

In the beginning, Xenophon admitted, he had been friendly with Seuthes and he had even thought of remaining in Thrace after the war. Their friendship ended over the issue of back pay for the army. Xenophon swore by the gods that he had not received even his own promised pay from Seuthes and he pointed to the Thracian king standing nearby and said that he knew the truth.

Xenophon related to the assembly that the small amount of pay he had received from Seuthes did not equal the pay of a captain, much less a general. He had been willing to support Seuthes while he struggled to gain the throne in the hopes that when Seuthes became king he would reward those who had stood by him. Xenophon admitted he had been deceived, and had only lately come to realize the limitations of this man who had hired them. It was hard for Xenophon to admit this because he had been deceived not by an enemy but by a man who professed to be his friend. Xenophon explained that the Greeks had upheld their obligations to Seuthes as mercenaries and supported him in his war. They had given no excuse to this man to deny them pay for the service they had rendered.

Then Xenophon reminded the Greeks of the state in which he had found them before they entered the service of Seuthes. The mercenaries had lost their cavalry and many of their peltasts during the retreat out of Asia. They had gone to Perinthus and found that Aristarchus the Lacedaemonian governor had shut the gates of that city against them. They were forced to remain on the Thracian coast, often without provisions, camped under the cold winter sky. Spartan war triremes prevented them from crossing back to Asia. By joining Seuthes the Greeks had saved themselves. They had found food in the Thracian villages and they had captured slaves and cattle. He reminded them that they had passed the winter with abundant supplies of food, warm quarters, and captive women. There had been little fighting and none of the Greeks had been killed or captured that winter. It had not been a difficult campaign and they had eaten well and kept warm. The Greeks should be thanking the gods at this moment instead of being angry with him.

As Xenophon stood before the assembly of the Greeks that day he found himself a man who was very alone. He was at odds with the powerful Lacedaemonian governor of Byzantium, and disliked by Seuthes, the Thracian king. The mercenaries he had led out of Persia were considering stoning him to death. He had no one to come forward on his behalf. When he left Greece nearly two years before with his friend Proxenus to join Cyrus he had been full of hope for his future. He had earned fame among the mercenaries for his service in Asia against the Persians and he had been praised and trusted by the Lacedaemonians. Now he was only a vessel of blame for misfortune.

He continued his speech and reminded the mercenaries how during their time of despair he had come forward to take command, and he had served them well. He had once been admired and praised by the men who now debated taking his life. He faced stoning by the very men who had once been his brothers, enduring common hardships and dangers. Xenophon recounted how when they needed him while marching through Persia and the mountains of Armenia many called him "father" and promised never to forget what he had done for their safekeeping. They had suffered difficult times together but now their fortune had changed once more. The Lacedaemonians, the powerful rulers of Greece, had come to enlist their services for pay. They would mount another campaign in Asia against the Persians. Now at the moment when their future looked the brightest they were preparing to put him to death. What, he asked the assembly, did they imagine the Lacedaemonian envoys, standing nearby and hearing every word, were thinking of these mercenaries who were turning on their commander? What was Seuthes thinking as he watched them debate the execution of the man who had sacrificed so much for them?

Charminus, one of the Spartan envoys, rose and spoke to the assembly. He told the mercenaries that the night before he had dined at the table of Seuthes. He had asked the Thracians about the character of Xenophon and they told him that Xenophon was a man who was "too good a friend" to the Greek soldiers. Then one of the mercenaries, Eurylochus of Lusi, rose and spoke. He proposed that the Lacedaemonian envoys seek from Seuthes the back pay due the mercenaries. Polycrates the Athenian rose and pointed to Heracleides, accusing him of having cheated them of their pay. He called Heracleides a thief and proposed that he should be stoned for cheating the Greeks. Then Polycrates turned to face Seuthes. Here was a Thracian, he told the assembly, a man who was not a Greek but a barbarian. They could understand such deceptive behavior from barbarians, but they would not accept it from fellow Greeks. The assembly now concentrated on Seuthes and Heracleides.

Heracleides became frightened by Polycrates' words and he moved closer to Seuthes and his bodyguard. He sensed that the mood of the assembly had changed and urged the new king to leave and return to the security of his own camp. Seuthes agreed and with Heracleides he mounted his horse and returned to his camp. Once in the safety of the Thracian camp Seuthes sent his Greek interpreter, Abrozelmes, to Xenophon. Abrozelmes urged Xenophon to remain behind with about a thousand of his best and most trusted hoplites after the army had departed. Seuthes renewed his earlier promise that Xenophon could have his own city on the coast of Thrace. The Thracian king also promised that when the campaign was finished Xenophon would receive all the back pay that was due him and a share in the spoils. Abrozelmes warned Xenophon of rumors that the Lacedaemonian commander Thibron was about to order his execution. The mercenaries had become a disturbing presence for the

Greeks on the mainland, especially after the incident at Byzantium. They were considered dangerously independent and often lawless. The prospect of their return home to mainland Greece where they might menace other cities was unsettling to the leaders of the city-states. The Lacedaemonians were looking for a way to disband the mercenaries and the execution of their leader seemed like a good start.

As was his habit in times of crisis, Xenophon turned to the gods for advice. Through the medium of sacrifice he sought guidance from Zeus, the father of the gods. Xenophon hoped for a sign that would help him decide if he should remain with Seuthes, depart with the army and take his chances with the Spartans in Persia, or return alone to Athens. The soothsayer held the sacrifice and advised Xenophon that the signs from the gods directed him to depart with the army for Asia.

When Seuthes learned that Xenophon would not remain with him in Thrace he moved his camp a greater distance away from the Greeks. The Greeks began to loot some nearby villages to secure provisions for their journey to the coast. Seuthes had given these villages to one of his generals, Medosades. When he learned that the Greeks were looting his villages he became angry and rode to the Greek camp with a bodyguard of about thirty horsemen. Medosades arrived at the perimeter of the camp and Xenophon went forward to meet with him with several captains as bodyguards. Medosades warned the Greeks to stop looting the villages under orders of Seuthes. If they did not stop and leave immediately for the coast they would be declared enemies and the Thracians would declare war on them.

Xenophon replied to Medosades that when Seuthes needed the Greeks to conquer this land, when he called the Greeks his comrades and friends, they were free to plunder and burn as they pleased. Seuthes and his nobles had hidden behind the Greeks when they first came to conquer this land and now that they no longer needed the Greeks, Seuthes sought to drive them away without their pay. Then Xenophon told Medosades that the Lacedaemonian envoys would lead the mercenaries out of Thrace and he had best address his concerns to them. The two Lacedaemonian generals, Charminus and Polynicus, were summoned to parlay with Medosades. Xenophon and his generals urged the Lacedaemonians to demand the back pay due the mercenaries before they agreed to leave Thrace. The Lacedaemonians approached Medosades, who became very submissive. He asked politely that the Greeks refrain from looting and burning the villages since harm toward the villagers, now subjects of Seuthes, was harm to Seuthes.

The Lacedaemonians replied that they were willing to put a stop to the plundering and prepare to leave for the coast once Seuthes had paid the mercenaries their back wages. The Spartan generals pledged to assist the Greeks in every way to obtain what was due them and to punish those who had betrayed them. They hinted that they would begin, if need be, with Medosades himself. Medosades urged the Lacedaemonians to go to Seuthes concerning the back pay due the Greeks and he suggested sending Xenophon to negotiate the matter. In the meantime he beseeched the Greeks to stop burning the villages.

Xenophon agreed to go to Seuthes with a bodyguard and negotiate the matter of the back pay. He rode to the Thracian camp where he urged the king to pay the Greeks their due. They had made him king of this land and he owed, before the gods and men, a just debt that must be paid. Xenophon warned Seuthes that now that he was king he must act in an honorable and fair manner if men were to regard him as just. There were six thousand Greeks who demanded their pay. Xenophon reminded Seuthes that the Greeks had trusted him when he had no money to pay them at the beginning of the campaign. The Greeks had believed his word and Xenophon had embraced him as a friend.

The sum owed the Greeks was thirty talents of gold, an amount worth far less than the price of the Thracian kingdom and the good name of its king. Xenophon reminded Seuthes that he ruled a kingdom that the Greeks had taken by force for him. The people of this land lived under his rule out of fear, not because they loved him. Unless fear restrained them they would struggle to be free once more. As long as the Thracian people saw that the Greeks honored Seuthes and would return to help him in time of need they would be more inclined to remain his subjects. If the day came when he had need of mercenaries again none would come because of his reputation for not paying what he had promised.

Xenophon pointed out that the Greeks had conquered this land not because its people lacked courage or numbers, but because they had no effective military leaders. When the Greeks had finished their business with the Spartans in Persia, and with the blessing of the Spartans, they would return to this land to finish their business with him. The Thracian people would rise up to join the Greeks against him. It would be cheaper for Seuthes to pay the Greeks what he owed than to try and drive them from his land later. If the Greeks returned to Thrace to wage war, he would need better troops than he had to fight them.

On a personal note, Xenophon recounted how he had considered Seuthes a friend. Seuthes knew that Xenophon had not taken a single gold piece from him that was given as pay for the Greeks. Nor did he ever accept money from Seuthes before his soldiers had been paid their due. He lectured the king of Thrace on the importance of honor. Xenophon explained that he had taken his friendship with Seuthes to heart. The Greeks had observed in Xenophon the affection he had toward Seuthes and this had made them suspicious of their leader. Seuthes had heard in the assembly how some of the Greeks accused Xenophon of caring more for Seuthes than for them. Xenophon had once seen in Seuthes the beginning of a friendship. Now that Seuthes had accomplished what he set out to do, he had turned on Xenophon and dissolved their friendship. Time would teach Seuthes to value friendship and pay what he owed to others. Pay to the Greeks what was owed them, he advised the Thracian king.

The sincerity of Xenophon's words moved Seuthes. He cursed the man who was to blame for not paying the Greeks, and his bodyguard in the tent looked toward Heracleides. Seuthes said he never intended to cheat the Greeks and then he agreed to pay what he could. Xenophon asked that Seuthes entrust him with the payment so he could personally bring it back to the army, thus restoring his status with the men. Seuthes again implored Xenophon to remain in Thrace with a thousand hoplites. He warned him again of the dangers he faced in the service of the Lacedaemonians. Xenophon thanked Seuthes for his generosity and friendship but said he would depart with the army for Asia. He would take his chances among the Greeks, for he could not live among barbarians.

Seuthes took stock of his resources and found he had only one talent of ready money but a large quantity of slaves, cattle, and sheep. He offered all these to Xenophon to discharge his debt to the Greeks. Xenophon laughed and wondered who the soldiers would think the single talent was for. If Xenophon returned to camp with herds of animals and slaves as payment, yet was personally carrying a talent of gold he feared he would be greeted with stones. Nevertheless, after staying the night in Seuthes's camp, Xenophon set out with all the payment Seuthes could provide, accompanied by Thracian herders and an escort.

Among the Greeks, rumors had begun to circulate that Xenophon had deserted the army to live with Seuthes and the barbarians. His enemies among the mercenaries were doing their best to turn the army against him, but when the soldiers caught sight of Xenophon on the road they left their tents and ran out to greet him. Nearly the entire army came out onto the road to escort him back to the camp. The two Lacedaemonian generals came forward and Xenophon asked them to take charge of the money and goods for distribution among the soldiers.

The Spartans appointed accountants to sell Seuthes's payment for conversion into money. All that day there was considerable arguing between the soldiers and the accountants over who was due what. There were charges that the distribution was being mismanaged and the soldiers became hostile toward the Lacedaemonians overseeing the operation. Xenophon prudently stayed to himself that day and prepared for his voyage home to Athens. He had decided not to follow the advice of the gods to remain with the army. He had secured for the mercenaries their wages, or at least as much as he could gather, and his obligations to them as commander had been discharged. Now he was tired and wanted to go home.

When word that Xenophon was leaving spread through the camp large numbers of the soldiers came to his tent and begged him to stay with the army. They asked him to remain their commander until they reached Asia Minor and entered the service of Thibron. Xenophon agreed to remain as commander and lead them as far as the coast where they would board ships for Asia Minor.

The army marched to the coast and boarded ships. Xenophon remained with them, and they sailed across the Hellespont to the port city of Lampsacus. There Xenophon tried to arrange passage home to Athens but he did not have enough money. He sold his horse and a few personal belongings in the marketplace and was able to raise enough money for the fare. The next day he went to the temple and sacrificed to Zeus with what little of his money remained. When the sacrifices were completed, he obtained favorable omens for his voyage home.

Bion and Nausicleides, two Lacedaemonian officers in the service of the Spartan general, Thibron, arrived at the temple searching for

Xenophon. They had a small quantity of gold they'd collected from the army. The two Spartans had been dispatched by Thibron to pay the mercenaries their first wages, and as they distributed the gold some of the soldiers told them Xenophon had sold his horse and weapons in the market. Some of the mercenaries knew that he was fond of the animal so they went into the marketplace and bought it back for him. Xenophon was touched by the gesture and returned to thank the soldiers. They prevailed upon him again to remain with them as their commander until they reached Thibron.

From Lampsacus, the mercenary army marched southeast through the interior of Lydia and crossed over Mt. Ida. They arrived at the city of Antandrus on the coast of the Aegean and from there proceeded farther south until they reached the plain of Thebe. They then made their way to the city of Pergamum, where they waited for Thibron. The soldiers and officers of his army, along with Thibron's officers, honored Xenophon for his service. He was given gifts of gold, horses, oxen, and slaves from what the mercenaries had looted on their way to Pergamum.

Xenophon made sacrifice to the gods and was preparing to sail for home when he learned that during his two-year absence he had been banished from Athens. Democracy had returned with a vengeance to the defeated city and Xenophon's close association with Cyrus, who had supported Sparta, and with the Lacedaemonians themselves had resulted in his exile. The fears for his well-being voiced by his teacher Socrates two years earlier had been justified. It was a dangerous time in Athens, for even Socrates had been condemned and executed that year on specious charges of impiety and corrupting the young. The old philosopher's dedication to questioning authority had grated against the resurgent wave of patriotism that aimed to restore Athenian power. Since Xenophon no longer had a home to return to, he remained with the mercenaries and entered Spartan service in Asia Minor.

Six thousand of the mercenaries had survived the long march from the original fourteen thousand who had started out with Cyrus in the spring of 401 B.C. At Pergamum they were assigned new officers and integrated into Thibron's Spartan army. They were promised that if they fought hard they could win fortune and glory warring against the Persians and return home to Greece wealthy men. These were promises they had heard before, but since they had no other prospects, they believed once again that they could find their fortunes in the East. At Pergamum, the mercenaries were fewer than a hundred miles from Sardis, where two years earlier they had begun their expedition with Cyrus.

During their march of nearly 3,000 miles to and from the heart of the Persian Empire, the mercenaries had endured burning heat and freezing cold, the ache of hunger and the sharp pain of wounds. They had staggered across vast plains and steep heights, braving antagonists from professional cavalry to wild mountain tribesmen at every step of the way. But they had found no succor upon returning to Greek territory in Europe. Warriors by profession, their homes a distant memory, they polished their armor and sharpened their weapons for another round of battle. They would wage war once more against the Persians, valued for their skills in the only profession they knew.

EPILOGUE

When the "Ten Thousand" returned to Asia in 399 B.C., exactly a hundred years had passed since the initial uprisings of the Ionian Greek cities against Persian rule. The intervening years, conveniently indicated in modern terms as the fifth century B.C., had seen total war waged between the Greeks and Persians, followed by an even more devastating conflict waged among the Greeks themselves. The century had witnessed the height of Greek cultural achievements as well as the height of the Persian Empire. And in 401–400 B.C. it concluded with the remarkable juxtaposition of an army of Greeks marching without a cause save an indefatigable commitment to individual freedom through the heart of the Persian Empire.

By the dawn of the fourth century B.C., the Ten Thousand were too dangerous to be allowed home, yet too valuable to be dispersed. They comprised the largest, most accomplished mercenary army ever to emerge from the Greek world (though only the first of many to come), but their homeland, still healing its deep wounds from the Peloponnesian War, was unwilling to take them back. During the winter of 400–399 B.C., the Spartans had halfheartedly offered to hire them to assist with a minor campaign in the Chersonese, but were just as pleased to see the mercenaries tread water elsewhere in the service of the Thracian king, Seuthes. In the spring of 399 B.C. the continued existence of such a large, experienced army proved invaluable to the Greek cause when war with Persia resumed.

Upon emerging from Asia after their great trek, the mercenaries had encountered Spartan forces in an uneasy peace with the Persians. Two years earlier, the Persian prince Cyrus had helped Sparta achieve its final victory over Athens. The Spartans had in turn assisted Cyrus in his huge gamble to seize the Persian throne. But now Cyrus was dead, his skull a trophy in Babylon, and the Spartans had inherited not only the former Athenian sphere of influence in Asia Minor but the bitter enmity of the Persian king, Artaxerxes II.

The king's loyal satraps, Pharnabazus and Tissaphernes, were reclaiming the western lands once ruled by Cyrus. The Greek cities of the Ionian coast, fearful of Persian rule and the satraps' revenge, had appealed to Sparta, the new controlling power of the Greek homeland, for protection. The Spartans, having gained a maritime capability in addition to the world's most formidable infantry, could hardly refuse the responsibilities attendant upon their victory over Athens. They would be the new protectors of "magna Graecia." Still, the army that Thibron had brought from the Peloponnese to Asia Minor, along with the troops he had summoned from the Ionian cities, was only strong enough to defend the coast. It was not until the Greek mercenaries— sometimes called the Cyreians—were recruited into the cause in the spring of 399 B.C. that the Spartans felt able to undertake offensive operations. Xenophon had all but booked passage home at this point, when he received word that he'd been exiled from his city-state. He would fight for five more years in the East before finally returning to the Greek mainland.

Xenophon may not have been surprised to learn of his banishment from Athens, which had been defeated but far from humbled. In response to Sparta's call for cavalry, the Athenians had dispatched knights who, like Xenophon, had supported the Thirty Tyrants. The Athenians thus continued to rid the city of its oligarchist elements while democratic fervor at home nourished the prospect of a return to former glory. The news of Socrates' execution must have given Xenophon pause to consider whether a return to Athens was even desirable in 399 B.C. If his former teacher, who was about 70 years old when put to death, had been considered such a threat to the Athenian polis, how would Xenophon, a proven general who had served Cyrus, Seuthes, and the Spartans have been received?

Xenophon's dream of founding a city of Greeks on the Black Sea had dissolved months before, as had his prospects of receiving a royal wife and city on the shores of the Propontis in Thrace. His property in Athens had been confiscated by the government, and his only option was to fall in with the Spartans. But this is not to say he greeted the prospect with dismay.

After its incredible march through the Persian empire—during which the mercenary army sometimes resembled less a military force than a mobile Greek city, voting on and debating decisions, veering between logic and mob fervor, and barely surviving the trek at all—Xenophon may have privately welcomed service under the Spartans. Like many in the Greek world, he had long admired the Lacedaemonian state's simple discipline in the service of patriotism, which often contrasted favorably with the emotional tumult of Athenian-style democracy. Here was the greatest power among the Greeks with a centuries-old constitutional system to guard against error or hubris. In addition, he would now be joining a pan-Hellenic army that even included Athens as a material, though sullen, contributor. With peace established in Greece by virtue of Spartan hegemony, it was time to serve against the common enemy—the barbarians.

In Spartan service, the mercenaries were offered regular wages as well as sustenance, and the greater possibility that they could enrich themselves by plundering the prosperous towns and cities of the enemy. Xenophon may have been interested in personal wealth—certainly the army, almost en masse, had suspected him of taking payment from Seuthes at its expense—but it is more likely that he was drawn to status more than money, and the prospect of serving as a key general under the Spartans held greater appeal for him than continuing to lead the rootless mercenaries in unsupported adventures, or even the prospect of returning home.

At Pergamum, the mercenaries were assigned new Spartan officers, and attached as a unit to the army of Thibron. The Spartans cautiously regarded them as a band of thugs, though experienced and skilled fighters. During their long months in the Persian Empire and their winter campaign in Thrace, their discipline had slipped more than a notch. The days when they elected officers, debated march routes and threatened to stone their generals were over. The new Spartan commanders put the mercenaries on wages, one daric a month for each soldier, and told the men that if they obeyed orders and fought hard they could win glory for themselves and either return home to Greece or settle in Asia Minor. These were familiar promises, but the majority of the mercenaries were impoverished men and had few other options. Xenophon was allowed to retain his position as commander of the mercenaries and was paid a general's wage each month. The Spartans began a campaign in Asia Minor against Tissaphernes in the south and Pharnabazus in the north.

The new round of wars between the Greeks and the Persians took place in Cyrus's old satrapy, with the object of controlling the Ionian Greek coastal cities and the straits leading to the Black Sea. The mercenaries had once more found their element. Much of the first year of the campaign was spent in looting, burning, and pillaging Persian-held villages and towns, some of them populated by Greeks—and the new Spartan commanders could not completely keep the mercenaries in check. When word reached Sparta of outrages in the theater of war, the ephors were displeased and Thibron was recalled. He was tried in Sparta and exiled for failing to discipline his army. The Spartans appointed a new commander in Asia Minor, Dercyllidas, who nevertheless retained Xenophon and the mercenaries in his service.

In the spring of 396 B.C., Agesilaus, a Spartan king, arrived to take command. Agesilaus's initial strategy was to create a buffer zone of rebel satrapies between the territory controlled by the Persians in eastern Asia Minor and the Greek coastal cities in the west and north. Toward that end he tried to encourage the satrap Pharnabazus in Phrygia to secede from Persia and establish a Spartan-supported kingdom that would include the area of Paphlagonia. Pharnabazus, who viewed Tissaphernes as a rival, was tempted by the offer but finally remained loyal to his Persian king. The war resumed on both fronts.

Xenophon greatly admired Agesilaus and the two men became close comrades during the war. After a series of maneuvers in 395 B.C., Agesilaus caught Tissaphernes' army near Sardis and dealt it a devastating defeat. As punishment, Tissaphernes was executed and his head was sent to Artaxerxes as proof of his demise. Tissaphernes had been hated by the Greek mercenaries, but he also had enemies at Babylon. His execution was one last stage of the revenge of the great king's mother, Parysatis, against those who had contributed to the death of her son, Cyrus.

Parysatis went on to poison her daughter-in-law Stateira at a common meal. The queen mother presented Stateira half of a small, succulent bird that had been prepared for the two women. While Parysatis ate one half to allay suspicion, she fed the poisoned half to Stateira. The manuscripts recount that Stateira died a particularly painful death from convulsions. The murder of his wife was too much for Artaxerxes to bear and he exiled his mother from the court. During his reign, the decadence that the Greeks had always suspected lay at the heart of the empire reached fruition. In the years that followed, Artaxerxes reconciled with his mother and married his daughter, Atossa. The gods were so offended by the incestuous union that they covered the body of the bride in leprosy. Artaxerxes eventually took 360 royal concubines and they bore him 115 sons. His greatest crisis had occurred in 401 B.C., when he defeated his younger brother Cyrus and the Greek mercenaries in battle. As it turned out, he ruled Persia until 359 B.C., and at forty-six years had the longest reign of all the Achaemenid kings.

Unable to subdue Agesilaus and the Spartans in Asia Minor, the Persians finally resorted to the tactic they had previously used to rid themselves of the Athenians. They began to funnel money to Sparta's enemies on the Greek mainland—this time, Corinth, Argos, Thebes, and, ironically, Athens itself. The result was the Corinthian War, in which an alliance of Greek city-states strove to overthrow Spartan hegemony in Greece. Agesilaus and his forces, including Xenophon, were recalled from the Ionian Coast in order to face the crisis at home.

In 394 B.C., Xenophon fought alongside Agesilaus at the battle of Coronea in Boeotia. The allied coalition included a contingent of Athenian soldiers and Xenophon found himself fighting against his own people. The Spartan victory did not produce strategic results and the war continued until 386 B.C., when it was finally brought to an end through diplomatic intervention by the Persian government. In the "King's Peace," the Spartans relinquished their claim to the Ionian Greek cities, which reverted to Persian rule. In turn, Sparta was made guardian of an agreement that all Greek city-states were to be strictly independent. Sparta thus gained Persian support for breaking up any new alliances that might form against her. Throughout its history, the Persian Empire's best weapon against the Greeks was the Greeks' own inclination to resist unity.

Xenophon's close friendship with Agesilaus, coupled with his years of service with the Spartans in Asia Minor, earned him the good will of the ephors. They provided him with an estate in Elis, the most western portion of the Peloponnese. He lived near the small town of Scillus that was situated only a few miles south of the Olympian plain. There the Olympic games were held every four years and athletes came from all parts of Greece to compete. The most magnificent among the temples in the plain at Olympia was the one dedicated to Zeus Olympius. The temple contained a colossal statue of the father of the gods, constructed of ivory and gold and adorned with precious stones. Considered one of the Seven Wonders of the ancient world, it had been designed and built by the greatest sculptor and statuary builder in Greece, the Athenian Phidias.

Xenophon took as his wife a woman named Philesia and spent the next twenty years in this quiet retreat, living among the Eleans as a country gentlemen and raising two sons. He entered into the autumn of his life with days spent hunting with his sons and writing. There is no evidence that Xenophon ever returned to his native city but there are indications that his exile from Athens was revoked in 369 B.C., when Sparta and Athens reconciled due to the sudden ascendancy of Thebes. Xenophon's two sons, Gryllus and Diodorus, fought in the new internecine war, and Gryllus was killed in operations leading to the battle of Mantinea.

Xenophon became a prolific writer in his retirement. Living in the tranquility of the countryside, he enjoyed nearly two and a half decades in which to reflect on his youth and all that he had experienced. He wrote about war, history, politics, and philosophy as well as about a number of practical matters such as hunting, farming, and raising horses.

Xenophon's most important work is the *Hellenica*, a seven-volume history of Greece from 411 to 362 B.C. He attempted to pick up where Thucydides, the father of history, had left off his account, at the end of the Peloponessian War in 404 B.C. Modern historians do not tend to rank Xenophon intellectually with Thucydides, and while Xenophon shows a skill for describing events in an exciting and lively manner, he is criticized for lacking the depth of a great historian.

His second most important work is the *Anabasis*, which relates the details of the campaign of the Ten Thousand while providing a rare glimpse into the Persian Empire at its height. The work stands as a travelogue and adventure story as well as a treatise on the art of ancient warfare, political science, and human psychology. And after twenty-three centuries it remains a classic text on the problems of tactical and strategic retreat.

The *Anabasis* has been criticized as a work of personal glorification that exaggerates Xenophon's role in bringing the Greeks out of Persia. Curiously, he published the work under a pseudonym, "the Syracusan Themistogenes," perhaps to lend a greater veneer of objectivity to his account. As with all Greek histories, the verbatim speeches attributed to principles reveal as much about the author's philosophy as his memory, and in the *Anabasis* most of the long speeches are by Xenophon. His words are invariably presented as the clear voice of reason, even when the other mercenaries are turning against him. If historians suspect Xenophon of polishing an image of his own virtue in the *Anabasis*, there is no reason to similarly doubt his details of the route, conflicts, and foreign peoples encountered during the campaign. Whether Xenophon exaggerated his role in the mercenary army is partly answered by the fact that, when they emerged from Asia, Xenophon was viewed by the Spartans as the leader of the Ten Thousand.

Another account of the Greek expedition was written by Sophaenetus of Stymphalus, one of the oldest generals on the march. In the four small fragments that remain of this work and in later writings that seem to have used it as a source, Xenophon is not mentioned. In the *Anabasis*, Sophaenetus is mentioned but does not come off well, at one point having been fined for neglect of duty and in another instance being timid in an attack, so it is possible that he and Xenophon were at personal odds.

Xenophon's *Cyropaedia* is an historical novel in eight books about the life of the foremost Persian king, Cyrus the Great. It concerns itself mostly with the topic of leadership and presents the model of a perfect ruler instituting the finest notions of Spartan authority, organization, and family life into his society. It is a virtual textbook on politics, the elements of leadership, and the art of war. Students of military science have read the book over the centuries because of its examination of the unchanging elements in the conduct of war. Scipio Africanus, the Roman conqueror of Hannibal, and Julius Caesar, who ended the Roman Republic, are both alleged to have carried the book with them and consulted it often. The forms of warfare in Xenophon's time were relatively simple compared to the technological complexities of today, but the essential elements that affect men in combat have remained unchanged over the centuries.

In the realm of philosophy Xenophon wrote four books that centered on the person of his old teacher, Socrates. The first was the *Memorabilia*, a lengthy description of Socrates' life and work. The *Oeconomicus* describes the views of Socrates regarding household management and offers lessons on proper behavior toward wives. The *Symposium* presents philosophically oriented dinner-table conversations involving Socrates, while the *Apologia* was a defense of Socrates

against the Athenian charges that led to his death and a description of
his conduct during and after his trial.

Xenophon went on to write a number of minor works. The
Hieron was a dialogue on the nature of tyranny in which he examined
the question of whether or not a tyrant could ever find happiness and
any measure of security so long as he ruled over his people using fear
and force. The *Agesilaus* was an historical biography of the Spartan
king with whom he had served in Asia Minor and had developed a
long and close friendship. *On the Constitution of the Spartans* was his
analysis of the Spartan constitution, and describes his admiration for
the stability it brought that society for so many centuries. *Ways and
Means* offered practical advice about raising revenue for the state
through taxation. In his work the *Hipparchicus,* Xenophon outlined
the proper duties for an Athenian cavalry commander, while in *On
Horsemanship* he wrote the oldest surviving complete work on the
topic of horsemanship. *On Hunting* was a treatise on hunting wild
boar and deer.

Xenophon's observations on the psychological elements of leadership in the military, especially in combat, are as valuable to an officer
or non-commissioned officer today as they were two thousand years
ago. The field commander, he wrote in an essay, the *Memorabilia,*
must be the perfect blend of nature and education. He must be a man
who is "ingenious, energetic, careful, full of stamina and presence of
mind." As well, Xenophon wrote that the commander in combat must
be "loving and tough" as well as "trusting and suspicious" of his men.
The most important quality of an officer, he wrote, is ambition.

Today, Xenophon has been praised as a writer of a plain, simple,
and unaffected Greek, but has not been widely admired as a philosopher. The *Hellenica,* his history of Greece following the Peloponnesian
War, and the *Anabasis,* his detailed account of the military expedition
into Persia, however, are seen as invaluable to our understanding of
the tumultuous Mediterranean world when the Greeks and Persians
vied for supremacy.

Xenophon's bucolic retirement ended when the Spartans were
defeated by the Thebans at the battle of Leuctra in 371 B.C. That battle ended Spartan hegemony on the Greek mainland. Among the many
provinces the Spartans lost was Elis, and Xenophon was forced to
leave the tranquility he had enjoyed for so long. Political circumstances forced him to move east to more secure accommodations at

Corinth. There he ended his days and died, according to sources, between seventy and seventy-five years of age.

The exact date of Xenophon's death, in the mid-350s B.C., is today unknown. But it closely coincided with the birth in 356 B.C. of a young prince named Alexander, who would follow him into the Persian Empire. First, this young man's country, Macedonia, would unite the Greek city-states—with the single exception of Sparta—into a united coalition. At the age of twenty-two he would lead a pan-Hellenic army in the footsteps of the Ten Thousand to the heart of the Persian Empire. He would defeat its king of kings in battle and forge, however briefly, a Greek empire fully as large as the Persians's. An entire body of humanistic and classical ideals associated with Greece would come to dominate the Mediterranean world. This young man, Alexander the Great, was schooled from childhood in the story of Xenophon's march. One man's legacy can lead to even greater achievements by another, and while today the Persian Empire appears as a shadowy relic of history, the legacy of the ancient Greeks continues to be taken up by succeeding civilizations.

BIBLIOGRAPHY

Primary Sources

Manuscripts in the Gallery Mazarine, Paris:

Parisinus, Anabasis of Xenophon. 1640
Xenophon. *La Retraite des Dix Mille de Xenophon*. Paris: 1695.

Manuscripts in the British Museum, London:

Xenophon, Fragment, third or fourth century A.D.
Xenophon, Anabasis, sixteenth century, A.D.
Xenophon, Life of, ninth century, A.D.
Xenophon, Scribe, thirteenth-century, A.D.
Xenophon. *The Historie of Xenophon*. London: J. Haviland, 1623.

General Reference Works

Cambridge Ancient History, Volumes V and VI, Cambridge: University Press, 1997.
Cary, M. *The Geographic Background of Greek and Roman History*. Oxford: Clarendon Press, 1949.
Delbruck, Hans. *Warfare in Antiquity*, Volume I. London: Greenwood Press, 1975
History of Herodotus. Tudor Publishing Co., New York: 1943 translated by George Rawlinson.
Olmstead, A.T. *History of the Persian Empire*. Chicago: University Press, 1948.

Select Bibliography of Secondary Sources

Ainsworth, William. *Travels in the Track of the Ten Thousand Greeks*. London: J.W. Parker, 1844.
Anderson, John Kinloch. *Military Theory and Practice in the Age of Xenophon*. Berkeley: University of California Press, 1970.

Cook, J.M. *The Persian Empire*. New York: Schocken Books, 1983.

Finley, M.I. (ed.). *The Greek Historians*. New York, Viking Press, 1959.

Freeman, Charles. *The Greek Achievement: The Foundations of the Western World*. New York: Viking, 1999.

Georges, Pericles. *Barbarian Asia and the Greek Experience*. Baltimore: Johns Hopkins University Press, 1994.

Gleason, Clarence Willard. *The Gate to the Anabasis*. Boston: Ginn & Company, 1894.

Grant, Michael. *The Founders of the Western World: A History of Greece and Rome*. New York: Charles Scribner's Sons, 1991.

Godolphin, Francis R.B. (ed.). *The Greek Historians*, Vol. II. New York: Random House, 1942.

Green, Peter. *Greco-Persian Wars*. London: Univ. of California Press, 1998.

Hirsch, Steven W. *The Friendship of the Barbarians*. Hanover: University Press of New England, 1985.

Keegan, John. *A History of Warfare*. New York: Alfred A. Knopf, 1993.

Martin, Thomas R. *Ancient Greece: From Prehistoric to Hellenistic Times*. New Haven and London: Yale University Press, 1996.

Maurice, Thomas. *Panthea, or the Captive Bride*. London: J.W. Galabin, 1789.

Mignan, Robert. *A Winter Journey Through Russia*. London: R. Bentley, 1839.

Stronk, Jan P. *The Ten Thousand in Thrace*. Amsterdam: J.C. Gieben, 1995.

Taber, Augustus (ed). *The Anabasis*. New York: Murray, Scott, Foresman and Co., 1914.

Toynbee, Arnold J. *Hellenism*. New York and London: Oxford University Press, 1959.

———. *Twelve Men of Action in Graeco-Roman History*. Freeport, NY: Books for Libraries Press, 1969.

Williams, John. *Two Essays on the Geography of Ancient Asia*. London: J. Murray, 1829.

Xenophon. *The Anabasis*. New York: Harper & Brothers, 1848.

Xenophon. *The Anabasis*. New York: Sheldon and Company, 1873.

Xenophon. *Anabasis Kyrou*. Oxford: Vincent, 1833.

Xenophon. *The Expedition of Cyrus and the Memorabilia of Socrates.* London: Translated from the Greek by J.S. Watson, G. Bell, 1880.

Xenophon. *The Expedition of Cyrus into Persia.* (n.p.) 1794.

Xenophon. *The Expedition of Cyrus into Persia.* Cambridge: J. Archdeacon, 1776.

Xenophon. *Expedition of Cyrus into Persia.* London: J. Davis, 1812.

Xenophon. *The Expedition of Cyrus.* London: Hunt & Clark, 1828.

Xenophon. *OEuvres de Xenophon.* Paris: Didot 1795.

Xenophon. *La Retraite des Dix Mille.* Paris: Librairie de la Bibliotheque Nationale, 1886.

Xenophon. *Anabasis* (Carleton L. Brownson, trans.). Cambridge and London: Harvard University Press, 1998.

INDEX